"The politics of the choices we make beyond basic methodological decisions are more meaningful today than ever before. It is vital for qualitative researchers to ask reflexive and critical questions of themselves, such as: who and what do/should we research, and why? How should we conduct that research? Where and when? Who are 'we' as researchers, and how do the ways in which we conceptualise our 'researcher identity' impact on our research? Anna CohenMiller and Nettie Boivin along with their colleagues effectively illuminate these issues, and provide real-world solutions to produce not only high-quality qualitative research, but also to generate transformative change addressing urgent issues of social justice and equity for our multicultural world."

— **Ronald J. Chenail, Ph.D.,** *Editor-in-Chief, The Qualitative Report*

"CohenMiller and Boivin have brought all of us in the field of qualitative methods to the table to better understand social justice practices in our research. Each chapter in the text has something to offer us given the many approaches and theories behind qualitative approaches to understanding the social world. Beginning, intermediate and experienced qualitative researchers will find something provocative to inspire them on the research journey."

— **Valerie J. Janesick, Ph.D.,** *author of Contemplative Qualitative Inquiry: Practicing the Zen of Research and "Stretching" Exercises for Qualitative Researchers*

"*Questions in Qualitative Social Justice Research in Multicultural Contexts* is an outstanding text for conducting social-justice oriented qualitative research in today's world. Special features such as "reflections for the field" written by leading researchers add a layer of depth to this book. Thoughtfully organized, well-written, with timely examples, this text will serve students and researchers well."

— **Patricia Leavy, Ph.D.,** *author of Research Design: Quantitative, Qualitative, Mixed Methods, Arts-Based, and Community-Based Participatory Approaches*

"*Questions in Qualitative Social Justice Research in Multicultural Contexts*, authored by Anna CohenMiller and Nettie Boivin, is a unique textbook that provides a much-needed guide to help researchers engage in reflexivity and criticality. By providing a resource for readers to arrive at thought-provoking questions, including questions that represent the 5W1H (also known as Six Ws), this dynamic and timely book will help researchers to identify their positionality, as well as to understand the role that it plays in their meaning-making processes. Further, by focusing on social justice, ethics, and online research, this book will inspire researchers to consider their roles, affect, and, above all, humanness during the research process. The section on Reflections from the Field, which appears in every chapter and which includes case studies and reflections provided by both well-known international scholars and emerging scholars, makes the book reader-friendly and far-reaching. Simply put, this inspirational book begins to fill a void in a way that will make a significant contribution to the literature."

— **Anthony J. Onwuegbuzie, Ph.D.**, *University of Cambridge, UK; Distinguished Visiting Professor University of Johannesburg, South Africa*

"*Questions in Qualitative Social Justice Researcher in Multicultural Contexts* will help novice researchers and those who teach them to understand foundational concepts essential for designing, enacting, and evaluating social justice research. The generative balance of academic text and reflexive researcher writings enlivens the text and teaches that research is embodied, political, and, that it can be transformative. Key concepts are explained in ways that illuminate their methodological and practical interconnections. This is an essential guide to developing research that can help to heal our hurting world, one study at a time."

— **Sharon M. Ravitch, Ph.D.**, *Professor of Practice, University of Pennsylvania Graduate School of Education*

"*Questions in Qualitative Social Justice Research in Multicultural Contexts* is the social justice thinking text for all qualitative researchers. In a field where answers are neither easy nor determinate, CohenMiller and Boivin offer a timely and essential resource for anticipating and thinking through the questions and issues that invariably arise in all multi-cultural qualitative research. Personably written and engaging, with reflective contributions from prominent qualitative scholars, this book will be the reflexivity companion text for doing qualitative social justice research."

— **Jennifer R. Wolgemuth, Ph.D.**, *Associate Professor of Educational Research at the University of South Florida and directs the Graduate Certificate in Qualitative Research*

Questions in Qualitative Social Justice Research in Multicultural Contexts

Questions in Qualitative Social Justice Research in Multicultural Contexts takes readers on an accessible and inspiring journey to critically self-reflect on current or future research practices to encourage and facilitate greater equity, inclusion, and social justice in qualitative research.

In a diverse world, "doing" qualitative research needs unpacking and developing awareness of interconnected perspectives and challenges. However, as researchers, there isn't always a chance to fully prepare or self-reflect on the processes and experiences. This book raises awareness of key multidimensional aspects of social justice, such as power, privilege, trust, insider-outsiderness, ethics, arts-based, co-produced, and decolonial research. The authors connect theory and conceptual constructs with practical in-field realities, guiding researchers through the dynamic, evolving steps to give voice to and promote social justice practices in research.

The book includes the following features to guide thinking for researchers and students:

- Bolded key terms and questions for self-reflection.
- Boxed case studies from top international and emerging scholars.
- Glossary of key terms.

This foundational book can be used as a jumping-off point to engage and critically self-reflect about research, moving us toward decolonizing research practice, creating more inclusive, equitable, and socially just research. It will be suitable for upper-level and postgraduate students and all researchers interested in qualitative methods in education and the social and behavioral sciences.

Anna CohenMiller is an arts-based qualitative research methodologist and award-winning educator, who examines issues of equity and inclusion in higher education in Kazakhstan and internationally.

Nettie Boivin is a decolonial multimodal, multisensory ethnographer who examines issues of diversity and inclusion for marginalized, transmigrant families and communities in Europe and internationally.

Questions in Qualitative Social Justice Research in Multicultural Contexts

Anna CohenMiller and
Nettie Boivin

LONDON AND NEW YORK

First published 2022
by Routledge
2 Park Square, Milton Park, Abingdon, Oxon OX14 4RN

and by Routledge
605 Third Avenue, New York, NY 10158

Routledge is an imprint of the Taylor & Francis Group, an informa business

© 2022 Anna CohenMiller and Nettie Boivin

The right of Anna CohenMiller and Nettie Boivin to be identified as authors of this work has been asserted by them in accordance with sections 77 and 78 of the Copyright, Designs and Patents Act 1988.

All rights reserved. No part of this book may be reprinted or reproduced or utilised in any form or by any electronic, mechanical, or other means, now known or hereafter invented, including photocopying and recording, or in any information storage or retrieval system, without permission in writing from the publishers.

Trademark notice: Product or corporate names may be trademarks or registered trademarks, and are used only for identification and explanation without intent to infringe.

British Library Cataloguing-in-Publication Data
A catalogue record for this book is available from the British Library

Library of Congress Cataloging-in-Publication Data
A catalog record for this book has been requested

ISBN: 978-0-367-25043-0 (hbk)
ISBN: 978-0-367-25040-9 (pbk)
ISBN: 978-0-429-28569-1 (ebk)

DOI: 10.4324/9780429285691

Typeset in Optima
by Apex CoVantage, LLC

To our students, participants, and children for showing us the questions needing to be asked.

Contents

List of contributors	xiv
Preface	xxiii
Acknowledgments	xxviii

How is social justice foundational in qualitative research? An introduction — 1
1. How is social justice foundational in qualitative research? — 4
2. What can we expect in this book? — 5
3. What are the origins of this book? Sharing about ourselves — 7
4. Adaptations as a result of the COVID-19 pandemic — 10

1 Owning our power — 13
1. How can we understand the changing nature of power? — 16
2. Do we understand ourselves? — 17
3. Who has the power? — 19
4. What's privilege got to do with it? — 20
5. How do we become more aware and reflective? — 22
6. How can we rebalance power dynamics? — 24
7. Are my practices amplifying or diminishing voice? — 27
8. What ethical dilemmas should we be prepared for relating to power? — 28
9. Reflections from the field: owning our power — 31
   Owning my power — 31
   KAKALI BHATTACHARYA

   A (3D) sensitivity . . . that's our (super)power! — 34
   POLINA GOLOVÁTINA-MORA AND RAÚL ALBERTO MORA

Contents

10. Engaging more deeply: concluding thoughts on owning
our power   37
Reflective questions about power   38

2   Unpacking the meaning and practice of trust   **46**
1. What is trust?   47
2. How to develop trusting relationships   51
3. What do we need to consider in building relationships?   53
4. How can I work with gatekeepers?   55
5. What ethical dilemmas should we be prepared for
relating to trust?   57
6. Reflections from the field: unpacking the meaning
and practice of trust   60
On the ethics of sharing power   60
JENNIFER R. WOLGEMUTH

*Co-constructing trust and working with multilingual,
multicultural, conservative,hard-to-reach families*   64
FATMA F. S. SAID

7. Engaging more deeply: concluding thoughts on
unpacking the meaning and practice of trust   66
Reflective questions about trust   67

3.   Uncovering the spectrum of insider-outsiderness   **73**
1. How can we understand our insider-outsider roles?   75
2. What is the changing nature of being an insider-outsider?   78
3. Are we seeing and understanding our roles?   81
4. What ethical dilemmas should we be prepared for
relating to the spectrum of insider-outsiderness?   83
5. Reflections from the field: spectrum of insider-
outsiderness   84
Inside the inside   85
LINDA TUHIWAI SMITH

Insider-outsider experience   87
ARCELI ROSARIO

6. Engaging more deeply: concluding thoughts on insider-
outsiderness   89
Reflective questions about insider-outsiderness   90

4. Awareness in social justice and transformative research — 96

1. Where does social justice fit? — 99
2. Why transformative research? — 102
3. What dilemmas of ethics can we consider related to social justice and transformative research? — 106
4. Reflections from the field: social justice and transformative research — 108

   Expanding social justice through transformative research? — 109
   DONNA M. MERTENS

   Researcher's reflexivity in a multicultural context: the role of framing and emotion work — 111
   TINEKE A. ABMA

   Reflections on teaching in English as a Second Language (ESL)classrooms: social inclusion and equity — 115
   NUPUR SAMUEL

5. Engaging more deeply: concluding thoughts on social justice and transformative research — 117

   Reflective questions about social justice and transformative research — 118

5 Crossing disciplinary boundaries within the research team — 123

1. Where are the disciplinary boundaries? — 125
2. Do we understand the implications of funding? — 129
3. Can we further extend our perspectives? — 131
4. What ethical dilemmas should we be prepared for relating to working across disciplines? — 134
5. Reflections from the field: crossing disciplinary boundaries — 137

   "It doesn't have to be hard work": finding common ideology and learning as an insider and outsider in cross-disciplinary research teams — 137
   AGNES ATIA APUSIGAH

   Reflecting on crossing disciplinary divides with academics and communities — 140
   AKMARAL SMAN

   Working across disciplinary and multicultural contexts — 142
   ROXANNE HENKIN, GOPAL KRISHNA SHARMA, PURVA GOPAL SHARMA, AND MASHABA MASHALA

Contents

6. Engaging more deeply: concluding thoughts on crossing
disciplinary boundaries   146
*Reflective questions about crossing disciplinary
boundaries*   147

6 Moving between face-to-face and online engagement   152
1. How can we understand the changing nature of
face-to-face and online engagement?   154
2. Do we understand online communication in multicultural
contexts?   155
3. What do we need to consider when collecting
data online?   158
4. What (other) ethical dilemmas should we consider
regarding online research?   160
5. Reflections from the field: moving between face-to-face
and online engagement   164
Is it possible to do meaningful interviewing online?   165
CAROLYN ELLIS

An equalities perspective applied to researching online   167
TAMSIN HINTON-SMITH

6. Engaging more deeply: concluding thoughts on moving
from face-to-face to online   171
*Reflective questions about moving from face-to-face
to online research*   172

7 Integrating the arts with collaboration and co-production   177
1. Arts in research   178
2. Arts as practice   180
3. Arts as knowledge   183
4. Arts as communication   187
5. What ethical dilemmas should we be prepared for
relating to using the arts in research?   191
6. Reflections from the field: arts in research with
collaboration and co-production   192
Reflection from the field   193
PATRICIA LEAVY

*"Sitting with the uncomfortable" as a research topic
and reflective praxis*   197
NADIA DRESSCHER-LAMBERTUS

7. Engaging more deeply: concluding thoughts on arts, collaboration, and co-production 199

Reflective questions about arts with collaboration and co-production 200

8 Applying social justice in research and practice in multicultural contexts 207

1. What have we learned? Uncovering rich answers and collective knowledge 209
2. Where do we go from here? Joining a journey for applying social justice in research and practice 211
3. Practical next steps: improving equity, inclusion, and social justice in research and practice 214
4. Reflection from the field: social justice in action 214

Black Lives Matter and humanizing methodologies for social justice 215

SHARON M. RAVITCH

5. Reflective questions on improving equity, inclusion, and social justice in research and practice 220

Glossary 223
Index 225

Contributors

Tineke A. Abma is Professor of "Participation and Diversity" in Amsterdam University Medical Centres, and Executive Director of Leyden Academy on Vitality and Ageing in the Netherlands. Formerly, she was an endowed chair in the field of client participation in elderly care. In 2013, she received an Aspasia laureate from the Dutch Council for Scientific Research (NWO). Her scholarly work is grounded in interactive and responsive evaluation and empirical ethics. She has been involved in many research projects focused on the participation and social inclusion of people with a marginalized position in society. Her work has been awarded for its high societal impact. She is the author/editor of a number of books, including *Evaluation for a Caring Society* (IAP Press, 2018) and *Participatory Research for Health and Social Well-Being* (Springer Nature, 2019).

Agnes Atia Apusigah is a professor of development sociology concentrating on gender, cultural, and education studies. She obtained her doctoral degree in cultural studies with curriculum studies from Queen's University Canada in June 2002. She took up a position in August 2002 in the University for Development Studies in Ghana until August 2019. She has published and presented her work in conferences, journals, and books both locally and internationally. She has also served as reviewer and editor of various journals. She currently holds a post-retirement position as Vice President of the Regentropfen College of Applied Sciences in Ghana.

Contributors

Kakali Bhattacharya is a professor in the Research, Evaluation, and Measurement Program at the University of Florida. Her work has made spaces in interdisciplinary decolonizing work and qualitative research, where creativity and contemplative approaches are legitimized and seen as gateways for cultivating depth, integrity, and expansive inquiry and discovering critical insights. Substantively, she explores transnational issues of race, class, gender in higher education. She is the 2018 winner of AERA's Mid-Career Scholar of Color Award and the 2018 winner of AERA's Mentoring Award from Division G: Social Context of Education. Her co-authored text with Kent Gillen, *Power, Race, and Higher Education: A Cross-Cultural Parallel Narrative*, won a 2017 Outstanding Publication Award from AERA (SIG 168) and a 2018 Outstanding Book Award from the International Congress of Qualitative Research. She is the 2020 winner of the Mary Frances Early College of Education Distinguished Alumni Award for research from the University of Georgia.

Nadia Dresscher-Lambertus is a sociologist and teaches in the Faculty of Arts and Science at the University of Aruba. She is a PhD candidate at the University of Amsterdam at Digital Methods Initiative (DMI) and the Amsterdam School of Cultural Analysis (ASCA). Taking the case of the island of Aruba, her doctoral research narrates the recalibration of small-island politics on Facebook by focusing on social networks, the co-production of political issues, and the modulation of political effects online while highlighting the cultural dynamics of small-island politics. She leans toward feminist new materialist ontologies that articulate the social as entangled in assemblages of human and non-human actors in constant flux of becoming, and she loves to experiment with creative methodologies that try to approximate the unfoldings of the self, the movements of the affective entanglements we are part of, and the changing structures of feelings.

Carolyn Ellis is Distinguished University Professor Emerita of Communication and Sociology at the University of South Florida. She has contributed to the narrative and autoethnographic study of human life through integrating ethnographic, literary, and evocative writing to portray and make sense of lived experience in cultural context. Her publications include *Revision:*

Autoethnographic Reflections on Life and Work (revised edition); *Final Negotiations: A Story of Love, Loss, and Chronic Illness* (expanded and revised); *Evocative Autoethnography: Writing Lives and Telling Stories* (with Arthur Bochner); and *Autoethnography: Understanding Qualitative Research* and *Handbook of Autoethnography*, both with Tony E. Adams and Stacy Holman Jones. She co-edits the Routledge book series Writing Lives: Ethnographic Narratives.

Polina Golovátina-Mora is an associate professor of Film and Media in Education at Norwegian University of Science and Technology (NTNU) in Trondheim, Norway. Her research, transdisciplinary by nature, intersects narratives, language, and power; the monstrous as a reflection of current societal issues; theoretical alternatives to traditional views of the nation-state; social and artistic processes in Central Europe; and nature and elements in folklore and their social and environmental meanings. Her research approach mixes elements from new materialisms, post-humanist theories, and duo-ethnography as entry points for a new form of sensitivity toward research phenomena. She has been visiting faculty in Poland and the Czech Republic and is actively engaged in different memory studies conferences and networks in Europe. As a researcher in Colombia, she has held the rank of Associate Researcher since 2019, awarded by the Colombian Ministry of Science, Technology, and Innovation.

Roxanne Henkin is a professor emeritus in the Department of Interdisciplinary Learning and Teaching at the University of Texas at San Antonio. She has published many articles and two books, *Who's Invited to Share: Using Literacy to Teach for Equity* and *Social Justice* and *Confronting Bullying: Literacy as a Tool for Character Education*, both published by Heinemann. She is a past-president of Literacies and Languages for All. She was also the lead co-editor of the journal *Voices from the Middle* (2006–2011). She has received many awards including the 2020 Literacies and Languages for All Lifetime Membership Award; the 2020 Distinguished Alumni Award from Niles North High School in Skokie, Illinois; and the 2020 NCTE LGBTQ+ Advocacy and Leadership Award. She created and is Director Emeritus of the San Antonio Writing Project. She has helped to create and teach writing projects in the United States, South Africa, India, the Philippines, and Kazakhstan.

Tamsin Hinton-Smith is a senior lecturer in higher education at the University of Sussex, England, where she is also Co-director of the Centre for Gender Studies. Her academic background is as a sociologist of gender and education, with particular interests around equality of opportunity. Tamsin's empirical research encompasses experiences around marginalization and belonging across diverse contexts and identities, from the family to the classroom. Her research is underpinned by a feminist, qualitative approach, with online and face-to-face methodologies that include co-production with schoolchildren and autoethnography with colleagues. Tamsin has particular methodological interests around exploring collaboration and equity in research processes, and the role of writing as a tool in research development. Tamsin's current research with international partners explores gender inclusion in higher education teaching across disciplinary and international contexts.

Patricia Leavy, PhD, is an independent sociologist and bestselling author. She has published over 30 books, earning commercial and critical success in both nonfiction and fiction, and her work has been translated into many languages. She is series creator and editor for ten book series with Oxford University Press, Guilford Press, and Brill/Sense, including the groundbreaking *Social Fictions* series. Recently, her novel *Film* won the 2020 American Fiction Award for Inspirational Fiction; her novel *Spark* won the 2019 American Fiction Award for Inspirational Fiction and the 2019 Living Now Book Award for Adventure Fiction; and her *Handbook of Arts-Based Research* won the 2018 USA Best Book Award for best academic book. She has received career awards from the New England Sociological Association, the American Creativity Association, the American Educational Research Association, the International Congress of Qualitative Inquiry, and the National Art Education Association. In 2018 she was honored by the National Women's Hall of Fame, and SUNY–New Paltz established the Patricia Leavy Award for Art and Social Justice. Her website is www.patricialeavy.com.

Mashaba Mashala is an academic literacies lecturer at the University of Mpumalanga, South Africa. She holds an MA in teaching English to speakers of other languages / applied linguistics with a focus on literacy, which she obtained from Iowa State University. She has taught English as a second language in the South African school system (both in primary and high school) for 19 years. In higher education, she has been teaching academic literacy modules and playing an active role in literacy student-support initiatives since 2015. She currently teaches academic literacy modules in several disciplines at the University of Mpumalanga. Her research interests include literacy, second language learning, and translanguaging.

Donna M. Mertens, Professor Emeritus at Gallaudet University, specializes in research and evaluation methodologies designed to support social transformation. She has authored or co-authored many methodological books related to social, economic, and environmental justice and human rights, most recently *Program Evaluation Theory and Practice* (2nd ed.); *Mixed Methods Design in Evaluation*; and *Research and Evaluation in Education and Psychology* (5th ed.). She has consulted with many international agencies including the Centers for Disease Control and Prevention, Johnson & Johnson Foundation, F3E, UN Women, Engineers without Borders Canada, and the W. K. Kellogg Foundation. She served as the editor for the *Journal of Mixed Methods Research* from 2010 to 2014. She was president of the American Evaluation Association in 1998 and served on the board from 1997–2002; and she was a founding board member of the International Organization for Cooperation in Evaluation and the Mixed Methods International Research Association.

Raúl Alberto Mora is an associate professor in the School of Education and Pedagogy at Universidad Pontificia Bolivariana, Medellín, Colombia. He teaches courses on critical theory, language teaching methods courses, and qualitative research. He also chairs the Literacies in Second Languages Project research lab at the university. His research interests combine the use of literacies research in second language contexts with a focus on Global South advocacy and a sociocritical, transformative perspective, favoring the use and remixing of multiple forms of ethnographic research to guide his work and the idea of "polyangulation" as the cornerstone of his data analysis. He is a founding member of the Transnational Critical Literacies Network (TCLN) and co-editor of *The Handbook of Critical Literacies* (Routledge, 2021). Since 2019, he has held the rank of Senior Researcher awarded by the Colombian Ministry of Science, Technology, and Innovation.

Contributors

Sharon M. Ravitch, PhD, is a professor of practice at the University of Pennsylvania's Graduate School of Education. Ravitch developed and is principal advisor to *Semillas Digitales* (*Digital Seeds*), a collaborative school-based initiative that integrates technology-rich instruction, social-emotional learning, immersive Freirean teacher education, and broader pedagogical innovation to improve the quality of education in coffee-producing communities in rural Nicaragua. She is Fulbright Fellow working with Dr. BMN College in Mumbai on equity and pluralism as well as the development of professional identity and agency for first-generation minoritized women. Her approach to sustainable, assets-based institutional and practice-based research is grounded in her decades-long experience collaborating with and serving as an advisor to educational leaders and practitioners as well as business, not-for-profit, and non-governmental organization leaders and policy makers, working to foster and support equitable change and transformation at the individual, community, state, and national levels around the globe.

Arceli Rosario has a PhD in education with a specialization in educational administration. She served as a high school teacher and principal, and as a vice president for academic affairs and college president. Presently, she is a professor and the chair of the Education Department of the Adventist International Institute of Advanced Studies in the Philippines. Her research interests are women leadership, educational administration, and church membership of the Adventist Church. She is the president of the Asian Qualitative Research Association, which advocates for the empowerment of qualitative researchers in Asia and beyond.

Fatma F. S. Said is an applied linguist currently appointed as Assistant Professor in applied linguistics in the Language Studies Department at Zayed University, United Arab Emirates. She teaches and researches mainly on bilingualism and multilingualism and issues of children and family language learning. Her research is centered particularly on the sociolinguistics of language learning, speakers' language ideologies, and how these affect the process within the home and educational domains. She obtained her PhD from Birkbeck, University of London (2015); held research posts at King's College London (2013–2015) and the University of York (2015–2018); and lectured in linguistics at Goldsmiths, University of London (2018–2019). She is currently a board member of *Multilingua* (De Gruyter) and member of the editorial panel of the *English Language Teaching Journal* (Oxford University Press). She is also the research coordinator of the Multilingual Childhoods/ Research into Early Language Learning group, European Early Childhood Education Research Association (EECERA).

Nupur Samuel is Associate Professor at the Centre for Writing Studies at O. P. Jindal Global University, Sonepat. From 2011 to 2019, she taught courses on multilingualism, language pedagogy, and academic English language to undergraduate and postgraduate students at Ambedkar University Delhi. Her research interests include writing pedagogy, inclusive education, critical thinking, English language assessment, gender education, and teacher education. Her doctoral work on dynamic assessment of writing explored the dialectic nature of assessment and teaching. In 2019 she was a visiting fellow at the Centre for Teaching and Learning Research, Sussex University, UK. She is an alumna of the International Visitor Leadership Program (2013) of the US Department of State's premier professional exchange program. Currently, she is engaged with an international research project, Gender on the Higher Education Learning Agenda Internationally: Co-constructing Foundations for Equitable Futures, funded by the British Academy.

Gopal Krishna Sharma is Assistant Professor in the Department of Computer Science at Dev Sanskriti Vishwavidyalya, Shantikunj, Haridwar, Uttarakhand, India. He focuses on education and research in the area of artificial intelligence and its multidisciplinary approaches. He is Guest Faculty for conducting Life Management and Scientific Spirituality Courses. He represented India in the Youth Delegation to China and also visited the University of Texas at San Antonio to take part in the Writing Project. He has traveled to more than 18 states in India in the past ten years for seminars, conferences, events, and awareness campaigns in rural, urban, and semiurban areas. He is an active volunteer of All World Gayatri Pariwar (AWGP), a socio-spiritual organization spread over 70 nations with over 5,000 centers worldwide and working for the greater good of humanity in various ways including education, environment protection, scientific spirituality, woman empowerment, de-addiction, health, and self-entrepreneurship.

Purva Gopal Sharma is Assistant Professor in the Department of Psychology at Dev Sanskriti Vishwavidyalya, Shantikunj, Haridwar, Uttarakhand,

India. She is a passionate researcher and academician working in the area of cyberpsychology. She is working closely with schools and education institutions to address issues associated with students with regard to internet addiction, game addiction, and other topics. She has traveled to several parts of India to provide sessions for students on subjects such as career counseling and stress management. She is a teaching consultant of the Haridwar Writing Project. She also took part in the San Antonio Writing Project at the University of Texas at San Antonio and has addressed the Academy of Teacher Excellence as an subject expert on life management.

Akmaral Sman, from Shymkent, Kazakhstan, earned her Master of Public Administration degree from Queen Mary University of London. She was the recipient of the prestigious Foreign and Commonwealth Organization (FCO) UK government Chevening Scholarship. She has served in various capacities to empower women and girls, including with UN Women, the United Nations Development Programme (UNDP), and the Food and Agriculture Organization (FAO) in Kazakhstan. She has supported UN entities in changing internal machinery and procedures to impact project results on gender equality. Additionally, she has contributed to the development of the Y-PEER youth volunteering network in Eastern Europe and Central Asia and is on the Advisory Board for the Consortium of Gender Scholars (Kazakhstan).

Linda Tuhiwai Smith, Ngāti Awa, Ngāti Porou, Tuhourangi, is a visiting fellow at the Spencer Foundation in the United States, a mentor for the Atlantic Fellows Programme out of the University of Melbourne, and an independent researcher. She has held a number of professorial positions at both the University of Waikato and the University of Auckland. She is a member of the Waitangi Tribunal. Linda has been recognized for her work as a leading Māori scholar and educationalist. She is a fellow of the American Educational Research Association, a fellow of the Royal Society of New Zealand, and has received the Prime Minister's Lifetime Achievement Award for Education. She was awarded a Companion of the New Zealand Order of Merit. She is known for her groundbreaking book, *Decolonising Methodologies Research and Indigenous Peoples*.

Jennifer R. Wolgemuth is Associate Professor of educational research at the University of South Florida, where she directs the Graduate Certificate in

Qualitative Research and serves as faculty advisor for the Student Organization for Qualitative Methodologies. Her research agenda focuses on ethics and validity in social science research. Drawing on critical, post-structural, and new materialist theories, she explores inquiry as an agential process that simultaneously investigates and creates lives and communities to and for which the researcher is responsible. Her qualitative work appears in journals such as *Qualitative Inquiry, Qualitative Research, Qualitative Health Research*, and *Educational Researcher*.

Preface

Questions frame research for social justice in multicultural contexts

Researchers are trained to ask questions that are worthy of inquiry. The focus in most research textbooks is on the development of research questions to guide data collection. In this unique contribution to qualitative research methodology, Anna CohenMiller and Nettie Boivin shift our gaze to questions that are foundational to good practice, especially when working in multicultural contexts with a goal of increasing social justice. The types of questions they ask prompt researchers to consciously assess their approach to research to avoid being complicit in sustaining an oppressive status quo and to rethink their roles as contributors to advance justice in marginalized and vulnerable communities.

CohenMiller and Boivin recognize the complexity and contextual situatedness of wrestling with questions that arise in research that attempts to advance justice. Their backgrounds, personal characteristics, and research experience lead them to describe challenges researchers face in many different marginalized communities, countries, and disciplines. Both authors are multiethnic and are from marginalized religious, ethnic, and cultural communities. For example, CohenMiller's family has roots in the Sephardic community (Spanish-Jewish), who were forced to flee their country during the Spanish Inquisition. Boivin comes from a mixed-race background including a francophone father in Quebec, a Chinese grandfather, and an Australian mother of color. Both CohenMiller and Boivin lived in a variety of countries and then found themselves drawn to working in Kazakhstan, raising children while conducting research in this multicultural context. They

Preface

extend the value of this book by including examples of qualitative studies that illustrate different aspects of research that focuses on promoting social justice. To add to the breadth of experience you will find in this book, they invited scholars from multiple disciplines and countries to share their reflections in their areas of expertise. One of the great strengths of this book is that the authors bring an ethical lens to the challenges that researchers encounter in research that focuses on socially just qualitative research in multicultural contexts that encourage inclusion and equity for communities who have been historically marginalized, colonized, and/or oppressed. They frame the book by raising questions about essential aspects of qualitative research: power, trust, insider/outsider status, crossing disciplinary boundaries, online engagement, transformative research, and arts-based research.

The issue of power in qualitative research has long been a topic of reflection. Who has power? How can researchers use their power in service to increase justice? How can studies be structured to consciously address power inequities? The authors identify these questions and discuss strategies researchers can use to engage in critical self-reflection while building relationships with community members. As part of that self-reflection, we are encouraged to challenge our own assumptions and stereotypes that come from our personal cultural lens. How do our own positionalities influence power sharing? Communities are not homogenous. How can researchers address intersectionality as a dimension of power? Working with participants, gatekeepers, and representatives of institutions with power such as governments, churches, and schools is part of the process. Acknowledging the privilege associated with Whiteness is relevant in most contexts. The call is for continuous self-reflection as well as seeking understanding of how we are perceived by community members. Other strategies to address power include creating teams of researchers that represent important characteristics of the community and using critical theoretical lenses such as feminist theory or Indigenous theories.

Trust is a second important issue in social justice research that follows on from addressing issues of power. The focus here is on questions such as: how can researchers build trust with participants and gatekeepers? What does trust mean in different cultural contexts? What strategies can be used to increase the trustworthiness of qualitative research? The importance of building trust is emphasized for social justice researchers premised on the belief that higher levels of trust will lead to more confidence in the results and use of those results to increase justice. Strategies are discussed, such as

xxiv

including cultural interpreters as part of the research team, member checks, peer debriefing, setting clear expectations, sharing data, and participatory data interpretation. A focus on social justice pushes researchers to engage with even more profound questions about who benefits from the research and how they benefit. How can I use my privilege to support agency for those with less privilege? How can we deal with situations in which we or our participants are exposed to risk?

The third topic examined in this book is the nature of the insider-outsider status of researchers. If I am an outsider in this community, I need to ask myself critical questions such as: how am I viewed by participants and stakeholders? How can researchers engage in co-construction of the research process and outcomes to avoid imposing their own cultural lenses on communities where they are outsiders? How important is matching specific identity markers such as race, ethnicity, and gender? Ethical issues arise when researchers assume that there is stronger similarity between themselves and participants than there is. Researchers need to allow the full story to emerge without making assumptions about their own understanding because of sharing similar experiences. Researchers should ask themselves: am I the right person to do this research, especially when they do not share a defining characteristic in a community, such as Indigeneity, disability, or deafness?

For me, key questions around research purportedly conducted to increase social justice and support transformative change are: why am I doing this research? Is giving voice to those who were previously silenced enough? How can I design my research so that it is transformative and contributes to increased social, economic, and environmental justice? It is important to acknowledge the synergy between environmental, economic, and social justice. Economic development can lead to increased jobs and poverty reduction. However, if environmental and social justice are not considered, an economic intervention can also lead to increased inequities and suffering. Researchers need to ask questions about structures and historical factors that support oppression. The researcher's role shifts to include that of social activist and to include community members as co-creators, co-researchers, and collaborators. Some designs, such as participatory action research and community-based participatory research, lend themselves to addressing issues of social, economic, and environmental justice. Researchers need to ask: how can I use these designs for transformative purposes? How do I address structural inequities, discrimination, and oppression? How can

Preface

I avoid being complicit in sustaining an oppressive status quo and contribute to transformative change?

The world is facing many wicked problems (i.e., those that are complex and for which there are no agreed-upon solutions). Problems such as the climate crisis, human rights violations, poverty, health care access, and conflict require reaching across disciplines to seek solutions. Because every discipline has a culture, working with groups that include multiple disciplines and communities that experience discrimination based on different characteristics multiplies the complexity in addressing these issues in a socially just way. Interdisciplinary work means researchers from different disciplines work together to intentionally integrate knowledge. Team members need to value diversity, be willing to understand their own and other's disciplinary cultures, and address power hierarchies. Competing priorities, cultural barriers, and organizational expectations further complicate this type of research. Researchers can ask themselves questions such as: which fields should I invite into my research study? Am I at risk of oversimplifying understanding a problem or a solution by taking a narrow uni-disciplinary approach? How do the assumptions associated with different philosophical paradigms influence our ability to work together respectfully?

Researchers have increasingly turned to the use of technology to take advantage of its potential to reach broader populations, record data, and disseminate results. The urgency of understanding the social justice implications of using technology has been increased by the COVID-19 pandemic, which began in 2019. The pandemic has heightened awareness of privilege and access in the use of technology. Questions arise about who is being included and excluded. How can issues of privacy be addressed? What differences does it make in which type of technology is being used (e.g., social media, texting, internet, discussion boards, virtual gaming worlds, forums, chatrooms)? How can communities of action be built using apps such as WhatsApp or texting or instant messaging groups? What is the comfort level with technology of different community members? How do participants understand privacy when they share through technology? Can researchers use publicly posted data without seeking permission or without awareness (e.g., Cambridge Analytics, Facebook)? Researchers need to consider potential adverse effects for participants from sharing their data, and from being exposed to hate speech, trolling, rude language, and threats. How can researchers conduct interviews, observations, or surveys in an ethical manner that addresses power differences? Guidelines for use of digital data

xxvi

are available, differ from country to country, and should be consulted before such data are used.

The final topic in the book is that of arts-based research and how to use it for social justice purposes. The use of arts-based strategies such as drawing, movement, video, music, photography, body mapping (drawing on a representation of the body), photovoice, poetry, storying, quilting, and weaving provide creative alternatives for data collection. This approach offers potential to provide opportunities for expression in communities in which language barriers might prevent inclusion. There are challenges in using this approach, such as: what if participants have anxiety about their lack of talent? How can participatory strategies, co-researchers, and co-producers be included? How can this approach to research focus on using research as a vehicle for social justice? From an ethical perspective, how can the researcher avoid imposing their own views and ensure that the research benefits the community? Performance and visual data also present challenges in terms of interpretation. This raises the age-old question: what is art?

CohenMiller and Boivin take us on a cognitive and emotional journey and provide us with an opportunity to reflect on important questions for researchers who work in multicultural contexts for social justice purposes. They provide insights from their own work, examples of other research, and reflections of experts. They acknowledge that there is no single correct answer to these difficult questions. However, they provide us with a body of literature and, through that, to a community of researchers who care about these issues. Appropriately, research is presented here as an ongoing reflective process with a community of kindred spirits where we can find support in our challenging times.

Donna M. Mertens, Gallaudet University

Acknowledgments

We would like to thank everyone who inspired, guided, encouraged, and offered insights. You have helped develop a text we hope will encourage critical self-reflection to speak to qualitative social justice research internationally. The process of writing this book has led us to more deeply see the community of qualitative researchers and the amazing way individuals come together with the goals of helping others and furthering social justice in research.

Thank you to those who have contributed *Reflections from the Field*, willingly sharing openly about your experiences and challenges faced in socially just qualitative research. It has been a pleasure to work with you: Tineke A. Abma, Agnes Atia Apusigah, Kakali Bhattacharya, Nadia Dresscher-Lambertus, Carolyn Ellis, Polina Golovátina-Mora, Roxanne Henkin, Tamsin Hinton-Smith, Patricia Leavy, Mashaba Mashala, Donna M. Mertens, Raúl Alberto Mora, Sharon M. Ravitch, Fatma F. S. Said, Nupur Samuel, Gopal Krishna Sharma, Purva Gopal Sharma, Akmaral Sman, Linda Tuhiwai Smith, and Jennifer R. Wolgemuth.

As we reflect further on the development of this book, we have a few words to share individually.

For Anna: Tracing the roots of this book, I am grateful for the early collaboration with Howard Smith when we developed a workshop for the first European Congress for Qualitative Inquiry, which provided a stepping-off point for this book. Thanks to that work I was discovered by Hannah Shakespeare, who became our insightful and dedicated editor who led us through the productive processes with reviewers and the full team at Routledge.

Acknowledgments

As we moved through proposal writing, thanks to a partnership between the Graduate School of Education at Nazarbayev University and the University of Pennsylvania, we had a chance to hear important critical reading suggestions from Matt Hartley and Peter Eckel on the proposal of this book and on the final manuscript, respectively. Others offering incredibly thoughtful feedback on the prepress manuscript included Samal Kadyrova, Donna M. Mertens, Sharon M. Ravitch, and Jennifer R. Wolgemuth. Thank you also to Donna, Jenni, and Patricia for their support and keen recommendations throughout the process, along with other valued guides, Valerie J. Janesick, Laura Perna, and Kathy Roulston.

Beyond the academic world, I consider the impact of personal networks and the home sphere, especially prevalent during a year of quarantine. Thank you to Catherine Hudgins for the ceaseless encouragement and support to find my voice, allowing me to explore new ideas and extend my work. For the steadfast care throughout the process across countries and even in lockdown, thank you to Douglas CohenMiller. Knowing he was available to listen, to help, and to create space was an irreplaceable form of help and love, thank you. And to my children, Elliot and Aurelia, I thank you for your example of growth and learning, from buoying my work in sitting next to me while working, offering ideas, and sharing special treats of love. I hope this book offers gentle guidance for making this world more equitable and inclusive for you and everyone.

For Nettie: I would like to thank the impetus and inspiration of my fellow colleagues who – through their support and modeling of ethical, socially responsible, and inclusive research practices – have paved the way for me in writing this book: my colleague Fatma Said, whose social justice and reflective practices inspire me; my research colleagues at Jyväskylä University, including Sari Sulkinen, Dmitry Leontov, and Sigurd D'hondt; and my co-research participants, Abdul, Hannele, Nael, Kamila, Jamilla, Sara, Ossi, Gloria, Somash, Mika, Ninna, and Tiina, who helped me with my research Building Bridges over the past three years. I would like to thank all the mothers, women, and families who over the years have shared, supported, and interacted with me and my research across the globe in Nepal, Japan, Guatemala, Malaysia, Singapore, the UK, Qatar, Finland, Canada, and Kazakhstan.

We are honored to have had the chance to bring together ideas and critical self-reflection about conducting research with participants and

xxix

Acknowledgments

communities to improve social justice and equity. In this process it has been incredible to feel immediate encouragement. As this book is particularly for those early in their careers, we thank you for your questions throughout the years and for fostering such a text. We encourage you to reach out to others – the qualitative research community is incredible and we look forward to hearing from you.

How is social justice foundational in qualitative research?
An introduction

As a researcher, have you ever wondered if you're doing your research **"right"**? *Have you ever wondered how many people you "need" to interview? Or maybe you have wondered about the "best" questions to ask your participants or sought out hoped to create the most effective way to gain your participants' trust?* If you are asking yourself such questions, you're on a good path. We know how that feels and have sought out answers. We have spent years exploring and addressing how to conduct qualitative research, how to engage with participants, and how to make research inclusive and equitable for communities to best voice their lived experiences. By asking questions of yourself and your research practice, you are being reflective and thoughtful about your qualitative inquiry and providing a means to make your research richer and more rigorous.

We often wish there were straightforward answers to these questions, as it could simplify our work. Yet, there aren't. And as it turns out, that's what makes qualitative research so rich. The responses will change depending on who you ask, when you ask them, and in what context or disciplinary field you approach the questions. For example, each year we review student ethics forms for conducting research for a program in education, commenting and providing feedback on potential ethical concerns. While we all work in the field of education, our viewpoints and backgrounds vary. For example, some faculty will notice potential risks with online communication, whereas others emphasize constraints with maintaining confidentiality. Both directions are important and valid. In other words, each of us has our own position and experience that can benefit our research. We can tap into these strengths by continuing to learn, ask questions, and reflect about ourselves and our research.

DOI: 10.4324/9780429285691-1

In this book, we focus on socially just qualitative research in multicultural contexts that encourage inclusion and equity for communities who have been historically marginalized, colonized and/or oppressed. We have benefited from those who have come before us in writing and thinking about researchers in diverse communities and multicultural contexts (Banks & McGee Banks, 2003; Court, 2017; Leavy & Harris, 2018; Mertens, 2020; Smith, 1999). For those who have been overlooked or silenced, as qualitative researchers we have an opportunity to help highlight and amplify voices of those glossed over. For qualitative researchers (here, we use the term broadly to also include ethnographic researchers) to work with others, it's essential to continually adapt and grow in awareness and critical self-reflection. So, **what is critical self-reflection?** Here's one perspective of the term that moves beyond reflecting on the past into a commitment to making positive change:

> *Critical self-reflection in qualitative research emphasizes reflecting on our work to purposefully become better researchers.*

Through such a reflective process, we have an opportunity to look at ourselves and our work. The process offers a chance to set aside judgment and become aware of where we are and where we want to go to move our research and practice in a constructive and beneficial direction.

Just as the way we define this term is not fixed, the ways we define **diversity** and **multiculturalism** can vary from a disciplinary perspective and region of the world. In some contexts, multicultural refers to differences in ethnicity, whereas in other contexts the emphasis may be linguistic or religious diversity presented as particularly salient. We consider multiculturalism as informed by the Canadian Rights and Freedoms Charter (2018), which reflects the cultural and racial diversity of society, acknowledging the freedom of all members of society to preserve, enhance, and share their cultural heritage. In this view, we see qualitative research across multicultural contexts as a step toward ensuring inclusivity and voice for all individuals that respects and values diversity. So, even within an outwardly *appearing* homogenous society can lie great variance of practice, perspective, and experience. For example, while residents may appear homogeneous based upon skin tone, multicultural aspects can remain, such as linguistic and ethnic differences. Becoming aware that our participants and communities

How is social justice foundational?

can present such varied experiences is fundamental to becoming a reflexive practitioner.

Other such differences that are not readily apparent include historical memory, such as experiences and family stories of forced migration and slavery. For example, centuries of colonialism affect countries around the world. Memories of fleeing one's homeland for fear of ethnic or religious retribution affect communities' lives today, and the process plays out today in other areas of the world. Because of these experiences and memories, participants' ability to be heard and seen in their community varies and requires a thoughtful, conscientious researcher.

In this book, we are using a multi- and interdisciplinary lens to raise awareness of multicultural contexts and also actual research practices. We explore the topics using questions to help us consider the dynamic internal and external issues confronted when working within and across multicultural contexts. The questions embedded throughout don't have specific answers, but instead are meant as jumping-off points for conducting socially just research and for the ways in which our steps are constantly evolving. From this perspective, we move beyond considerations of *culture* as a blanket term and instead unpack the multiple perspectives and identities increasingly experienced in a globalizing world.

Broadly then, our primary goals in sharing with you are the following:

1   To raise awareness of the multidimensional aspects of researching within/ across multicultural contexts through self-examination and reflection on the research process during planning and implementation.
2   To connect theoretical and conceptual concepts with practical in-field examples of qualitative research within/across multicultural contexts.
3   To encourage researchers to move beyond simple classifications of individual and community identification (e.g., culture, ethnicity, language, religion, gender), to better describe the complexity of the human experience.

As qualitative researchers, it's useful to think about our research and those we want to work with. As you read through these chapters, you will be encouraged to be critically reflexive as you are presented with real research and the challenges qualitative researchers have and are grappling when with working across multicultural contexts to create socially just inclusive and equitable research. Across the chapters, relevant issues of ethics are presented and offer ways to think deeper and more rigorously about your current or future research.

1. How is social justice foundational in qualitative research?

Social justice provides a framework throughout this book. Just as with large-scale questions, defining social justice does not have one "right" answer. For instance, your disciplinary perspective may emphasize social justice as equalizing economic and social distribution as key factors for social justice, such as by creating "equitable redistribution, knowledge, and empathy" (Salvador & Kelly-McHale, 2017, p. 7). Or for example, in counseling, an emphasis is placed on social justice as related to serving clients and "ending the silence about oppression" (Dollarhide et al., 2016). Social justice may also align with researchers focused on sustainable change through socio-cultural, transformative education (Rodriguez & Morrison, 2019), whether starting within the classroom or outside.

From the perspective of multicultural counseling, social justice includes six key themes: "(a) ongoing self-examination, (b) sharing power, (c) giving voice, (d) facilitating consciousness raising, (e) building on strengths, and (f) leaving clients with the tools for social change" (Goodman et al., 2004, p. 798). Researchers often emphasize the importance of *systemic change* as a foundational aspect of social justice (see Ratts, 2009). In this book, we integrate an interdisciplinary understanding of **social justice**:

> *Social justice in research is the purposeful commitment and advocacy to address systemic and systematic issues of equity and inclusion in particular for marginalized and oppressed peoples.*

In other words, social justice research can address inequities by actively engaging all participants, all of whom have a stake in the research, to the forefront of the discussion. This type of research can help unpack historical and current systems of injustice and instead place at the center of our work the essential nature of working, hearing, and amplifying the voices of diverse sets of communities, especially those who have been historically marginalized. This approach enables engagement to actively humanize and decolonize research (see Pak & Ravitch, 2021). Utilizing a social justice lens provides us with tools to widen our perspective to be open to seeing, understanding, and thus addressing inequalities in research and practice.

2. What can we expect in this book?

This book can help you find the voice and process that works best for your qualitative research project. Yet, it is not a textbook on *how* to conduct research. It won't detail the process of interviewing or conducting focus groups. Instead, we provide methodological approaches and address how power relations are overtly and covertly embedded in multicultural research contexts. You will have a chance to expand your awareness, to connect theoretical and conceptual concepts, and to be encouraged as researchers to move beyond simple understandings to complexity. Throughout, you will find questions embedded to encourage critical self-reflection for the dynamic nature of your research and the related answers. In this way, the questions can be used iteratively over time as you develop new awareness, insights, and experiences.

When you read through these chapters, you will have a chance to become more aware of having both unconscious and unintentional inherent perspectives and beliefs that can impact your research. There is the opportunity to reconsider and retrain ourselves, learning about ways as researchers we can undo and learn new ways of thinking and seeing. We highlight practices that have worked well and emphasize social justice and decolonial practices. Throughout the book, you will find questions embedded and at the end of each chapter to encourage and guide critical self-reflection and a deeper examination of socially just research practices.

You can read this book consecutively from beginning to end or you can skip around. The first four chapters emphasize broad theoretical and conceptual topics: power, trust, insider-outsiderness, and social justice and transformative research. The following three chapters then focus on more pragmatic approaches including crossing disciplinary teams, moving to online engagement, and using the arts with collaboration and co-production. The final chapter brings together the more theoretical and conceptual topics with practical applications. Incorporated is a current real-world example drawing from principles of the Black Lives Matter movement followed by a set of mindful reflective questions to inventory our growing research practices.

Throughout you will find certain words bolded, which will either be further defined in the glossary or listed in the index to see where it's discussed in other sections. We encourage you to enjoy and explore the topics and delve into those that speak most to your current interests or needs. You will see some common themes throughout the chapters, including an exploration of how power can be understood across multiple disciplinary perspectives within a multicultural and diverse research context. Embedded within each chapter are discussions around providing voice for communities. We focus on social justice emphasizing conducting research in multicultural contexts addressing issues of equity, diversity, and inclusivity, with attention to online research and ethics.

We want to encourage everyone to engage in qualitative research, to recognize your potential to effect positive change through helping voice the experiences, needs, and insights of multicultural communities around the globe. So, **how do we as qualitative researchers find our path forward in an increasingly diverse world?** A simple response is, we take it step by step and see what we can learn from others and where our growing awareness and critical self-reflection can enhance qualitative inquiry and social justice.

Organization of chapters. Each chapter's organization includes questions to guide the reading process, followed by theoretical or conceptual constructs, and *Reflections from the Field.* For these latter sections, we have invited both well-known and emerging scholars from around the globe to submit case studies and reflections on their work. Each chapter includes a discussion of aspects related to social justice, ethics, and online research, and ends with questions for critical self-reflection. The book includes the following chapters:

- Chapter 1: Owning Our Power
    - *Reflections from the Field* from Kakali Bhattacharya and from Polina Golovátina-Mora and Raúl Alberto Mora

- Chapter 2: Unpacking the Meaning and Practice of Trust
    - *Reflections from the Field* from Jennifer R. Wolgemuth and from Fatma F. S. Said

- Chapter 3: Uncovering the Spectrum of Insider-Outsiderness
    - *Reflections from the Field* from Linda Tuhiwai Smith and from Arceli Rosario

How is social justice foundational?

- Chapter 4: Awareness in Social Justice and Transformative Research
  - *Reflections from the Field* from Donna M. Mertens, from Tineke A. Abma, and from Nupur Samuel
- Chapter 5: Crossing Disciplinary Boundaries within the Research Team
  - *Reflections from the Field* from Agnes Atia Apusigah, from Akmaral Sman, and from Roxanne Henkin, Gopal Krishna Sharma, Purva Gopal Sharma, and Mashaba Mashala
- Chapter 6: Moving between Face-to-Face and Online Engagement
  - *Reflections from the Field* from Carolyn Ellis and from Tamsin Hinton-Smith
- Chapter 7: Integrating Arts with Co-creation and Co-production
  - *Reflections from the Field* from Patricia Leavy and from Nadia Dresscher-Lambertus
- Chapter 8: Applying Social Justice in Research and Practice in Multicultural Contexts
  - *Reflection from the Field* from Sharon M. Ravitch

3. What are the origins of this book? Sharing about ourselves

To give a bit more insight about ourselves, the following is a brief overview of our positionality, how we see the world, the disciplinary background that led to this work, and our experiential work. Within each chapter, we share some about our research as it relates to each topic. Broadly, we are both multiethnic from marginalized religious, ethnic, and cultural communities with an overt presence as motherscholars (CohenMiller, 2014, 2015, 2016, 2018; CohenMiller & Demers, 2019; Matias, 2011). We recognize the ways our identities can interrelate with our participants.

We are also both from fields in language and education, including from multi-perspectival disciplinary backgrounds. For example, Anna started her research with linguistics and anthropology, integrating multimedia and Spanish as key elements and expanding into multicultural education, identity, interdisciplinarity, and in-depth study of qualitative research, in particular, arts-based approaches to support voice. Nettie started with theatre, shifting to social justice and outreach theatre, language teaching overseas, psychology, literacy, and then ethnography of marginalized families, children, and communities (refugees, immigrants, multiethnic and multicultural contexts).

As Anna explains:

> If you were to just look at me, from appearances, you might say that I am a "White" or maybe "Hispanic" woman. To understand more, you could talk with me, learn where I grew up, see my identity, and perhaps how I developed my social justice, inclusion, and equity lenses. I am a Sephardic (Spanish-Jewish) cisgender woman. I pass as "White" in the US, but often felt like an outsider, having to prove to others who I was. I was frequently the only Jewish student in my class or workplace and regularly faced hearing, seeing, and experiencing discrimination. My history extends to the Spanish Inquisition, where stories were frequently told about our ancestors who had to flee the Iberian Peninsula as refugees, for fear of their lives. Another part of my family is also connected to oppression, avoiding persecution in Germany, Hungary, and Russia. Concerns over our safety and well-being about being "different" were, and are, realities. Today I am a mother of two young children, I speak Spanish to them and we have raised them Jewish. We live in Kazakhstan in Central Asia and we are exposed to Kazakh and Russian languages and over 100 nationalities in the country. These historical memories and current realities have led to my commitment to addressing issues of equity, inclusion, and social justice, and to the writing of this book.

And as Nettie explains:

> If you were to look at me, you would struggle to recognize the mixed-race religion, language, and background I grew up in and lived with as a transnational woman. I grew up in a less tolerant time in Canadian immigration policy. I lived through the Front de libération du Québec (a terrorist organization) and the marginalization of Quebeckers and of my francophone father. I saw my Chinese grandfather denied citizenship and was impacted by my mother experiencing the Australian color bar, which prohibited Asians from entering except with special permission; she was a Canadian-born citizen because her father was born in China. My multicultural experiences included celebrating Christmas, Ukrainian Christmas, New Year's Day, and

How is social justice foundational?

Chinese New Year. These lived experiences, along with living and sharing Chinese New Year in Malaysia, the UK, Canada, Kazakhstan, and Qatar, imbued a clear awareness and importance of food and multisensory discourse resource (MDR) analysis (Boivin, 2020a, 2020b), providing differences for transnationals and migrants. For the past 20 years I have taught, lived, and researched globally, including in Japan, Malaysia, Nepal, Qatar, Kazakhstan, the UK, Finland, and Canada. And I am a single mother of a biracial, bilingual, transnational child. The issues faced in living and working in multicultural contexts is deeply rooted.

This book emerged from questioning our thought processes and wondering, *How do I do my work better? How do I show or prove or provide evidence that I'm doing all I can to conduct socially just research with the communities I work with?* In working with master's and doctoral students, teaching research methods and guiding them through their research, these same questions bubbled up for many of them. They too wanted to know the recipe, the formula for doing good, ethical, socially just work. In working across communities worldwide, we were continually confronted with the fact that there was more to be said, learned, and shared about working across teams, especially in multicultural contexts.

We have eagerly engaged in writing this book and have learned a lot about ourselves as researchers in the process. Along the way, we have many people to thank for their contributions to the process of writing this book and affording us the time and space to deeply engage in such work. For those interested in staying in touch or with ideas for collaboration or comments, we welcome your thoughts and look forward to hearing from you. We hope you will enjoy the book and will likewise take the time to reflect on your own research process in an ever-globalizing multicultural world.

Together, our backgrounds highlight the journey we as researchers and authors took in creating and writing this book. They also illustrate that our positionality is intrinsically linked to an experiential background that favors inclusion, diversity, and social justice. We have a wide framework that integrates the fields of language, education, cultural anthropology, social justice, gender, and identity. We see that many researchers are inherently utilizing multidisciplinary perspectives. And through reflection, seeing others practice and bringing together diverse ideas and disciplinary perspectives, challenging questions can lead to socially just steps forward.

9

4. Adaptations as a result of the COVID-19 pandemic

While we were writing this book, the COVID-19 pandemic also hit the world. The pandemic affected many aspects of people's lives, including those conducting research. We saw the changes needed to adapt research for socially distanced qualitative inquiry. Our students conducting theses and dissertations found that their planned qualitative data collection would no longer work. Their observations, interviews, and focus groups were no longer possible in the same manner. For example, one of Anna's graduate students had planned to conduct interviews face-to-face but found herself in a countrywide quarantine that did not allow people to leave their homes easily. So, a solution was found – in this case, a simple one: to interview participants online using Zoom.

But for other students, the pandemic meant greater changes. For example, a graduate student planning to observe instructional practices (focusing on differentiated instruction, the practice of adjusting teaching to each student's varied learning needs) in secondary school found herself no longer able to enter the schools because of quarantine. Instead, the schools were teaching online and the class periods were now only 20 minutes long within a virtual classroom. The ability to observe interactions between educators and students was no longer possible. Even community observations were limited due to the restrictions. Instead, a new solution was found to refocus her thesis to emphasize and to help uncover best practices for differentiated instruction during the quarantine period. In this way, her thesis research focused on participants' voices and provide ideas and solutions for online teaching and learning – a topic of great importance. We discuss ways to think and reflect about conducting socially just online qualitative research, which can entail many embedded, interrelated aspects (e.g., anxiety, physical and mental health constraints, technology access). And in particular, due to the recent health crisis, the need is even more evident to address the potential of socially distanced research, and the interrelated issues of inequities and injustice, to continue being critically self-reflective to enhance socially aware and socially just qualitative research.

References

Banks, J. A., & McGee Banks, C. A. (2003). *Handbook of Research on Multicultural Education* (2nd ed.). San Francisco, CA: Jossey-Bass.

Boivin, N. (2020a). Multisensory discourse resources: Decolonizing ethnographic research practices. *Journal of Multilingual and Multicultural Development*. https://doi.org/10.1080/01434632.2020.1841215

Boivin, N. (2020b). Homescape: Agentic space for transmigrant families multisensory discourse of identity. *Linguistic Landscape Journal, 7*(1), 37–59. https://doi.org/10.1075/ll.19019.boi

Canadian Rights and Freedom Charter. (2018). Retrieved January 28, 2021, from www.justice.gc.ca/eng/csj-sjc/rfc-dlc/ccrf-ccdl/rfcp-cdlp.html

CohenMiller, A. S. (2014). The phenomenon of doctoral student motherhood/mothering in academia: Cultural construction, presentation of self, and situated learning [Doctoral dissertation]. University of Texas at San Antonio. ProQuest Dissertations Publishing.

CohenMiller, A. S. (2015). The Motherscholar Project. www.motherscholar.org

CohenMiller, A. S. (2016). Artful research approaches in #amwritingwithbaby: Qualitative analysis of academic mothers on Facebook. *LEARNING Landscapes, 9*(2). Special Issue, *Artful Inquiry: Transforming Understanding Through Creative Engagement, 9*(2), 181–196. https://doi.org/10.36510/learnland.v9i2.770

CohenMiller, A. S. (2018). Creating a participatory arts-based online focus group: Highlighting the transition from DocMama to Motherscholar. *The Qualitative Report, 23*(7), 1720–1735.

CohenMiller, A. S., & Demers, D. (2019). Conflicting roles of mother and academic? Exploring the use of arts-based self-care activities to encourage wellbeing. *Art/Research International: A Transdisciplinary Journal.* https://journals.library.ualberta.ca/ari/index.php/ari/article/view/29391

Court, D. (2017). *Qualitative Research and Intercultural Understanding: Conducting Qualitative Research in Multicultural Settings.* London, UK: Routledge.

Dollarhide, C. T., Clevenger, A., Dogan, S., & Edwards, K. (2016). Social justice identity: A phenomenological study. *Journal of Humanistic Psychology, 56*(6), 624–645. https://doi.org/10.1177/0022167816653639

Goodman, L. A., Liang, B., Helms, J. E., Latta, R. E., Sparks, E., & Weintraub, S. R. (2004). Training counseling psychologists as social justice agents: Feminist and multicultural principles in action. *The Counseling Psychologist, 32*, 793–837.

Leavy, P., & Harris, A. (2018). *Contemporary Feminist Research from Theory to Practice* (1st ed.). New York: Guilford Press.

Matias, C. E. (2011, April). *Paying it Forward: Mother Scholars Navigating the Academic Terrain.* Paper presented at the American Educational Research Association (AERA), New Orleans, LA, AERA Division G Highlighted Panel.

Mertens, D. M. (2020). *Research and Evaluation in Education and Psychology: Integrating Diversity with Quantitative, Qualitative, and Mixed Methods* (5th ed.). Sage.

Pak, K., & Ravitch, S. M. (Eds.). (2021). *Critical Leadership Praxis for Educational and Social Change*. New York: Teachers College Press.

Ratts, M. J. (2009). Social justice counseling: Toward the development of a fifth force among counseling paradigms. *Journal of Humanistic Counseling, 48*, 160–172.

Rodriguez, A. J., & Morrison, D. (2019). Expanding and enacting transformative meanings of equity, diversity and social justice in science education. *Cultural Studies of Science Education, 14*, 265–281. https://doi.org/10.1007/s11422-019-09938-7

Salvador, K., & Kelly-McHale, J. (2017). Music teacher educator perspectives on social justice. *Journal of Research in Music Education, 65*(1), 6–24. https://doi.org/10.1177/0022429417690340

Smith, L. (1999). *Decolonizing Methodologies: Research and Indigenous Peoples*. London, UK: Zed Books.

Tran, T. V., Rhee, S. Y., & Shen, C. (Eds.). (2016). *Research Methods & Data Analysis for Multicultural Social Work and Human Services*. San Diego, CA: Cognella Academic Publishing.

Owning our power

What exactly is my power in a research study? How can I negotiate and mediate it in the research process? Many people haven't thought about these questions directly. As researchers, we are powerful. Therefore, we can reflect on the notion that the choices we make involve consequences for those we work with. For instance, have you ever filled out a survey and wondered what would happen with your answers? Maybe you have feelings of worry, curiosity, or general interest. Have you ever wondered if somebody might share the information you post online in ways that make you feel uncomfortable or vulnerable? Our potential participants could be feeling the same way. So, what do we do about that? **How do we help our participants feel better, feel as relaxed and comfortable as possible, feel okay to participate in a study with us?** The answers come from building a relationship based on a space of agency and voice that is not one-sided. Instead of researchers taking information from participants, we can work *with* participants. In critically self-reflecting, we have opportunities to conduct research differently – to enter into a socially just process involving, for instance, a dialogical process that is a two-way reciprocal relationship of co-creating, co-implementing, and sharing knowledge.

As socially aware qualitative researchers, it's important to be mindful of power imbalances. For instance, Western researchers have institutionalized embedded colonial power. The institution of academia contains embedded power structures. English-speaking Western academics maintain greater status than non-Western institutional researchers. And non-academic researchers, such as social justice artists or Indigenous researchers, are marginalized outside the institutional machine and the direct access to funding, policy makers, and other forms of power typically embodied in Western academia.

DOI: 10.4324/9780429285691-2

So, we can work toward becoming more aware. Despite our decolonizing or social justice–minded intentions, the invisible hierarchy of universities still binds us (Bell & Pahl, 2018). As we increase our awareness and critical self-reflection, we can better adapt ourselves to the communities we seek to serve.

Thus, we can also improve our understanding of participants and community needs, in contrast to applying external ideas and assumptions. Imagine this scenario about making assumptions. One day you walk out of your home and trip, falling gently to the ground. It just so happens that when you lost your footing, you put your hands down and got dirt on them. As you are brushing the dirt off your hands, someone sees you with dirty hands and now clothes that are a bit muddied. What might they think of you at that moment? Maybe they can deduce you had just fallen. Perhaps they offer to help. Or perhaps they think you don't know how to keep yourself clean, or that you don't have enough money to buy new clothes, or – more extreme – that you don't have clean water to wash with.

While this is a hypothetical story, we as researchers may enter a new environment and make assumptions about the community. We have an idea of what *they* need. Yet, the goal is to become aware that we make assumptions and inferences all the time. These are based on embedded normative values, beliefs, and practices from growing up in specific cultures and societies. So, how do we see assumptions and listen instead to the voices of those we want to work with? This chapter can enable us to become proactively aware of these assumptions to avoid them.

Fieldwork in itself is personal, and our positionality (e.g., gender, class, ethnicity) plays a role, as external and internal experiences shape who we are (Palaganas et al., 2017, p. 428). By moving away from the traditional role of objective investigator, we can embrace our position in the academic institutional structure and address any "conflicting responsibilities as researchers/protectors and activists/exposers" (Baez, 2002, p. 36). For instance, Foucault (1982) reminds us that power is not an object of possession that can be traded or given to individuals or groups; instead, it exists within relations, including those between individuals and groups. Power is an inherent aspect of researching in a multicultural, globalized context. It's not just the power of the policies, laws, ideologies, and practices but the relationship between the researcher, community, individual participant, and the intent of the research aim and objectives. Therefore, being aware of power differences between individuals and communities, organizations, institutions, cultures, communities, and societies is central when researching multicultural contexts.

So, what do we do? **How do we embrace our research while appropriately recognizing our power?** *And how can we best negotiate and mediate the effects of our power?* Let's take a step back to understand what it means to negotiate and mediate power. Here's one way to define these concepts for research:

- *Negotiating our power as a researcher is an ongoing process of critical self-reflection to understand ourselves relating to those we work with.*
- *Mediating our power as a researcher is an iterative process (one that occurs again and again) to try to reduce adverse effects of an imbalance of power.*

While negotiating and working to mediate our power between the expectations of funding bodies and participants' needs in diverse contexts, it's useful for qualitative researchers to purposefully critically self-reflect and push for participant agency and voice to overcome power structures. Until recently, qualitative researchers have struggled with who owns the knowledge from research (Lepore et al., 2020; Court & Abbas, 2013).

Overall, this chapter deals with concepts stemming from the idea of owning our power. Power relationships change as we relate to other stakeholders, whether with other researchers, participants, community members, or institutional members. Other topics within the chapter highlight trends in emancipatory research and decolonizing knowledge to facilitate participant voice in multicultural contexts (Mertens, 2020). For example, when researching with children, there are necessary steps to consider to avoid imposing adult concepts and theories, thus impeding children's voices (Robson & McCartan, 2016).

As you read, you can learn about power as a concept and how disciplines have explored it from theoretical and practical approaches. In an era of globalization, transnationalism, and multiculturalism, we want to develop skills to not inadvertently use our power against others, whether in face-to-face or online interactions. You will hear from researchers about their negotiation with power and ownership of it. Overall, this chapter explores how we, as qualitative researchers in multicultural, multilingual, and diverse contexts, can confront our power head-on. One such direction involves learning to critically reflect on our **positionality** and address our own power ethically.

1. How can we understand the changing nature of power?

Power infiltrates research and our lived worlds, affecting each of us and our interactions with one another. So, **what is power?**

> *Power is a concept, a cultural construct, and a process that affects interactions and relationships with others.*

Most academics study within a particular discipline that provides ideas and definitions about the world. In anthropology, for instance, the field associates power with two different schools of thought: one stemming from Franz Boas's concept of cultural anthropology in the United States and one from British social anthropology. Power is an inclusive part of the cultural construction of society and was often not discussed systematically (Duranti et al., 2003). In the British concept of social anthropology, power focused on "social order and this implied a special interest in social forces like political power" (Schoenmakers, 2012, p. 49). And yet, we can move beyond a purely disciplinary perspective in how we define and understand power in qualitative research, as Bhattacharya (2020) suggests in "hybridized interdisciplinary work." (We will further discuss crossing disciplinary boundaries in Chapter 5.)

Power is particularly noticeable when we are confronted by difference. For instance, a researcher conducting a study with young children who are also homeless would immediately notice an age difference and status difference. Other differences, though, may be less noticeable. One of our first steps as socially just researchers is to become aware of our power. We can ask ourselves what our relationship is to other people and institutions. We can ask ourselves what our relationship is to the communities we participate in and research within. For instance, you can think about your own life and ask yourself, **do I have a role where others look up to me? In my family, school, or workplace?**

Now think about stereotypes about where you live (e.g., region of the world, country, city, area of town). Are these **stereotypes** positive, negative, neutral? In what ways? You can think about how you present yourself. **What do other people tend to think when they see you?** Think here about how you present your gender, what your height suggests, or your skin tone as some ways to start thinking about your positionality and power within a community. By continually asking ourselves questions relating to the concept of power, we are taking steps in understanding, negotiating, and meditating challenges of power in qualitative research.

2. Do we understand ourselves?

Our background, the purpose of our research, and our agenda, affects our research. Another way to say this is that our **positionality** influences inquiry and those we work with. For qualitative researchers, particularly those working in multicultural, multilingual, and diverse communities, there are significant assets to expanding upon the research from the past to be aware of their positionality both as individual and group researchers. Our positionality, which includes our gender identity, class, and ethnicity, continually plays a role, as we are shaped by external and internally personal experiences (Palaganas et al., 2017, p. 428). As qualitative researchers, we can aim to understand ourselves and our positionality. Many qualitative researchers will attempt to "identify with a group based on shared experience, gender, sexuality, ethnicity, race, and so on. This issue confronts both researchers who are members of the group they are studying and those who are not, for there are costs and benefits to each status" (Baez, 2002, p. 57). As we better understand ourselves and our positionality, our research can also improve.

Researcher positionality cannot be separated and objective from the research process. Instead, as Palaganas et al. (2017) mention, it's important to remain in constant dialogue with participants, and to challenge perspectives and assumptions both of the social world and oneself. However, this will not always be easy. While some qualitative researchers may aim to present a position of **objectivity**, many have argued this is not realistic. The lives participants are living are not objective. Research conducted in communities inherently deals with topics, issues, and challenges that consciously or unconsciously contain moments of emotionality or affect. Therefore, we must be aware of this subjectivity and open to negotiating the messy moments of life.

For example, during Nettie's two-year collaborative arts–based ethnography, Building Bridges (Boivin, 2018), there was an unexpected moment of emotion. Nettie explains that when Sofia, a transitory migrant (without residency) participant, explained how to make an Iranian food dish, she began to cry. The translator, Shania, eventually asked why she was sad and they spoke for a while. Then Shania informed us that Sofia was remembering her brother and how he used to love her cooking; she was remembering people she had lost. This moment was emotional, and a powerful example of allowing a participant to feel their truth. Again, it was a moment of "messiness" in qualitative research. As a researcher, we can negotiate our power to allow emotions to exist, not to contain or infer from them, but instead to care for the participant (van der Riet, 2012).

Not only can understanding our positionality help us with research but so too does becoming aware of our **bias**. Power and bias go hand in hand. While quantitative researchers may aim to have no bias, qualitative researchers tend to see the importance of recognizing that we all have bias due to growing up in a particular society and culture (Duranti et al., 2003). Bias is a natural component of being human that can either lead us to become more self-aware or, if not explored, to negatively affect others. For example, within feminist scholarship we could examine the increasing identification of race, class, and gender as closely intertwined and see how forms of stratification need to be studied in relation to each other (Dervin, 2012). Such an understanding occurs through co-encouraging and co-interaction of all individuals. It suggests and even requires us to consciously remain reflexive throughout the research process with all those involved. In this process, stakeholders can become aware of the multiple categories that exist in and around power and positionality to promote inclusiveness.

As researchers, we want to keep the notion of **intersectionality** in mind when developing research relationships related to multicultural groups, particularly those that are marginalized or oppressed. We can ask ourselves: What are the intersections of race, ethnicity, gender, age, ability, sexual orientation to consider for the people I want to interact with? **How can I better understand the intersections of those I want to develop a relationship with?**

Within intersectionality there are many layers. For example, an Australian Muslim researcher who identifies as a White woman may want to study a community of Middle Eastern Muslim women in the same country. On the surface, the study would require understanding various religious, socioeconomic, and perhaps political and historical backgrounds. On deeper reflection, it would also be useful to recognize that while religious background provides similarities, there are privileges the researcher embodies in a culturally global position. Thus, when conducting qualitative research with those of apparent similar background and experience – in our backyard (Galam, 2015) and home institution (Malone, 2003) – it's useful to ask yourself, **what experiences do we share, what varies, and where are the commonalities?**

Intersectionality signifies the importance of including the perspectives of those who are marginalized at multiple levels, such as women of color. Intersectionality looks beyond the individual levels of inequality and instead recognizes how numerous aspects (e.g., gender, ethnicity, ability) multiply inequity (Choo & Ferree, 2010, p. 131). We can look to gender theory as an example of theorizing of the intersection of multiple inequalities. In feminist research, for example, many have moved toward the theoretical recognition of the importance of the intersection of various inequalities, although there remain significant differences as to how this should proceed (Alexander-Floyd, 2012; Collins, 1998; Windsong, 2018; Yuval-Davis, 2006). Intersectionality uses concepts such as cosmopolitanism (Beck & Sznaider, 2006), multiculturalism (Phillips, 2009; Berry, 2013; Vora et al., 2019), hybridity (Gilroy, 2004), and identity and nationalism (McLeod, 2020). The notion of intersectionality highlights that research is a process that is not fixed or structured but rather a daily, shifting, fluid process. As a qualitative researcher, it's valuable to co-construct research and raise questions. The goal, then, is to remove inequalities for participants, to hear their voices better.

3. Who has the power?

While researchers hold power by being in that role, there is also power of those who are part of a study – stakeholders. **Participant power** is embodied through such directions as controlling entrance into their world. Sometimes the potential participant is choosing their participation. At other times, they are acting as a **gatekeeper**, making decisions about the inclusion of a whole community. The struggles with balancing power must include allowing participants to own their unique role in the power relationship. It's important to consider who to include within a study. You have an opportunity throughout the research process to help nourish the legitimization of participants' power. For instance, are you conducting a study within a school? Perhaps you want to talk to teachers about their practice. Have you thought about how to incorporate the leadership, administration, students, parents, or others involved at the school? Perhaps you're conducting a study within another

Owning our power

type of community. You can then ask yourself, **who is being prioritized in terms of nation-states, language, and culture?**

Institutional power can be seen in many ways, such as how governments identify power and provide labels about groups of people. Today, it's recognized that researching in multicultural contexts requires working *with* the community instead of *on* them. The importance of researching *with* others is central to qualitative research, delineating a process forward to conduct inclusive research. As a related sidenote, Anna reflected on a recent talk she had with her nine-year-old about research, explaining the difference between researching *with* versus researching *on* or *about*. She explains:

> My child wanted to understand more, so I asked them, "Imagine a researcher wants to understand what it's like to be a kid today. What if they didn't talk to any kids?" My child was surprised. "That doesn't make any sense! The researcher should talk to kids to understand us." Absolutely. If you want to understand the lived experiences – thoughts, ideas, perspectives, experiences – of other people, it's important to hear their voice and unpack what is important to them.

It's not just the power of the researcher, policies, laws, ideologies, and practices, but also the relationship between the researcher, community, individual participant, and the intent of the researcher that informs who has power. Recognizing inequality is a first step to see the nature of the relationship between yourself as a researcher and those you want to work with. Imagine you are an able-bodied person and want to study infrastructure in city parks for those with a physical disability. **What types of inequalities do you see in connection to your community and your potential participants?** Inequality needs to be realized and reflected on before unpacking the nature of the relationship between stakeholders' unequal social relations. Therefore, being aware of power differences between individuals and communities, organizations, institutions, cultures, communities, and societies is essential when embarking on research in multicultural contexts.

4. What's privilege got to do with it?

Power stems from position and privilege. There are various forms of privilege – such as economic, political, and social (ethnicity, race, religion, identity) – which shift and change depending upon the culture, community, and society. For example, those who identify as women are in a lower position than those who identify as men in most Western societies. However, in those same societies, being a woman of color is yet a lower status than a White woman. Evidence of the privilege of being one race or gender versus another can be demonstrated by looking at the wage gap, especially as related to people of color. In the United States, women on average earn 82 percent of what men make, with the intersectionality of gender and race compounding the inequality. Black women in the United States earn 63 percent of what non-Hispanic White men make (AAUW, n.d.). Regardless of one's positionality in society, we must acknowledge, understand, and negotiate around our researcher privilege and power. The subject of race, a socially constructed concept, has deep roots and consequences drawing from such massive structures as colonialism and capitalism.

Across disciplinary perspectives, power and privilege are discussed and addressed in different ways. For example, in education, one approach may discuss inclusivity and diversity in the classroom and potentially draw connections to the "homescape" (Boivin, 2020). Those in education may research from social justice positions and may examine curriculum and policy documents and how these negate voice for students and communities. Sociologists and anthropologists tend to view the wider socioeconomic and political aspects within their studies (De-Sardan, 2005). Consequently, when researching from a particular field, it's significant to understand the configuration of power for our own disciplines.

Whiteness in itself is a power structure that's useful to recognize in research. For instance, McClaren (2000) explains it this way:

> Whiteness in the United States can be understood largely through the social consequences it provides for those who are considered to be nonwhite. Such consequences can be seen in the criminal justice system, in prisons, in schools, and in the boardrooms of corporations.
>
> (p. 150)

Such power structures play key roles when we think about our own power and working with others across and within multicultural contexts. Whiteness is a sociohistorical power identity, constructed during the intersection of capitalism, colonial rule, and the emergent relationships among dominant and subordinate groups (Collins et al., 2009; Grosfoguel, 2002; Leonard,

2016). Being othered suggests being treated economically, politically, and socially in obstructive ways to a person's life. In other words, those who are othered experience a "politics of difference" (Dervin, 2012). As a qualitative researcher, for example, going into the field as a White English speaker can create linguistic difficulties when researching in non-English-speaking communities. Yet this same status can at times prompt a hierarchical position that promotes access. For example, in Adu-Ampong and Adams's (2020) study in Ghana and Malawi, the community members looked to see if the researchers could be allowed access. In their case, community members reviewed their status. The researchers' use of local language practices and their enrollment in international universities helped provide outward articulation of their credibility to conduct research. Therefore, certain power identities can often unfold an invisible cloak of privilege, one that we can work toward becoming more aware of in our qualitative inquiry in multicultural contexts. So, you can ask yourself, **what types of power do I embody?** *And how might these be useful or harmful in working with others?*

5. How do we become more aware and reflective?

In conducting qualitative research in multicultural contexts, **reflexivity** is a useful tool to understand ourselves, the research process, and our effects on others. In the development of postmodernism (Boswell, 2020), the notion of reflexivity became central. Some researchers view reflexivity as sociological **praxis** (Shadnam et al., 2020), while others emphasize introspection and subjectivity (Hesse-Biber, 2017, p. 17). As a concept and process (Dowling, 2006), reflexivity is a relevant and "elusive" aspect of qualitative research (Palaganas et al., 2017, p. 427). As qualitative researchers, we can work toward being willing to critically think about this ongoing process of how our research participation affects the outcome.

Reflexivity is the concept and process of critical self-reflection to better understand ourselves and our effects on the research process.

We can recontextualize reflection and assess our role and the project outcomes in terms of *future learning,* instead of using the language of extremes such as good or bad, and success or failure. By reevaluating and applying future learning, we can reposition our relationship with participants not in static, fixed outcomes but in inclusive, collaborative, and constructive positions.

For qualitative researchers, better understanding their participants can occur through self-reflexive practices (Athanases et al., 2019). Therefore, to create a more intersectional research process, we can use a methodology that pushes past a comparative view of each participant at a particular fixed time and see the fluidity of experience and identity. Reflexivity can be conceptualized in various forms, such as from a position of epistemological or a feminist approach. By centering on theoretical assumptions or gender experiences, as researchers we would want to reflect on who we are, where we come from, where we want to go, and with whom will we take the journey (Palaganas et al., 2017, pp. 429–430). Reflexivity and awareness of outcomes, such as continuously working toward a fair distribution of results and benefits in a transparent and fair manner, offers a step to maintain ethical standards. We can check and recheck our commitment to the study and the participants by asking ourselves questions. There are multiple forms of reflexive research practice, including personal, epistemological reflexivity, critical, and feminist.

In **personal reflexivity**, as researchers, we can focus on contemplating our belief systems, political values, and other perspectives. From this perspective, we would understand that research is interpreted, analyzed, and even collected in ways informed by beliefs and prior experiences. You could ask yourself such questions relating to personal reflexivity as, *who am I? What are my intentions?* In **epistemological reflexivity**, there is an emphasis on constant reflection and reviewing of personal assumptions and theoretical influence (Ackerly & True, 2010). You could ask yourself such questions relating to epistemological reflexivity as, *is this process ethical for all? How does my background help me understand the participants (e.g., what do we share in common)?*

In **critical reflexivity**, we would emphasize recognizing that the production of knowledge is entrenched in sociopolitical and cultural contexts. We would then work to unravel such political and social construction within the research. You could ask yourself such questions relating to critical reflexivity as, *whose knowledge is being validated? Am I respecting the participants' expertise?* In **feminist reflexivity**, we can work toward reciprocity in research, highlighting how gender-based differences shape the research process (Palaganas et al., 2017). You could ask yourself such questions relating to feminist reflexivity as, *does my research enable equality, equity, and inclusion? Am I aware of whose identity is involved in the process? Does the research perspective encourage awareness of marginalized voices?*

How then can qualitative researchers utilize reflexivity as a tool to create more inclusive research projects? As qualitative researchers, we can consider the power and privileges we have, especially in working in multicultural contexts. Privilege in and of itself is not something to be ashamed of, but instead is often a matter-of-fact aspect of life. However, if we do not acknowledge our privileges, such as economic, ethnic, political, and cultural powers, then we're doing a disservice to our research participants, our project, and even ourselves.

6. How can we rebalance power dynamics?

There are several research paradigms supporting working in multicultural contexts. Positioning oneself provides metacognitive awareness regarding the power relationship with participants. For instance, there are **non-positivist paradigms** (e.g., post-positivism, constructivism, critical theory, postmodern). These paradigms, such as in constructivism, view research knowledge as co-produced between participant and researcher (Murdoch, 2001; Duff, 2002). The invisible barrier or "fourth wall" (Boivin & Cohen-Miller, 2018) of objectivity between research and subject is blurred, and control over the research narrative is increasingly a co-constructed, shared relationship (Gergen, 2000). While we discuss co-production in depth in Chapter 7, it's noteworthy to discuss the relationship of research design incorporating co-production to power as well. In this connection between researcher and participant, there is a need to balance developing a relationship, such as negotiating research with friends as a form of research method (CohenMiller & Demers, 2018; Hesse-Biber & Leavy, 2006). Moreover, in researching with refugees whose life context is tenuous and can shift at any moment, consistently checking in with them and ourselves, asking ourselves questions about our awareness of our position in relation to participants is quite relevant. Researchers can often feel the emotional pain and loss experienced by a participant when receiving such news as a decree to return to their home country.

The choice of research design can act as a means to **decentralize power**, or conversely, to emphasize power hierarchies (Mertens, 2020).

It might be part of a methodological strategy to consider how a design will denaturalize hegemonic relations, particularly by drawing attention to the unmarked categories where power and class clusters, thus creating research methodologies that work to decolonize the institutional structural inequalities in the global hierarchies, which serve to continue a global narrative of misrepresentations perpetuating social injustices (Smith & Smith, 2018).

An example of a research design to decentralize power is duo-ethnography (Lund & Nabavi, 2008; Meier & Geldenhuys, 2017). In duo-ethnography, two or more researchers work in tandem to critically juxtapose stories from their lives in relation to a similar phenomenon, creating a process of inter-rogation – not reification – of personal critical sites or socially relevant issues such as race, ethnicity, and sexuality (Meier & Geldenhuys, 2017, p. 1). Another approach to build rapport is to use our own stories when talking with participants to encourage empathy and "foster" openness (Berger, 2001). Or, for instance, when researching across a multicultural context, a team of individuals with varied backgrounds that align with the community can encourage trust through discussion and address multiple perspectives and language backgrounds (Boivin et al., 2014; CohenMiller et al., 2017).

Mixed race or mixed ethnic teams may deliberately construct and create sociocultural capital that balances power differences and can enhance the overall research process (Lund & Nabavi, 2008). (A further discussion of integrating views from across perspectives and disciplines can be found in Chapter 5.) In such multicultural and multilingual groups, there will likely be multiple decisions to be made. For instance, *how am I presenting myself, such as in linguistic register (e.g., academic, personal)?* As a dynamic social circumstance, there is no fixed way forward but regular decisions and adaptations (Grosjean, 2015; Meier & Geldenhuys, 2017, p. 8).

The choice of research designs can enhance participation or marginalize certain groups. There are several types of research paradigms aiming to shift power relationships. (More can be read about some of these research practices in Chapter 7, which addresses social justice and transformative research.)

1   *Decolonizing research* is an approach used to challenge Eurocentric research methods that undervalue, underrepresent, and overlook local knowledge and experiences of marginalized communities (Smith, 2013).

2 *Feminist research* (including intersectional, postmodern/poststructural-ist, and multiracial **feminism**) has a dual objective to seek new knowledge and contribute to social change (Hamad, 2020; Christensen & Jensen, 2012).
3 *Rights-based research* focuses on a core emphasis with respect to the human rights of participants during the research process (Pittaway et al., 2010).
4 *Participatory research* recognizes that people have expert knowledge and deep insight into their own lives (Wallerstein et al., 2020).

Power is not an object of possession that can be traded or given to individuals or groups; instead, it exists within relations, including those between individuals and groups. Understanding our power is central in researching in multicultural, globalizing/globalized contexts. Multiple theories and paradigms exist that address power and research. For instance, a critical theory paradigm speaks to central concepts of power, specifically transformation, emancipation, restitution, and critique (Guba & Lincoln, 2005).

From a **postmodern** perspective, a researcher may attempt to illustrate the power structure and push past traditional normative structures (Stewart et al., 2020). In postmodernism, the emphasis is on understanding the researcher's context (gender, class, ethnicity, etc.) as part of narrative interpretation (Angrosino, 2005). We can then acknowledge the power relationship we have with participants and seek to become vulnerable as a step toward speaking to issues of social justice, such as in academia (Bhattacharya, 2015; Diversi & Moreira, 2016). We can then aim to overcome "traditional" power roles of the unbiased, "objective" researcher and "subject." Understanding relationships between different social groups and between projects that shape each other are important (Walby et al., 2012, p. 225). Thus, instead of seeking objectivity, as a qualitative researcher, you can work toward uncovering your positionality, seeing inequality, and working toward equitable and inclusive research in multicultural contexts with *participants*, whether in your community or much further afield. So, you can ask yourself, **how does your positionality affect the power relationship in your research (think about positive, negative, and neutral effects)?**

7. Are my practices amplifying or diminishing voice?

How do we balance our need to assess objective data and our desire to be more inclusive? Balancing all modes inherent in communication rather than valuing language over other modes of communication is a progressive step (Pennycook, 2018). Language is power, and the language of Western academics tends to benefit the colonizers rather than the colonized (Atalay, 2006; Denzin et al., 2008; Gill et al., 2012; Smith, 1999, 2013; Swadener & Mutua, 2008). Observations investigating questions of who, how, and why often contain unconscious inferences and biases of marginalized, colonized, and underrepresented groups/people (Denzin et al., 2008). Among many researchers, there is an attempt to create agency for all participants (Latour, 2004). For example, until recently, qualitative researchers have struggled with the issue of who *owns* the knowledge emerging from research participants, such as in an interview (Court & Abbas, 2013).

A research approach not fully embracing agency and voice of the participants can create a false narrative from the results – a narrative that researchers control, not the participants. This "helicopter" (superficial) research approach is in many cases unintentional, yet it still must be addressed (Knoblauch, 2005). While navigating between the expectations of funding bodies (rigorous scientific control, objectivity, social impact in outcomes) and participants' needs in diverse contexts, qualitative researchers can aim toward meta-cognitively and reflectively pushing for agency and voice, and to overcome power structures for participants and communities. You can ask yourself, *am I trying to spend time to discover the truth, or trying to just conveniently obtain data?*

Many cultures perceive **colonization** as a continual experience (Smith, 2013). For instance, for many Indigenous peoples, colonialism is still ingrained within institutions (Smith, 2013). Therefore, at present, we are not in a post-colonial period and must consider invisible and embedded institutional mechanisms that create power gaps and inequalities when working across and within cultures. Researching in a cultural context you are not familiar with is possible, but often requires in-depth learning about the community first (Alfred & Corntassel, 2005). For example, in working with Indigenous communities, it's critical to recognize how societal and relational networks are shaped (Snipp, 1989, p. 322). As researchers, then, we would want to view power relationships through the lenses used in the multicultural context we are exploring in order not to impose our conceptualizations on others (Davidson-Hunt, 2006).

Often researchers enter a community with good intentions regarding facilitating and raising awareness of how groups are marginalized. However, sometimes intentions and outcomes get lost if we forget the past, glossing over historical and systemic abuse that has occurred in underrepresented communities. We may unwittingly treat a marginalized community as "needing our help," or we may have forgotten or missed unpacking important shifts in historical and political discourse and practices. For example, those who had durable states prior to conquest and colonization, such as the Mongolian peoples, or who fight for modern state recognition, such as the Kurdish diaspora (in modern-day Turkey, Syria, and Iraq), can be classified as ethno-nationalists rather than Indigenous peoples.

Global colonial powers have attempted to marginalize Indigenous communities by imposing political/legal policies often at odds with Indigenous practices. Language has created and perpetuated class divides across societies, creating "linguicism" (Flores & Rosa, 2015) that embodies inherent power relationships. Therefore, the institutions may indirectly or directly impose normative practices aimed at diminishing the narratives of Indigenous. Thus ethnic identity, embedded racism, and language intersect and further complicate power dynamics and deepen biases (Flores & Rosa, 2015).

8. What ethical dilemmas should we be prepared for relating to power?

Ethical dilemmas permeate the heart of socially aware qualitative research. We can continually ask and critically reflect on how best to approach an interaction, a relationship, a partnership, or a community – ethically. For instance, there are fundamental aspects of power to consider when working across and within cultures regarding intercultural communication (Phipps, 2013) and when we move from face-to-face to online environments. (We discuss more about engaging online for qualitative research in Chapter 6.)

The following list provides some key points to consider, with some questions being quite concrete and others requiring deep introspection:

1   *Are there incongruities in power relationships of micro-ethics of equality* (Thompson, 2012) in the research relationship and the macro context? For example, in medical institutions or educational institutions where researchers have inherent power and privilege, what inequalities exist if the researcher is a doctor and the participant a patient?
2   *What data am I sharing with whom, and for what purpose?*
3   *Am I reinterpreting the data analysis based on participants' review of initial findings?*
4   *What terms am I using to classify or identify participants?* Who determined these terms? For example, the language utilized in labeling and identifying participants creates an ethical dilemma. Are we describing the person we have interviewed as informer, subject, participant, co-researcher, co-participant, or collaborator? Each of the terms to describe participants carries a differing description of power and implications for disciplinary and cross-disciplinary research.
5   *Have we taken into account the sociocultural significance of the different types of informed consent?* For instance, are we researching within a cultural context where fluid and continually informed consent is needed? Or are we in a context where signing a written informed consent would challenge participation, whereas oral informed consent would allow for ease of sharing experience?

One way to further wrap our minds around ethics is to become literate in **societal ethics**, which helps us see our positionality. Through these steps, we can work to understand concepts such as hegemony, cultural hegemony, structural inequality, and various other types of power. Societal ethics supports all stakeholders to have space to participate in change toward more inclusivity, social justice, and equality (Brown, 2006). Hegemony is a commonly understood and accepted practice allowing certain people to maintain power in a culture (Thompson, 2012). **Cultural hegemony** is the dominant powers' control achieved by spreading beliefs, assumptions, and values through social institutions, such as schools, churches, courts, and cultural media (Gramsci, in Ransome, 1992). These institutions socialize people through embedded normative practices of dominant social group practices, such as celebrating Christmas or Father's Day. Knowledge of these ideas as embedded practices and norms can help qualitative researchers become aware of our position within a dynamically changing landscape. By exploring these ideas, we can start to see new insights about ourselves and those around us.

Yet, there are still issues to address globally. As some Indigenous researchers and scholars point out, there are concerns about how to decentralize power and be post-colonial and modern if a large portion of the global population still exists in a colonial structure (Denzin et al., 2008; Smith & Kauanui, 2008). To move past normative power relations, we can develop greater awareness of the language utilized, the degree of participation, and the types of reflection and reflexivity throughout the research process. Moreover, considering these processes and practices can become commonplace throughout the research stages, and the aim may be to democratize power relations, you can ask yourself, **what can I do to help democratize power relations in your research study?**

Perhaps you can consider how you can share control over data, or choices during data collection and interpretation? Integrating member checking and including participants in viewing or hearing about data interpretation can allow for greater voice and inclusion within the research process. Moreover, this process can provide an opportunity to decrease power and privilege within the research relationship. As you consider how to bring in participants in a more participatory, collaborative format, you will come back to ethical questions, such as **How am I researching with the various stakeholders? Are my practices providing space?** *Have I confirmed, clarified, and triangulated all the data with the participants?*

At each stage, there is an inherent risk to address by working to clarify participants fully understand the meaning of the study. Helping participants understand the ethical risks of participating in your study may involve multiple steps of returning to participants regularly to clarify and explain, especially if you are working across linguistic and cultural contexts. Qualitative researchers can make extra efforts to facilitate the voice of participants, such as through a rigorous process of asking additional questions (Boivin & CohenMiller, 2018); member checking; or incorporating the arts (Ajodhia & CohenMiller, 2019; Bell & Pahl, 2018; Boivin, forthcoming; CohenMiller, 2018; CohenMiller & Demers, 2019). The research must provide participants with a benefit of participation, and it's part of our job to understand what that could be. Overall, the key is to avoid doing harm, whether intentionally or unintentionally. The use of participants' own language and contextualization is at the heart of ensuring we as researchers are presenting our participants in a proper light. So, you can ask yourself, **how can I provide participants with a benefit of participation?**

9. Reflections from the field: owning our power

In the following *Reflections from the Field*, we asked a few researchers to consider how they engage in issues of power in their research and what it means to them. In the first reflection, Kakali Bhattacharya, from the University of Florida, speaks to the internal power guiding and challenging her in qualitative research. Through a story of her experience and critical reflection, she provides recommended practices useful to address issues of power when conducting qualitative research. Specifically, Bhattacharya notes that qualitative researchers can work to accept themselves and move into ethical research and critical compassion through the four practices of journeying and imagination, shadow work, metamorphosis and impermanence, and letting go of expectations and community building.

Owning my power

Kakali Bhattacharya

When I think of owning our power, I do not think of power that comes with rank, money, or visibility, and/or other external indicators. Instead, for me, power is internal, imaginal, that manifests outwardly in external relations and practices. I consider myself a creative, critical, contemplative scholar. What that means for me is that I engage in inner journeys to explore my own fears and shadows, and I cultivate an understanding of self in relation to others, to the world, environment, sentient and non-sentient beings, and to the universe. I seek guidance from wisdom traditions and lean on contemplative practices such as meditation, mindfulness, writing, movement, and art. My criticality stems from understanding that we live in a national and global cultural landscape that is intersected by multiple power structures such as colonialism, patriarchy, Islamophobia, privileged Whiteness, ableism, classism, racism, and xenophobia. Therefore, even in contemplation of possibilities of liberation or liberatory agendas, I have an ethical obligation to be mindful of the daily suffering people experience and attend to possibilities of relief from suffering, instead of enacting acts of spiritual bypassing. The human spirit is a life force, with enormous power. My work and understanding of power comes from engaging, activating this life force that is within all of us.

Owning my power, then, comes with an understanding that the level of reality and consciousness from which oppression is created cannot really offer a comprehensive range of solutions for suffering. This is akin to Audre Lorde's statement that the master's tools cannot break the master's house. Therefore, for me, the path of owning power comes with the following four practices:

Journeying and imagination
I engage in a practice of journeying and imagination that includes journeying within and to other realms via meditation, writing, art-making, movement, and stillness. Through these acts, I am able to cultivate an expanded consciousness that exceeds the level of consciousness in which suffering and oppression are created. From this space, I am inspired by insights that I might not have had without such journeys. I have used these insights to bring to my research and relationship with participants, where we might have collaboratively created art pieces or had kitchen table conversations that are genuine, with vulnerability and transparency with each other. Being open to imagination alleviates the restrictions we feel in our daily lives that are norm bound. Imagination allows border crossing, seeing things in a new way, or cultivating a curiosity, or wonder, and yet remaining humble that all that is to know will never be fully known.

Shadow work
Inner journeying work can lead to lighting up parts of ourselves within that we might fear, or feel could be dark. Yet this practice of engaging in shadow work, leaning into experiencing that which we fear can create deep insights for ourselves and empathy for a collective fear that can allow relatability and bridge building with those we are in relationship as community members, research participants, or fellow human beings.

Metamorphosis and impermanence
Engaging in any relationship, professional or personal, especially for someone who is introspective, is also an investigation of what acts

are not working and what might be more constructive in moving forward. Such acts require a transformation, a metamorphosis of sorts, where one would be able to leave a previous version of self behind in favor of a shift, transformation, and elevated wisdom and insight. Remaining open to the possibility of letting go and transformation, one can be responsive to the ways in which relationships are formed with others including research participants, mentees, students, and colleagues. In this way, we become accepting of shifts in selves and others and impermanence. We can then live with our own contradictions and those that show up in our research participants without being unsettled or judging participants, or worse, insisting that they offer consistent answers to our queries.

Letting go of expectations and community building: *Nishkam Karma*
In Hinduism, there is a saying, *Nishkam Karma*, which means that one would engage in actions because of their righteousness, without expecting anything in return. In other words, I would have to have integrity with myself, with my environment, other beings and non-beings, and inform my actions. After I act, I would not expect any form of benefit or reward for doing what felt right or ethical. In relationships with participants, this approach can create a sincere interest in their lives while remaining humble. I do not expect that I have a right to know anything, except for what the participant is willing to offer. I remain genuinely curious, imaginative of possibilities of their life paths, and carve allyship, if invited to do so, without any expectations. In this way, I build community with those within my cultural group and beyond.

These four practices allow me to cultivate a sense of power and understanding for myself that facilitates bridge building and perspective taking, and to engage in actions that are informed by radical interconnectedness of our collective existence. I am able to accept my mistakes, especially when I am complicit with oppressive power structures, as that is inescapable. Further, with practices that cultivate imagination, introspection, curiosity, humility, and community building, and that allow me to look at my fears and failures, I am able to let go of the restrictions that are imposed on me via multiple oppressive

Owning our power

structures. I own my power when I am not guided by fear, disciplinary apparatuses, or surveillance. I own my power when I accept that parts of me that are wounded from experiencing trauma, and I can look at those parts and walk through the dark forest in my journeying to arrive at a clearing with insights and wisdom. I own my power when I can activate my life force to engage in actions that are non-transactional, reflecting ethical moves that are in integrity with my being. From there, working with participants, colleagues, researchers, and students in academia and beyond seem to come from a space of being in flow, interconnected, and in critical compassion with each other.

In the next reflection, Polina Golovátina-Mora and Raúl Alberto Mora, from the Universidad Pontificia Bolivariana in Colombia, critically self-reflect on what research in multicultural contexts means to them. They describe the ways they stay connected to their own sensitivities about the world – considering the power and flaws of superheroes – moving inward. To imagine the growing potential of our research in our mind's eyes, Golovátina-Mora and Mora provide us with an accessible tool for socially just qualitative research.

A (3D) sensitivity . . . that's our (super)power!

Polina Golovátina-Mora and Raúl Alberto Mora

Polina:

Tony Stark, Iron Man from the Marvel Universe, looks at the flat city model, inherited from his dad (Favreau, 2010). He feels that something is there, but it is just an urge, he does not see it yet. Tony searches for the right perspective: limit, then broaden it. Some details are hidden; some are in plain sight but obscuring the others. Flatness of the surface does not help. It is that impeding limitation that hides rather than reveals (Sousanis, 2012, p. 3). Tony takes the flat model to his workplace, asks Jarvis to scan it, transforms it to a 3D projection. With his hands,

> he opens it up and sets it around him. He is inside it, part of it; the glowing blue projection casts its light on him. He is almost there. He deletes some hiding details of the plan and there it is: the new energy element.

That was my mind's reaction to the call and its question of the super-power that a multicultural inquiry experience grants. This scene from Marvel's Iron Man 2 (Favreau, 2010) visualizes the hypermodal assemblage (Ulmer, 2015) – multiple massive and microscopic, existing already and existing potentially interconnecting among multiple beings – which we do not just design (Lemke, 2002), but of which we are part (Barad, 2007). In intra-active performativity (Barad, 2007) or as "an aparallel evolution" (Deleuze & Guattari, 2005, p. 11), they/we rearrange these interconnections and transmute them/ourselves within them. Culture is such a sensible matrix/rhizome and assemblage, a linear, ever-mutating multiplicity rather than a centric structure as it is often perceived.

The sensitivity to feel this deterritorialization requires overlooking the borders or looking beyond and through them, not even seeing them. It simultaneously requires and stimulates the extrasensory vision of Heimdall, the guardian of gods and the Bifrost, the entrance to their realm Asgard (Encyclopedia Britannica, 2021). Heimdall "can see and hear as far as creation" (Marvel Database, n.d.).

This sensitivity feels like superpower – or like a superflaw from the perspective of the unidimensional world – while in fact it is just a sensitivity to the life force. This sensitivity favors open-ended structures and dwells on recognition of the mobile nature of the world and its beings. The absence of anything certain and fixed does not destress it, but the imposition of the static does. In more practical terms, command of languages, knowledge of different disciplines, ideally those in the humanities and natural sciences, and the recognition of multiple media as the valid source of knowledge contribute to this sensitivity. This gives more freedom to one's movement, revealing the incoherence of the static impositions, and (as if in an opening gesture of the arms) expanding the projections of the flat surfaces around us.

Raúl:

There is always this one thing I do when I'm drafting my research: I need to visualize it, I need to feel it, I need to know what is out there. You can call this a multimodal (Kress, 2010) or even synesthetic (Kalantzis & Cope, 2012) approach to the research phenomenon. I also associate it with Stake's (2010) idea of the vicarious experience: only if I can see and feel the research event can I say it exists. This is already part of my research rituals and it has also become part of my work as a research methods instructor.

My graduate students have already gotten used to the moment: I lean back in my chair and I see in my mind what probably looks closer to what Cassandra Cillian from *The Librarians* (Devlin et al., 2014–2018) used to do. In my case, instead of mathematical formulae, I see research problems. As I start talking to my research teams, our dialog begins to bring those shapes: I can see them, I can feel them. When I am talking to my graduate students, both my mentees and those in my research methods classes, I can only say there is a researchable problem if I can see it growing (and glowing) in my mind.

I don't conceive research as unidimensional either. I see it as embodied and linked to who we are, not detached from our own selves and our own senses. I sometimes worry how some people have turned research methods classes into a how-to manual, just giving out instrumental tips, overlooking that the instrumentality without reflexivity (Mora, 2014) does not lead to real change. I have to visualize the act of research in my path to discover its raison d'être; otherwise it's just a mechanical act that is just utilitarian and short-lived. Part of finding that reason lies in that synesthetic moment when I can see the research flowing in my mind; I can move it around with my hands and think of the different dimensions that begin to emerge. I don't do research just for the publications. I do it because, as Sheldon Mopes said in *Death to Smoochy* (DeVito, 2002), "You can't change the world, but you can make a dent." And maybe visualizing all the possible dents that we can make in the world can ultimately change it.

References

Barad, K. (2007). *Meeting the Universe Halfway: Quantum Physics and the Entanglement of Matter and Meaning*. Durham, NC: Duke University Press. https://doi.org/10.1177/1077800413482102

Deleuze, G., & Guattari, F. (2005). *A Thousand Plateaus: Capitalism and Schizophrenia*. Minneapolis, MN: University of Minnesota Press.

DeVito, D. (Director). (2002). *Death to Smoochy* [Film]. Warner Bros.

Devlin, D., Roskin, M., Wyle, N., & Rogers, J. (Executive Producers). (2014–2018). *The Librarians*. Electric Entertainment. Atlanta, GA: Turner Network Television (TNT).

Encyclopedia Britannica. (2021). Heimdall. www.britannica.com/topic/Heimdall

Favreau, J. (Director). (2010). *Iron Man 2* [Film]. Marvel.

Kalantzis, M., & Cope, B. (2012). *Literacies* (1st ed.). Cambridge, UK: Cambridge University Press.

Kress, G. R. (2010). *Multimodality: A social Semiotic Approach to Contemporary Communication*. London: Taylor & Francis.

Latour, B. (2004). How to talk about the body? The normative dimension of science studies. *Body & Society*, *10*(2–3), 205–229.

Lemke, J. L. (2002). Travels in hypermodality. *Visual Communication*, *1*(3), 299–325. https://doi.org/10.1177/147035720200100303

Marvel Database. (n.d.). Heimdall. https://marvel.fandom.com/wiki/Heimdall_(Earth-616)#Abilities

Mora, R. A. (2014). Reflexivity. *Key Concepts in Intercultural Dialogue*, *21*. https://centerforinterculturaldialogue.files.wordpress.com/2014/06/key-concept-reflexivity.pdf

Stake, R. E. (2010). *Qualitative Research: Studying How Things Work*. New York: Guilford Press.

Ulmer, J. B. (2015). Photography interrupted. *Qualitative Inquiry*, *22*(3), 176–182. https://doi.org/10.1177/1077800415605052

10. Engaging more deeply: concluding thoughts on owning our power

Who has power and who doesn't stems from multicultural sociocultural contexts we embody and those of our participants. Thus, within the field of qualitative research, regardless of discipline, it's important to deconstruct these positions. Despite shifts in perspective and understanding, there

Owning our power

remains a question of how to work *best* with individuals and communities. In the last 20–30 years, the term "subject" has been replaced with "participant," recognizing researchers are *not* studying *on* individuals but *with* them. **How can we work to allow and facilitate other people's *own* voices without inadvertently imposing our own prejudices, authority, and power on another set of people?** One answer is to critically reflect on power. Ryen (2019) asks in a study of institutional structures in academia for immigrant students, *why do we do what we do? Is our work relevant?* Across qualitative research studies, researchers question their practice. We have moved in and out of various theoretical approaches. It would be hard to find a qualitative text where a researcher did not question themselves and their work, and consider the ways to improve.

As qualitative researchers in globalized, transnational, and multicultural contexts, it's important to be aware of how others view themselves and their identities. We can work to understand our own positionality, our power, and privilege, and reflexively engage in a process to conduct equitable and inclusive research. Through continually questioning ourselves and our practice, it can become more apparent the varied ways people identify and experience life. Even such terminology that may seem potentially obvious, like "multicultural" or "globalization, or "societal and cultural practices," can contain and shape researchers' bias and inferences, offering places to question our practice. Thus, embarking upon relationships in a qualitative research context requires facing and negotiating how one is perceived, viewed, and framed themselves. Phipps (2013) suggests asking ourselves about our methods and including others: "Were such methods decolonizing and restorative in their approach, did they work towards a decentering of the researcher? (p. 17). In questioning our research process in a socially just manner, we can emphasize moving away from colonization and into decolonization across and within diverse contexts.

Reflective questions about power

The chapter raises several questions for researchers to critically reflect upon regarding their personal power, that of the communities, and the overt and covert power dynamics that these studies illustrate. We've discussed the challenges and, at times, the messy experience of working with others during qualitative research. There is a lot to consider and reflect upon as we go into our research. Also, we explored considerations of various questions related to each topic. Now, here are a few questions to guide you through thinking about these ideas as a whole as related to power, equity, and inclusion in qualitative research in multicultural contexts as related to your own research study.

Topic	Questions
Considering power in community. Think of a community you are familiar with.	• Who has power? How do you know? • How would you define/classify the types of power? • Where is knowledge centered in the community? • What types of knowledge are present? Which type(s) are respected, and by whom?
Language. As you go into the research planning, consider what language is used in the research study.	• How are we classifying "participants," and why?
Us vs. them. As researchers, we are often set up in a position of duality between "us" (researchers) and "them" (participants).	• What degree of participation do the participants have, and why? • How might we improve our communication/interaction with participants to bridge this unnecessary duality?
Critical self-reflection	• How are we critically reflecting throughout the development and implementation of the study?
Position and power. Now, think about your own position in the community.	• What type of power and knowledge do you have? • How does this intersect or diverge from the community itself? • What action can be taken to reposition participants in an active position of power or agency?

References

AAUW. (n.d.). Black women & the pay gap. *Workplace & Economic Equity*. Retrieved December 29, 2020, from www.aauw.org/resources/article/black-women-and-the-pay-gap/

Ackerly, B., & True, J. (2010). Back to the future: Feminist theory, activism, and doing feminist research in an age of globalization. *Women's Studies International Forum*, *33*(5), 464–472. https://doi.org/10.1016/j.wsif.2010.06.004

Adu-Ampong, E. A., & Adams, E. A. (2020). "But you are also Ghanaian, you should know": Negotiating the insider – outsider research positionality in the field-work encounter. *Qualitative Inquiry*, *26*(6), 583–592. https://doi.org/10.1177/1077800419846532

Ajodhia, A., & CohenMiller, A. (2019). Can arts-informed pedagogy facilitate communities of learning and belonging for minoritised early years children? An integrative review of research. *International Journal of Early Years Education*. https://doi.org/10.1080/09669760.2019.1685467

Alexander-Floyd, N. (2012). Disappearing acts: Reclaiming intersectionality in the social sciences in a post–black feminist era. *Feminist Formations*, 1–25. www.jstor.org/stable/23275087

Alfred, T., & Corntassel, J. (2005). Being Indigenous: Resurgences against contemporary colonialism. *Government and Opposition*, *40*(4), 597–614.

Angrosino, M. V. (2005). Recontextualizing observation: Ethnography, pedagogy, and the prospects for a progressive political agenda. In N. K. Denzin & Y. S. Lincoln (Eds.), *The SAGE Handbook of Qualitative Research* (pp. 729–745). Thousand Oaks, CA: Sage.

Atalay, S. (2006). Indigenous archaeology as decolonizing practice. *American Indian Quarterly*, *30*(3/4), 280–310. www.jstor.org/stable/4139016

Athanases, S. Z., Banes, L. C., Wong, J. W., & Martinez, D. C. (2019). Exploring linguistic diversity from the inside out: Implications of self-reflexive inquiry for teacher education. *Journal of Teacher Education*, *70*(5), 581–596. https://doi.org/10.1177/0022487118778838

Baez, B. (2002). Confidentiality in qualitative research: Reflections on secrets, power and agency. *Qualitative Research*, *2*(1), 35–58. https://doi.org/10.1177/1468794102002001638

Beck, U., & Sznaider, N., 2006. Unpacking cosmopolitanism for the social sciences: A research agenda. *The British Journal of Sociology*, *57*(1), 1–23.

Bell, D. M., & Pahl, K. (2018). Co-production: Towards a utopian approach. *International Journal of Social Research Methodology*, *21*(1), 105–117. https://doi.org/10.1080/13645579.2017.1348581

Berger, L. (2001). Inside out: Narrative autoethnography as a path toward rapport. *Qualitative Inquiry*, *7*(4), 504–518. https://doi.org/10.1177/107780040100700407

Berry, J. W. (2013). Research on multiculturalism in Canada. *International Journal of Intercultural Relations*, *37*(6), 663–675.

Bhattacharya, K. (2015). The vulnerable academic: Personal narratives and strategic De/Colonizing of academic structures. https://doi.org/10.1177/1077800415615619

Bhattacharya, K. (2020). Nonsense, play, and liminality: Putting postintentionality in dialogue with de/colonizing ontoepistemologies. *Qualitative Inquiry*, *26*(5), 522–526. https://doi.org/10.1177/1077800418819624

Boivin, N. (2018). *Building Bridges – Collaborative Arts-Based Research*. Conference Paper presented at Taking Risks in Applied Linguistics, British Association for Applied Linguistics (BAAL), York St. John University, York, UK.

Boivin, N. (2020). Homescape: Agentic space for transmigrant families multisensory discourse of identity. *Linguistic Landscape Journal, 7*(1), 37–59. https://doi.org/10.1075/ll.19019.boi

Boivin, N. (forthcoming). Transmodalities: Co-constructing agency for transmigrant children. In J. Ennser-Kananen & T. Saarinen (Eds.), *(New) Materialist Approaches in Language Education*. Cham, Switzerland: Springer.

Boivin, N., & CohenMiller, A. S. (2018). Breaking the "fourth wall" in qualitative research: Participant-led digital data construction. *The Qualitative Report, 23*(3), 581–592.

Boivin, N., Yashawanora, Y., & Mohammad, H. (2014). External factors influencing the co-constructing of experiential learning between Afghanistan participants and Malaysian lecturers. *International Journal of Teaching and Education, 2*(4), 1–16.

Boswell, M. (2020). *Understanding David Foster Wallace*. Columbia: University of South Carolina Press.

Brown, K. M. (2006). Leadership for social justice and equity: Evaluating a transformative framework and andragogy. *Educational Administration Quarterly, 42*(5), 700–745.

Choo, H. Y., & Ferree, M. M. (2010). Practicing intersectionality in sociological research: A critical analysis of inclusions, interactions, and institutions in the study of inequalities. *Sociological Theory, 28*(2), 129–149.

Christensen, A. D., & Jensen, S. Q. (2012). Doing intersectional analysis: Methodological implications for qualitative research. *NORA-Nordic Journal of Feminist and Gender Research, 20*(2), 109–125. https://doi.org/10.1080/08038740.2012.673505

CohenMiller, A. S. (2018). Visual arts as a tool for phenomenology. *Forum Qualitative Sozialforschung/Forum: Qualitative Social Research, 19*(1). https://doi.org/10.17169/fqs-19.1.2912

CohenMiller, A. S., & Demers, D. (2018). *Friendship as Methodology: A Multimodal Cogenerative Study of Motherscholar Wellbeing*. The 9th Annual Qualitative Report (TQR) Conference, Ft. Lauderdale, FL.

CohenMiller, A. S., & Demers, D. (2019). Conflicting roles of mother and academic? Exploring the use of arts-based self-care activities to encourage wellbeing. *Art/Research International: A Transdisciplinary Journal*. https://journals.library.ualberta.ca/ari/index.php/ari/article/view/29391

CohenMiller, A. S., Faucher, C., Hernández-Torrano, D., & Brown Hajdukova, E. (2017). Practical steps for using interdisciplinary educational research to enhance cultural awareness. *International Journal of Research and Method in Education, 40*(3). https://doi.org/10.1080/1743727X.2017.1310834

Collins, P. (1998). *Fighting Words: Black Women and the Search for Justice* (Vol. 7). Minneapolis, MN: University of Minnesota Press.

Collins, P., McLaughlin, A., Higginbotham, E., Henderson, D., Tickamyer, A., MacDonald, V. M., . . . Dance, L. J. (2009). *Emerging Intersections: Race, Class, and Gender in Theory, Policy, and Practice*. New Brunswick, NJ: Rutgers University Press.

Conrad, D., & Sinner, A. (Eds.). (2015). *Creating Together: Participatory, Community-Based, and Collaborative Arts Practices and Scholarship Across Canada*. Waterloo, ON: Wilfrid Laurier University Press.

Court, D., & Abbas, R. (2013). Whose interview is it, anyway? Methodological and ethical challenges of insider – outsider research, multiple languages, and dual-researcher cooperation. *Qualitative Inquiry, 19*(6), 480–488.

Court, D., & Abbas, R. (2013). Whose interview is it, anyway? Methodological and ethical challenges of insider – outsider research, multiple languages, and dual-researcher cooperation. *Qualitative Inquiry, 19*(6), 480–488. https://doi.org/10.1177/1077800413482102

Crowe, M., Inder, M., & Porter, R. (2015). Conducting qualitative research in mental health: Thematic and content analyses. *Australian & New Zealand Journal of Psychiatry, 49*(7), 616–623. https://doi.org/10.1177/0004867415582053

Davidson-Hunt, I. J. (2006). Adaptive learning networks: Developing resource management knowledge through social learning forums. *Human Ecology, 34*(4), 593–614.

Denzin, N. K., Lincoln, Y. S., & Smith, L. T. (Eds.). (2008). *The SAGE Handbook of Critical and Indigenous Methodologies*. Los Angeles, CA: Sage.

Dervin, F. (2012). Cultural identity, representation and othering. *The Routledge Handbook of Language and Intercultural Communication, 2,* 181–194.

Diversi, M., & Moreira, C. (2016). *Betweener Talk: Decolonizing Knowledge Production, Pedagogy, and Praxis*. London: Routledge.

Dowling, M. (2006). Approaches to reflexivity in qualitative research. *Nurse Researcher, 13*(3). https://doi.org/10.7748/nr2006.04.13.3.7.c5975

Duff, P. A. (2002). The discursive co-construction of knowledge, identity, and difference: An ethnography of communication in the high school mainstream. *Applied linguistics, 23*(3), 289–322.

Duneier, M. (2001). On the evolution of sidewalk. *Contemporary Field Research: Perspectives and Formulations, 2.*

Duranti, A., Ahearn, L., Cook Gumperz, J., Gumperz, J., Darnell, R., Hymes, D., . . . Duranti, A. (2003). Language as culture in US anthropology: Three paradigms. *Current Anthropology, 44*(3), 323–347.

Flores, N., & Rosa, J. (2015). Undoing appropriateness: Raciolinguistic ideologies and language diversity in education. *Harvard Educational Review, 85*(2), 149–171.

Foucault, M. (1982). The subject and power. *Critical Inquiry, 8*(4), 777–795.

Galam, R. G. (2015). Gender, reflexivity, and positionality in male research in one's own community with Filipino seafarers' wives. *Forum Qualitative Sozialforschung, 16*(3), article 13.

Gergen, K. J. (2000). Qualitative inquiry: Tensions and transformations. In N. Denzin & Y. S. Lincoln (Eds.), *The SAGE Handbook of Qualitative Research* (pp. 1025–1046). Thousand Oaks, CA: Sage.

Gill, H., Purru, K., & Lin, G. (2012). In the midst of participatory action research practices: Moving towards decolonizing and decolonial praxis. *Reconceptualizing Educational Research Methodology, 3*(1).

Gilroy, P. (2004). *After Empire: Melancholia or Convivial Culture*. London, UK: Routledge.

Grosfoguel, R. (2002). Colonial difference, geopolitics of knowledge, and global coloniality in the modern/colonial capitalist world-system. *Review (Fernand Braudel Center)*, 203–224.

Grosjean, F. (2015). Bicultural bilinguals. *International Journal of Bilingualism, 19*(5), 572–586.

Guba, E. G., & Lincoln, Y. S. (2005). Paradigmatic controversies, contradictions, and emerging confluences. In N. K. Denzin & Y. S. Lincoln (Eds.), *The SAGE Handbook of Qualitative Research* (3rd ed., pp. 191–216). Thousand Oaks, CA: Sage.

Hagan, W. (1985). Full blood, mixed blood, generic, and Ersatz: The problem of Indian identity. *Arizona and the West, 27*(4), 309–326. www.jstor.org/stable/40169479

Hamad, R. (2020). *White Tears Brown Scars: How White Feminism Betrays Women of Colour*. London: Hachette UK.

Hesse-Biber, S. N. (2007). The practice of feminist in-depth interviewing. *Feminist Research Practice: A Primer, 111148*, 111–138.

Hesse-Biber, S. N. (2017). *The Practice of Qualitative Research: Engaging Students in the Research Process* (3rd ed.). Thousand Oaks, CA: Sage.

Hesse-Biber, S. N., & Leavy, P. (2006). *Emergent Methods in Social Research*. Thousand Oaks, CA: Sage.

Knoblauch, H. (2005, September). Focused ethnography. *Forum Qualitative Sozialforschung/Forum: Qualitative Social Research, 6*(3).

Latour, B. (2004). How to talk about the body? The normative dimension of science studies. *Body & Society, 10*(2–3), 205–229.

Latour, B. (2013). Reassembling the social. An introduction to actor-network-theory. Oxford, UK: Oxford University Press..

Leonard, P. (2016). *Expatriate Identities in Postcolonial Organizations: Working Whiteness*. London: Routledge.

Lepore, W., Hall, B. W., & Tandon, R. (2020). The Knowledge for change consortium: A decolonising approach to international collaboration in capacity-building in community-based participatory research. *Canadian Journal of Development Studies*. https://doi.org/10.1080/02255189.2020.1838887

Lund, D. E., & Nabavi, M. (2008). A duo-ethnographic conversation on social justice activism: Exploring issues of identity, racism, and activism with young people. *Multicultural Education, 15*(4), 27–32.

Malone, S. (2003). Ethics at home: Informed consent in your own backyard, *Qualitative Studies in Education, 16*(6), 797–815. https://doi.org/10.1080/0951839031000163215 3

McClaren, P. (2000). Unthinking whiteness: Rearticulating diasporic practices. In P. P. Trifonas (Ed.), *Revolutionary Pedagogies: Cultural Politics, Instituting Education, and the Discourse of Theory* (pp. 140–173). Psychology Press; London, UK: Routledge

McLeod, J. (2020). *Beginning Postcolonialism*. Manchester, UK: Manchester University Press.

Meier, C., & Geldenhuys, D. J. (2017). Co-constructing appreciative inquiry across disciplines: A duo-ethnography. *SA Journal of Industrial Psychology, 43*(1), 1–9. http://dx.doi.org/10.4102/sajip.v43i0.1400

Mertens, D. M. (2020). *Research and Evaluation in Education and Psychology: Integrating Diversity with Quantitative, Qualitative, and Mixed Methods* (5th ed.). Thousand Okas, CA: Sage.

Murdoch, J. (2001). Ecologising sociology: Actor-network theory, co-construction and the problem of human exemptionalism. *Sociology, 35*(1), 111–133.

Olivier de Sardan, J. P. (2005). Mediations and brokerage. *Anthropology and Development: Understanding Contemporary Social Change*, 166–184.

Palaganas, E. C., Sanchez, M. C., Molintas, V. P., & Caricativo, R. D. (2017). Reflexivity in qualitative research: A journey of learning. *Qualitative Report, 22*(2).

Pennycook, A. (2018). Posthumanist applied linguistics. *Applied Linguistics, 39*(4), 445–461.

Phillips, A. (2009). *Multiculturalism Without Culture*. Princeton, NJ: Princeton University Press.

Phipps, A. (2013). Intercultural ethics: Questions of methods in language and intercultural communication. *Language and Intercultural Communication, 13*(1), 10–26.

Pittaway, E., Bartolomei, L., & Hugman, R. (2010). "Stop stealing our stories": The ethics of research with vulnerable groups. *Journal of Human Rights Practice, 2*(2), 229–251. https://doi.org/10.1093/jhuman/huq004

Ransome, P. (1992). *Antonio Gramsci: A New Introduction*. Hemel Hempstead, Hertfordshire: Harvester/Wheatsheaf.

Robson, C., & McCartan, K. (2016). *Real World Research*. Hoboken, NJ: Wiley & Sons.

Ryen, A. (2019). Fighting the crocodiles: Immigrant students and their perilous routes at campus. *Qualitative Inquiry, 25*(7), 615–624. https://doi.org/10.1177/1077800418806616

Schoenmakers, J. H. (2012). *The Power of Culture: A Short History of Anthropological Theory About Culture and Power*. Groningen, the Netherlands: University of Groningen.

Shadnam, M., Bykov, A., & Prasad, A. (2020). Opening constructive dialogues between business ethics research and the sociology of morality: Introduction to the thematic symposium. *Journal of Business Ethics*, 1–11.

Smith, A. (2006). Indigenous feminism without apology. *New Socialist, 58*, 16–17.

Smith, A., & Kauanui, J. (2008). Native feminisms engage American studies. *American Quarterly, 60*(2), 241–249. www.jstor.org/stable/40068531

Smith, G. H., & Smith, L. T. (2018). Doing indigenous work: Decolonizing and transforming the academy. In E. McKinley & L. T. Smith (Eds.), *Handbook of Indigenous Education* (pp. 1075–1101). Singapore: Springer. http://doi.org/10.1007/978-981-10-1839-8_69-1

Smith, L. T. (1999). *Decolonizing Methodologies: Research and Indigenous Peoples*. London: Zed Books.

Smith, L. T. (2013). *Decolonizing Methodologies: Research and Indigenous Peoples* (2nd ed.) London: Zed Books.

Snipp, C. M. (1989). *American Indians: The First of This Land*. Thousand Oaks, CA: Sage.

Sousanis, N. (2012). The shape of our thoughts: A meditation on & in comics. *Visual Arts Research*, *38*(1), 1–10. https://doi.org/10.5406/visuartsrese.38.1.0001.

Stewart, G. T., St. Pierre, E., Devine, N., & Kirloskar-Steinbach, M. (2020). The end of the dream: Postmodernism and qualitative research. *Qualitative Inquiry*. https://doi.org/10.1177/1077800420971867.

Swadener, B. B., & Mutua, K. (2008). Deconstructing the global postcolonial. *Handbook of Critical and Indigenous Methodologies*, 31–43.

Thompson, S. (2012). The micro-ethics of everyday life: Ethics, ideology and anti-consumerism. *Cultural Studies*, *26*(6), 895–921.

van der Riet, P. (2012). Reflexivity: A mainstay in promoting rigor and trustworthiness in qualitative research. *Philippine Journal of Nursing*, *82*, 28–32.

Vora, D., Martin, L., Fitzsimmons, S. R., Pekerti, A. A., Lakshman, C., & Raheem, S. (2019). Multiculturalism within individuals: A review, critique, and agenda for future research. *Journal of International Business Studies*, *50*(4), 499–524.

Walby, S., Armstrong, J., & Strid, S. (2012). Intersectionality: Multiple inequalities in social theory. *Sociology*, *46*(2), 224–240. https://doi.org/10.1177/0038038511416164

Wallerstein, N., Oetzel, J. G., Sanchez-Youngman, S., Boursaw, B., Dickson, E., Kastelic, S., . . . Parker, M. (2020). Engage for equity: A long-term study of community-based participatory research and community-engaged research practices and outcomes. *Health Education & Behavior*, *47*(3), 380–390. http://doi.org/10.1080/08038740.2012.673505

Windsong, E. A. (2018). Incorporating intersectionality into research design: An example using qualitative interviews. *International Journal of Social Research Methodology*, *21*(2), 135–147. http://doi.org/10.1080/13645579.2016.1268361

Yuval-Davis, N. (2006). Intersectionality and feminist politics. *European Journal of Women's Studies*, *13*(3), 193–209.

Unpacking the meaning and practice of trust

What does it mean to develop trust within a research study? Trust is a complex and multilayered concept that can make or break a research study. Trust is the process of developing a relationship with the participants, stakeholders, and community. It can start with a relationship with a gatekeeper whose introduction can be foundational to laying the initial layer of trust. It includes several intersecting relationships such as school administrators or other institutional guardians, community stakeholders, research assistants, translators, or ethical review boards. If any of these relationships fray, trust can be impacted or affected negatively (Bancroft, 2015).

When we enter a community and are unsure of cultural norms and practices, trust becomes even more critical and affects how we can engage in socially aware and just research. It's built, developed, and negotiated between people. Trust can be based on a reciprocal relationship (see Opsal et al., 2016; Tracy, 2010) rather than a concept of "taking" data or knowledge from another. For instance, Marie Keta Miranda conducted an ethnographic study of girls in gangs in Los Angeles, USA. After much work to build trust with her participants, proving she could maintain their anonymity in the public sphere, she saw their roles change. Miranda's (2003) participants were becoming researchers in their own right, speaking for themselves instead of through her as the researcher. (You can learn more about co-produced research in Chapter 7.) How trust is constructed between the researcher and the participants can indicate a study's findings' strength and authenticity. Miranda (2003) used detailed and extensive descriptions of her research in the ethnographic tradition of thick description (Geertz, 1973).

In addition to building trust with participants and community members, there's also the concept of trustworthiness of a study itself. For Guba and

Lincoln (1981), trustworthiness became central to suggesting methodological rigor in a study. It's not just believing or trusting the researcher, but a concept and process throughout the research.

So, what can trust look like throughout the overall research process? Here are a couple ways to think of trust in qualitative research:

- Trust offers an opportunity to establish and nourish a belief in research, especially when investigating marginalized and diverse communities.
- Trust is composed of parts creating the notion of someone or something as being trustworthy, and not just the connection one has with people.

This chapter begins with an overview of trust. It then moves into perspectives on the role and nature of trust in qualitative research, with questions for you to consider throughout your own practice. We touch upon concepts from the previous chapter about positionality and power, highlighting considerations for multicultural and diverse research contexts and how we can work with gatekeepers. We conclude with *Reflections from the Field*, where two scholars critically reflect on their practice and intersect trust with ethics. Throughout, you can consider how socially just research is seen through the lens of trustworthiness and rigor in qualitative inquiry studies.

1. What is trust?

As qualitative researchers, one of our goals is to build relationships grounded in trust and create research that you can "trust and have confidence in the results" (CohenMiller & Saban, forthcoming). This means that at times when we talk about trust, we are referring to the others' reading and understanding the "telling" of the research "tale" (Stahl & King, 2020), the protocol used to create trustworthiness in the study (Amankwaa, 2016), or trust as developed and negotiated with participants in the study. An entire issue of trust, or the lack thereof, relates to understanding how the quality of the relationship impacts the research quality. Lincoln and Guba (1985), in their classic work on naturalistic inquiry, explained how to trust connections to qualitative research rigor: "How can an inquirer persuade his or her audiences (including self) that the findings of an inquiry are worth paying attention to, worth taking account of?" (p. 290). An answer is **trust**, which is referred to as **trustworthiness** in some aspects of qualitative research. For example, if one enters an Indigenous community, not fully aware of different social interactions, great offense can occur, which is then perceived as a *lack* of trust. Here's one way to consider trust in qualitative research:

Trust in qualitative research is a sense of confidence in the researcher's dependability and authenticity.

Trust goes hand in hand with an understanding of cultural norms or a willingness to acknowledge a need to learn more. For example, what one culture views as normative, another might view as offensive, such as the distance between a researcher and the participant. **Should I shake the hand of your participant?** For some participants, a touch of any sort is a breach of trust, whereas for others it helps create an encouraging environment. Thus, we can return to the idea of learning about the norms of your community and participant. By becoming aware of potential trust issues, you are on the right track. Only in awareness can we work to make any meaningful change.

According to Guba and Lincoln's (1981) model, there are four key components of trustworthiness relevant to qualitative research: truth value, applicability, consistency, and neutrality. Let's explore these. The first is **truth-value**, or **credibility**. Credibility can come in multiple forms, such as how participants view you and how audiences view your research. For instance, being authentic can display credibility as a researcher. A person can often project an aura of credibility, but it is more likely that credibility comes over time. For researchers, we can ask ourselves, **how can we gain credibility with participants and communities?** There are several research practices that enable a sense of trustworthiness as related to credibility with stakeholders. Some examples of strategies used to establish credibility include the practice of reflexivity, member checking, and peer debriefing or peer examination.

Likewise, in describing data, using clear and accurate details can be a means for portraying credibility. It allows others to recognize the experiences contained within the study through the interpretation of participants' experiences. Achievement of credibility can occur by checking for the representativeness of the data as a whole. "A qualitative study is considered credible when it presents an accurate description or interpretation of human experience that people who also share the same experience would immediately recognize" (Krefting, 1991, p. 218).

Another component of trustworthiness is **applicability**, or **transferability**. We can ask ourselves, **how do the data findings apply to other settings?**

The meaning and practice of trust

How are they transferable? Like credibility, transferability can be considered in different ways. There is applicability related to how the study affects those potentially involved. For instance, if the stakeholders view the researcher or research itself as coming from a place relevant to their needs, participants are more likely to embrace the research (Hennink et al., 2020). This can occur by co-creating with participants, such as by discussing the expected details of the context, participants' roles, and engagement of communities bridging what the researchers wish to investigate. This depth of knowledge and understanding of the community can reflect trustworthiness. Without an understanding of the sociocultural context, as researchers, our work can appear superficial and irrelevant.

A third component of trustworthiness is **consistency**, or **dependability**, often centered on the research process rather than the people. However, for consistency to be created, researchers can project a sense of consistency in their actions, intent, and beliefs throughout the research (Guba, 1981). This includes involving stakeholders in the process and communicating effectively with them through various communication strategies (e.g., linguistics, signs, visuals, symbols).

For diverse communities to allow outsiders (researchers) into their lives, the research practices must be reliable. For this to occur, you can ask yourself, **what strategies am I using, or plan to use, to incorporate trustworthiness into my study?** *How are my practices facilitating social justice or hindering them?* One strategy might include incorporating participants in the analysis process. This facilitates voice and creates a purpose for the participants. Another strategy could be to provide a detailed description of the research methods to participants. Allowing the participants behind the curtain and involving their opinions in the process enables trustworthiness in the process to be created.

Another component of trustworthiness is **neutrality**, or **confirmability**. It's relevant to demonstrate to others the idea that the research process can be believed. However, in qualitative research, neutrality does not translate to complete objectivity, rather it highlights that the process itself does not have an agenda. To improve the research agenda's neutrality, we can employ the strategy of **reflexivity** throughout the research process (Nowell et al., 2017). As discussed in the last chapter, the term reflexivity requires a self-critical approach on the researcher's part about how one's own preconceptions affect the research. Allowing participants to witness reflexivity in the research process can help facilitate the trustworthiness of the overall

49

process (Heath et al., 2010). For instance, you can show your reflexivity by talking with your participants about any issues or challenges they face or asking yourself how we are feeling at the moment.

Breaking trust. While these examples provide insight into how to create trustworthy research processes as well as terminology to describe your rigorous process, let's also talk a bit about what breaking trust might look like. One such example could include not providing, or not appearing to provide, enough information or responses to their participants. For example, an Indigenous participant reflected on second thoughts about sharing information with a researcher:

> A researcher came. In a cultural way he was sitting too close, in my face. . . . our knees were nearly touching. He was a little bit negative . . . coming back with very little answers. This information, that's been passed on for a very long time, was not valued. He said things weren't special that I was telling him, that they happen everywhere. He inferred that all Aboriginal people are the same. . . . Us Mob are different from all other Aboriginal people: different language, custom, culture, songs and dances. When I first met him just a little gap was open . . . like a little door or gap. Then, when he wasn't listening – the little door shut. . . . I shut myself off. I regretted giving the information. It made me think "Why did he come here in the first place? What was he after?" He didn't explain to me properly what he was researching. It made me confused. They need to explain themselves before they come.
>
> (Woodward & Marrfurra McTaggart, 2016, p. 135)

This reflection speaks to how one must continually cultivate trust through both actions and words. In this way, trust can be connected to the idea of showing respect for individuals and cultures. This was demonstrated by dismissing and belittling the information the participant provided, by not engaging her in conversation or seeking to understand further what she was saying, and by a lack of cultural awareness by sitting too close and directly opposite her. Moreover, the lack of paralinguistic cultural understanding as noted in the reflection, connects to the discourse around respectful language of a culture (Zhu, 2013). Moving forward in your study, you can ask yourself, **am I taking from a culture or providing voice for one?**

2. How to develop trusting relationships

Trust in relationships can be further developed, or forged, through extended interactions. To fully understand a community requires time. Time enables better sociocultural knowledge sharing. Such sociocultural knowledge is essential to create effective recruitment and, more importantly, a transparent and trusting research relationship (McLean & Campbell, 2003; Rugkasa & Canvin, 2011, p. 136). If there's not enough time to engage in deep relationship building and forging of trust, then you will want to state that as a limitation explicitly.

For research taking place in short bursts, the one-time interview of a person within a community, though, will not have the benefit of time. For example, disseminating information doesn't always have to consist of academic channels (e.g., journals, reports, conference presentations). Information sharing can take place both formally and informally. Another aspect of communicating with communities during the initial recruitment stage is understanding how communities communicate. Research has shown that non-personal recruitment methods, such as newsletters or handouts, are often reported to be less effective than face-to-face recruitment (Kondowe & Booyens, 2014). Being present and meeting the participants, showing who you are, is a way to highlight trusting research practices. Yet, with socially distant research and expanding use of digital research, the feeling of trust can be nourished through communication. Consider for yourself, **which social media format do I feel most comfortable interacting with?** *Who do I tend to communicate with the most in those formats? Do I feel comfortable responding to someone's post who I don't know? How might I feel more comfortable joining a research study?*

Thinking beyond insider/outsider. Trust is not solely about whether someone is an outsider or insider but about building a kind of research partnership. Vulnerable and marginalized groups often have a harder time trusting (Baser & Toivanen, 2018). While building partnerships occur over time, often we do not have the luxury of time. Therefore, we must investigate how we can build a partnership in the short term. Ethnography, similar to a case study, requires deep trust: "intensive excursions into their [participants] lives, which use more interventional as well as observational methods to create contexts through which to delve into questions that will reveal what matters to those people in the context" (Pink & Morgan, 2013, p. 352).

Trust and positionality. Building trust through negotiating and renegotiating differences in positionality is another direction. McAreavey and Das (2013) highlight research within minority communities: "Ethical research in minority communities requires cultural sensitivity, an open-minded and non-judgmental attitude that respects the opinions of others" (p. 119). For example, McAreavey and Das (2013) shared the negotiations and ethical concerns arising during their research on the sensitive topic of divorce (p. 116). There are practices and strategies one must consider when entering diverse and marginalized multicultural communities. These are often based on multiple, often interrelating factors, such as status (e.g., job, family name, heritage, economic status, education); age (e.g., deeply ingrained respect for elders); gender (e.g., lack of respect for women); personality type (e.g., too friendly, too aggressive, rude); past historical position (e.g., colonialist, Indigenous); and perceived aim of the research (e.g., governmental, university, policy). These factors become particularly relevant when aiming to conduct socially just research across and within multicultural contexts.

Bicultural recruiters and cultural brokers. Within multicultural communication contexts with linguistic and sociocultural diversity, another useful approach is to involve researchers who can navigate communication nuances. For researchers entering into multicultural contexts, this could include hiring a translator or interpreter to facilitate understandings during the recruitment process. These approaches can provide essential steps for building trust (Eide & Allen, 2005; Hall & Kulig, 2004). Incorporating bicultural recruiters can be useful when we don't share the same culture as your participants or when the research is sensitive or political (Culley, 2006; Kokanovic et al., 2009).

However, there also can be issues to consider around trust with translators. For example, in research conducted by Nettie, she found that her Farsi-speaking translator was not trusted because of their age: the community considered them to be too young. Another one wasn't trusted because he was male. Another translator wasn't trusted because she was Iranian with particular cultural perspectives of Afghanistan Farsi speakers. And for Anna's research with Russian and Kazakh translators, age, status, gender, dialect, and region of the country came into play regarding how well the person was trusted. Thus, we can see that age, gender, ethnicity, and other identity markers can all play a role in building trust, or the lack thereof.

Allowing research assistants, translators, and others in the process who present similar identities to those we are building relationships with is

The meaning and practice of trust

a strategy in showing faith in building authentic and respectful relationships (Jacquemet, 2015). Bicultural researchers who perform a "bridging role" might help vouch for researchers' credibility and trustworthiness and improve their cultural competence by contextualizing, for example, nonverbal communication (Rugkâsa & Canvin, 2011, p. 135). As a student, you may not have such access to others working on a team, or perhaps your team has limited funding. In those cases, you can consider self-reflective questions such as, **what do I know about the cultural context I want to research within? How can I learn more?** *What do I know about the socio-cultural background and experience of those I want to talk with or observe? How can I learn more? Who can help provide insight, introductions, and/ or linkages with the community/people I'm interested in?* By considering such questions and approaches, we can show respect for and sensitivity to others' cultures.

3. What do we need to consider in building relationships?

Researching in minority communities can be tricky. There are many ways to consider relationship building in qualitative research. When viewing partnerships, part of the problem lies in the different cultures surrounding those doing research and the participants engaged in a community (Lomas, 2018, p. 236). The philosophy of "linkage and exchange" is a promising way to increase the relevance and use of research (Lomas, 2018, p. 236). The linkage and exchange philosophy starts at the top. Linkage highlights the relationship between government institutions and policy makers through funding, whereas exchange illustrates the need for researchers to create a relationship to communicate to decision makers how they can use the results of a particular piece of research in policy formulation. One such way to consider building relationships and partnerships is to consider social capital. According to Lin (2002), there are three components of social capital that connect to access and trust-building. Such awareness is important prior to building relationships. Creating a connection in one component can build trust more broadly:

1 *Relationships and memberships* include understanding how relationships in the community are built. Consider, *how long does it typically*

take to build a relationship? How is membership in the group granted, and by whom?

2 *Types and quality of interactions and social identities,* including short-term, long-term, gender, age, and status in a sociocultural interaction are important to comprehend. For instance, these aspects could include language, communication practices, cultural and social practices, norms, and values that occur and are expected during interactions. For example, how women present themselves varies due to cultural, religious, and ethnic perceptions and can vary based upon many factors. You can ask yourself, *do communities have expectations regarding types of social identities?*

3 *Potential or real support and access to valued resources* include online resources and engaging with community institutions and policy makers. You can ask yourself, are there resources in the community that could be utilized for research? And what type of resources might these be? What are the needs and constraints of a community (such as access to digital technology and other resources)?

For researchers, highlighting social capital that participants inherently possess, that which is valuable to society, can help bridge differences. For instance, you can ask yourself, *what capital can I offer to the stakeholders or explain to participants how the research can benefit them?* If we are unable to enter a community, we cannot do research. Bourdieu's concepts of social fields and social capital can provide insights into understanding the extent to which someone who on a variety of levels is considered "at risk" is or is not able to access necessary resources to achieve her desired ends in a range of different social contexts (Allard, 2005, p. 64). As Bourdieu (1993) defines it, social capital is "contacts and group memberships which, through the accumulation of exchanges, obligations and shared identities, provide actual or potential support and access to valued resources" (p. 143).

Some researchers argue that the first aspect of a relationship is the most important in the creation of trust: "Shared norms, a sense of trust, reciprocity, civic responsibility, and links between voluntary and state institutions are all domains of social capital" (Allard, 2005, p. 65). This means believing the researcher and team are there for the benefit of participants. Therefore, as researchers, we must find ways to create a feeling that participants are wanted, are supported, and have control. One way to encourage these feelings and ownership is to allow participants to participate in the research process. However, it's important to note that not all ethical review boards or university committees will understand such an approach. In that case, you can explain the process and communicate how a participatory approach can better benefit the university.

4. How can I work with gatekeepers?

When entering a community where you could be perceived as an outsider, there are always relationships to consider, particularly with any gatekeepers. Let's think for a moment about who might be gatekeepers for your study. The **gatekeeper**, a person coordinating access to the research, can hold tremendous power to allow ease of access or present major challenges. Key aspects of building a relationship of trust with gatekeepers involve negotiating differences in positionality and power and being reflective on many aspects of the relationship. When entering into a relationship with a community gatekeeper, there are several aspects to consider, such as articulated by McAreavey and Das (2013): "This includes evaluating gatekeepers' motives, how routes of access affect research participation, and how the relationship between a gatekeeper and researcher is established and maintained" (p. 112). So, a gatekeeper could be a school principal, the community leader, or a parent in a family. When working with gatekeepers online, we have additional considerations. For instance, *what is the best way to contact someone in leadership? Will they take my email or phone call? Do I need to get access to the gatekeeper through someone else – another gatekeeper?* The gatekeepers are those that you want to understand your study and help allow you to talk to others. If you're considering research that requires talking to a gatekeeper first, you can ask yourself, **how do they know me and why should they trust me?**

Working with local community groups. While gatekeepers can be individuals (e.g., the principal of a school allowing access to study the school environment), we can also conceptualize a gatekeeper as an entire community group. In diverse and multicultural contexts, it's particularly useful to ask questions and spend time understanding the day-to-day realities of a context as a central component of building trust. In this way, we can think about the community and work with them to produce (and ideally co-produce) research. (Co-production of research is further discussed in Chapter 7.) You can ask yourself, **how can I better appreciate and become**

aware of the community? According to Alvarez et al. (2006), workers in community organizations (e.g., newspaper sellers, wait staff) are often well placed to have greater awareness of community issues, needs, and concerns.

Strategies for gaining access through gatekeepers and issues of researcher positionality have been examined by researchers (Clark & Sinclair, 2008; Clark, 2011; Yancey et al., 2006; Yu, 2009). Nevertheless, there appears to be limited literature on "real-life" ethical dilemmas that might provide insight into practical strategies for dealing with issues of participation and working with gatekeepers. Communities of refugees or migrants, regardless of their religious, ethnic, or political backgrounds, do not have permanent status, and they often feel particularly vulnerable. Gatekeepers tend to be aware of their emotional and stressful situations. Therefore researchers must tread carefully, as these communities are particularly susceptible to power imbalance and marginalization. Minority and migrant groups increasingly face issues of marginalization, exclusion, identity, and citizenship (Berry, 2011). Migrants have enshrined rights, not necessarily identical to those of national citizens but significant nonetheless, and indicative of similarities to minority groups (Rugkâsa & Canvin, 2011, p. 135). Thus, building a relationship of trust includes building confidence, security, and faith in the researcher and the process.

Gatekeepers control access to a particular community or institution, and as a result, researchers are reliant on their input. It's generally recognized that gatekeepers play an important role in social research (McAreavey & Das, 2013), particularly for researching communities that do not trust mainstream research and are seldom heard, or for research involving sensitive subjects (McAreavey & Das, 2013; Yancey et al., 2006). Gatekeepers have the power to deny access to the researcher and they may also influence whether individuals opt in or out of a process. By negotiating directly with prospective research participants, gatekeepers facilitate the recruitment process (Levkoff & Sanchez, 2003). By acting as cultural mediators, or brokers (McAreavey & Das, 2013), gatekeepers can also help the researcher become more culturally competent, acting as guarantors of the researcher's legitimacy within the community (Whyte, 2012) and saving the researcher time and resources (Rugkâsa & Canvin, 2011, p. 134). Participants' ethical concerns can often be appropriately represented by gatekeepers, who are respected members of their communities (Sanghera & Thapar-Björkert, 2008).

So, **what does trustworthiness mean in the field when conducting research?** Let's look at an example from research I (Anna) conducted in schools in Kazakhstan. I worked with a team to understand the gendered nature of schooling (Durrani et al., 2020, 2021). We had a few contacts of school principals as initial gatekeepers, but we could not spend time at the site (the school) until we had permission to enter the campus. Even though it could have helped to understand more of the school campus's day-to-day reality, without the initial acceptance of the principal we wouldn't have been able to enter the school. In this way, we took small, typical steps of sending out information via email and then following up with phone calls about the study. We were then invited, by some schools, to come and meet to discuss the research further. Only after that meeting – the face-to-face time where we talked through the research, showing ourselves as trusted researchers – were we then allowed to take the next steps of scheduling interviews and observations with various participants. For your own work, you can ask yourself, *who do I have a relationship with that can allow me entrance into a space to build an initial relationship of trust?*

5. What ethical dilemmas should we be prepared for relating to trust?

It's significant to recognize how our actions can inadvertently affect communities we work within a multicultural diverse world. As Smith (2012) explains of Western researchers coming to research within Māori communities:

> The West can extract and claim ownership of our way of knowing, our imagery, the things we create and produce, and then reject the people who created and developed those ideas and seek to deny them further opportunities to be creators of their own culture.
>
> (p. 1)

The concept of taking from those we research, especially in diverse contexts, remains to be a major issue and one that decolonizing approaches, transformative approaches, and social justice can help address (Mertens, 2020). Asking questions to engage community members collaboratively can facilitate trust-building. Such questions we can consider to move through potential issues are, *what kind of experiences count? How do we extend this knowledge to what academics want to do? How can co-production expand what and how we research?*

Exploring gender and trust. Sexuality and gender roles can be forgotten when building trust. For example, when Nettie was a single mother, raising a mixed-race second-language dyslexic child while working on her PhD, she explained that other mothers who were part of her study on language maintenance, social language, and literacy practices and identity connected with her about guilt over not always being available for their children, as well as struggles with time, money, and best intentions (Boivin, 2015). As a mother, Nettie's gender and identity connected her to several of her participants, building a commonality based on gender roles and identity. As Botterill (2015) notes, the interview process is a relationship where "trust and rapport are actively negotiated through layers of cultural norms and expectations in the interview encounter" (p. 10).

In some cultures, a woman cannot discuss certain issues with a man, even if he is her husband. For example, to best understand Iranian female participants' experiences, Nettie's team had to employ female translators when interviewing female participants; however, male translators were better for male participants (Boivin, forthcoming). As Bhopal argues (2010): "By constantly questioning our own positioning and our own expectations, research with women by women can have positive benefits for both the respondent and the researcher" (p. 194). While self-identification as a man or woman may limit some research across gender lines, if we reflect on our limitations and possible constraints, we can best develop trust in a research relationship.

Race, religion, and ethnicity. Race, religion, and ethnicity are areas that can connect and divide participants. As researchers, to overcome any division we must reflect on building trust through non-hierarchical, co-participatory co-construction of the research process. During the interview process, we must be aware of how interviews can marginalize and exploit certain communities if we do not first build trust between stakeholders. Bhopal (2010) "emphasized how a shared experience of racism between the researcher and the interviewee may affect the research relationship more significantly than shared gender, language, religion and culture can" (p. 188). Bhopal (2010) explains that research/interview relationships should be non-hierarchical, non-exploitative, and reciprocal. Moreover, we must aim to build on a "participatory model" in which the researcher shares their own biography with the researched (Bhopal, 2010, p. 188). Knowing who the researcher is, where they came from, and how our common pains connect us is an important part of the process.

Empathy is key to building a trusting relationship. Understanding the plight of one's participant is key. For example, there was a critique against early feminist research for focusing on White, middle-class women's experiences while neglecting the issues relevant for those of Black, working-class women (Bhopal, 2010; Carby, 1982; Hill Collins, 1991; Phoenix, 1987). White feminists, for instance, appeared to have overlooked the effects of "race" on the interview process and the complexities involved in this (Bhopal, 2009), such as the commonalities and differences between the researcher and the researched. Campbell and Wasco (2000, p. 783) note that the aim of feminist research is "to capture women's lived experiences in a respectful manner that legitimates women's voices as sources of knowledge." Shared gender was crucial in building trust and rapport with minority communities (Bhopal, 2010, p. 190). Moreover, the interrelationship of factors such as "race," class, and gender can construct and reproduce differences in the research process (Hill Collins, 1991; Phoenix, 2001). Additional aspects of positionality and trust (e.g., age, status, minority participants) will be explored further in the chapter on the spectrum of being an insider and outsider.

Researching ethnic, linguistic, racial, and gender issues requires becoming as aware as possible, expanding our understanding. However, issues of vulnerability and trust will vary, even when one's role or identifier matches those of our participants. For instance, coming from the same ethnicity may be useful in some studies, but in other research contexts socioeconomic status, education, or gender may be a priority. For example, researching across gender affords chances for reflexivity and considerations on how to move forward in establishing trust (Galam, 2015). In these cases, we can see an overlap between negotiating trust and insider-outsider roles (see Katyal & King, 2011; Morosanu, 2015). (In the following chapter, we explore the spectrum of insider-outsiderness in detail.) As qualitative researchers, we can aim toward a participatory model incorporating empathy, reflection, and trust-building as central to our research process. To that end, you can ask yourself, *how can my privilege provide agency for those with less privilege?*

6. Reflections from the field: unpacking the meaning and practice of trust

In the following *Reflections from the Field*, two researchers discuss how they have sought to build or struggle with issues of trust in qualitative research. Jennifer R. Wolgemuth, a qualitative methodologist at the University of South Florida, discusses in her critical self-reflection how ethics, trust, and power intersect. Wolgemuth opens up about how she struggled to manage a surprising instance of abuse experienced by a student conducting interviews. Through her honesty and open sharing, we are provided with insight into issues of trust, power, and ethics within the research that can emerge in unexpected spaces. She concludes by critically self-reflecting about her own practice and suggests steps for others to consider regarding ethics and power.

On the ethics of sharing power

Jennifer R. Wolgemuth

Emily Mahoney was visibly excited about her upcoming research project (see Mahoney, 2020). On presentation day in my summer Qualitative Research class, she stood beaming next to her artfully crafted research poster, which depicted elements of her narrative case study design: an image of a young man in combat uniform with an artificial limb; a self-portrait of herself working with veteran students; and a reflection on her upbringing as an Asian American woman, the daughter of a Chinese mother and White veteran father.

Emily gushed, "I've found the most amazing veteran for a case study on thriving after losing a limb in combat. I wrote him last week and he agreed to be interviewed! I can't wait to hear and share his story!"

In class that summer, we'd read Roulston's (2010) *Reflective Interviewing* and learned about different theoretical approaches to interviewing. Emily knew that not all interviews are the same. She knew that both the questions she planned to ask and the way she planned to ask them were important to practice and reflect on in advance. She read literature on interviewing vulnerable populations, sensitive topics,

The meaning and practice of trust

and across cultural differences. She wanted to make sure her participant was comfortable, that he felt safe to share, and that he could trust her. She emphasized building rapport and trust and expected to share her experiences as a biracial woman, as a college counselor who supported veterans to return to civilian life, and as the devoted daughter of a veteran – all to foster empathic connections with her participant.

She had crafted well-worded interview questions that I advised her to consider straying from, to conduct the interview like a conversation between friends. I suggested she let him take the lead and tell the story he wanted – he would be her guide to his culture and experience. I knew she was well prepared to share power in the interview.

Sometimes power doesn't behave the way we expect it to. Despite extensive training, experience, and preparation, it is not possible to anticipate all the ways power might circulate in multicultural research. In fact, when power runs counter to its usual flows, it may very well be our extensive training that cements assumptions about power's directionality and invites aporias – moments when the right thing to do is neither obvious nor sufficient to the task. Who researchers think should have power (themselves) and who they should be sharing it with (participants) can render them incapable of coming to terms with their own powerlessness.

"He kissed me," Emily shared in my office two months later.

I laughed. "He did what?! That's ridiculous. Who would do that?"

Emily caught me completely off guard. Being kissed by a participant seemed unthinkable, totally absurd. Maybe that's why I laughed – a knee-jerk reaction cut off way too late when I noticed the pain in her eyes. The kiss had been more than one, and more than a kiss. He refused to answer questions. He turned off the recorder. He put his hand on her throat and chest. She felt trapped. He was persistent. He grew frustrated when she insisted she was there for the interview. That this was unprofessional. That she was a researcher. He cut the interview/assault off early and tried to give her money for an Uber ride home. These were details that would emerge only finally in her dissertation. An unwanted kiss was all she could share with me in my office, in that moment.

"Do you think I can still use the data? That interview was such a failure."

It's normal for victims to blame themselves. This was what triggered, finally, my more appropriate reaction: "I believe you. It's not your fault. How can I help?" But Emily's genuine concern about her data, what she considered the failure of her first research project, was what made me most uncomfortable . . . and culpable. What did it say about my relationship with her, my power as a professor, my responsibility to students, the way I teach about research, that her primary concern was not her own trauma and healing, but the shame of reporting a failed interview to her research professor?

There is nothing Emily (or I) could have done to prevent her assault. It wasn't her fault. It wasn't my fault either. Yet Emily's story (Mahoney, 2020), which is now the focus of her dissertation, has dramatically shifted the way I plan for, conduct, reflect on, and teach about research into cultures, cultural identities, and cultural experiences that are both the same and different from my own.

First, I emphasize self-care more. Research can break your heart. It can also shred the fabric of your life. Graduate school is a culture in and of itself and, for many graduate students, a disempowering one. It is important to have good supports, perspectives, and strategies for coping when learning and doing research that always risks going awry. No one can anticipate what will happen and how they will react, but cutting yourself a bit of slack is an important skill to master alongside all other research techniques.

Second, I understand power and researching within and across cultures and cultural differences, differently. Our cultural identities and the meanings of a research encounter are never fully our own to determine. Bodies are not neutral objects but active communicators of culture; the shape, style, and color of researchers' bodies matter in research. Interview contexts and materials also matter. The recording device, for example, is a cultural artifact that can be an object of power, rather than just a passive mechanism to record interview talk.

Power itself is not a cultural given, fixed before the research encounter. Power emerges in the encounter and is contingent on predictable and unpredictable embodied cultural assumptions – assumptions, for example, about what it means to be a man, about the purpose of an in-depth conversation, about the role and place of Asian women in US society, about disability, about good research, about heterosexuality, about sharing power. Even as it is a multicultural research ethic to share power, build rapport, engage participants and communities as co-researchers, and so on, these techniques are part of a Western attempt to undermine science's (present) history of colonial (and gendered, classed, raced. . .) oppression. Enacted, these techniques will not – cannot – be read the same way across the multiple cultures and cultural identities that manifest in each research encounter, nor do they automatically guarantee the ethicality of research.

Learning from Emily's story, I double down on my efforts to sensitize myself and students to the unpredictability of research, encouraging us to focus on how so much of research is done in the moment. This includes being aware of both the material and discursive (cultural) contexts of research and being willing to let go of well-learned assumptions about how research should be conducted – the assumed power of the researcher. While I am not sure tuning ourselves to power as emergent within research's varying cultural milieus will make us better researchers – whatever that might mean – I am sure I will be less surprised and kinder to myself and students when research hurts.

References

Mahoney, E. E. (2020). The gentle artist: Empowering warrior-scholars through the physical feminism of Jiu-Jitsu (Publication No. 27830083) [Doctoral dissertation]. University of South Florida. ProQuest Dissertations Publishing.

Roulston, K. (2010). Considering quality in qualitative interviewing. *Qualitative Research, 10*(2), 199–228. https://doi.org/10.1177/1468794109356739

Fatma F. S. Said, at Zayed University in the United Arab Emirates and the University of York in the UK, delves into the connections between participatory research and trust. Said discusses the co-construction of trust across both multilingual and multicultural communities, speaking specifically to challenges faced and suggestions when working with those who are from areas that are "hard to reach."

Co-constructing trust and working with multilingual, multicultural, conservative, hard-to-reach families

Fatma F. S. Said

Building trust with participants is a fundamental condition in qualitative work (Kvale & Brinkman, 2009), and without a doubt it allows for access to unique data and inevitably the introduction of new knowledge for the betterment of humanity. In addition to robust rigorous theoretical and methodological plans for the study, the researcher must also reflect on how they intend to build trust with the *researched*. Indeed, it is the foundation of any strong research project (Guillemin et al., 2018), and without participants' trust, researchers often lose great opportunities to learn about the human condition (Horn et al., 2011).

As researchers, we occupy a privileged status in society, and such a position is central to relationship building, power dynamics, and cultivating trust (Parson, 2019; Råheim et al., 2016). We gain access to people and are able to investigate or learn about them (Connelly, 2016; Krefting, 1991) because of our "professional citizenship" (Association of Social Anthropologists, 2018). In my experience, conducting research with multilingual families presents an added challenge in that families do not take part until they decide that trust has been established. They require the researcher to conduct data collection in a manner that suits them and for assurances that the final results will reflect a true picture and not an essentialized – or in my case, orientalist – narrative of their truths (Said, 1994). The fine art of establishing trust is further magnified when working with conservative, often hard-to-reach families who do not easily take part in research or wish to put their private lives on display.

My research focus

My research investigates bilingual acquisition of Arabic and English in multilingual families (Crespi et al., 2018; Li, 2009; Sengstock, 2001). The focus of the work endeavors to understand how Arabic, a minority language (Williams, 2013), is learned and used alongside English. The work is qualitative in nature (Heath et al., 2010) and is based on recording (audio and visual) interactions of family members within the home domain (or the classroom) and often includes parental/teacher interviews, questionnaire responses, and diary entries (Kvale & Brinkman, 2009). My aim is to understand the ideology(ies) the family members hold about their language(s) and how such beliefs affect language learning (see Said & Zhu, 2017, 2019; Said & AlGhamdi, 2018).

Co-constructing trust

The first way I build trust with my participants is through clear communication in terms of what their role in the research is and what I would prefer them to do in order to offer information I need. As a researcher who often shares the same background as the participants I research, I have to constantly be acutely aware of how I can use knowledge about the group to gain trust, but also be prepared that they may also refuse to engage with me. To aid this problem, I offer the participants two ways in which they can offer me data: either video record their conversations or audio record them and either allow me to be present or simply send me the data files. When I respect and accept their decision, this creates an interesting outcome: an almost binding, yet unspoken commitment that they feel they have to offer the data. Such delicate decisions build trust on part of the researcher and the researched and make for a successful data collection cycle.

The second way I build trust is through clearly and openly informing participants how the data they provide for the project will be used. To seal this co-constructed relationship of trust, I share raw data files as well as final reports. In all, participants like to see what they have provided, and this usually makes for an interesting discussion because they have the opportunity to see themselves in a new light.

References

Crespi, I., Giada Meda, S., & Merla, L. (Eds.). (2018). *Making Multicultural Families in Europe: Gender and Intergenerational Relations*. London: Palgrave Macmillan.

Heath, C., Hindmarsh, J., & Luff, P. (2010). *Video in Qualitative Research: Analysing Social Interaction in Everyday Life*. Thousand Oaks, CA: Sage.

Kvale, S., & Brinkman, S. (2009). *Interviews: Learning the Craft of Qualitative Research Interviewing*. London: Sage.

Råheim, M., Magnussen, L. V., Sekse, R. J. T., Lunde, A., Jacobsen, T., & Blystad, A. (2016). Researcher-researched relationship in qualitative research: Shifts in positions and researcher vulnerability. *International Journal of Qualitative Studies in Health and Well-Being*, *11*. https://doi.org/10.3402/qhw.v11.30996

Said, E. W. (1994). *Orientalism: Western Conceptions of the Orient*. London: Penguin Books.

Said, F. (forthcoming). The challenges of presenting multilingual data in sociolinguistics: A focus on Arabic-English data. In B. L. Samuelson & S. Silvhiany (Eds.), *Learning to Do Research Multilingually*. Bristol, UK: Multilingual Matters.

Said, F., & AlGhamdi, F. (2018). *Development of Minority Language Literacy at Home: The Case of an Arabic-English Speaking Family*. Paper presented at the Fourth Intergenerational Transmission of Minority Languages Symposium: Language and Identity, Uppsala University and University of Canterbury. http://ikt.edu.uu.se/jhlm/?p=415

Said, F., & Zhu, H. (2017). The strategic use of address terms in multilingual interactions during family mealtimes. In A. De Fina, D. Ikizoglu, & J. Wegner (Eds.), *Diversity and Super-Diversity: Sociocultural Linguistic Perspectives* (pp. 81–96). Washington, DC: Georgetown University Press.

Said, F., & Zhu, H. (2019). "No, no Maama! Say 'Shaatir ya Ouledee Shaatir'!" Children's agency in language use and socialisation. *International Journal of Bilingualism*, *23*(3), 771–785.

Sengstock, M. C. (2001). Multicultural families-what makes them work? *Sociological Practice*, *3*(1), 1–17.

Williams, C. H. (2013). *Minority Language Promotion, Protection and Regulation: The Mask of Purity*. London: Palgrave Macmillan.

7. Engaging more deeply: concluding thoughts on unpacking the meaning and practice of trust

Trust requires reflexivity, awareness, dialogue, a commonality of purpose, and empathy based on similar experiences. The concept of trust in qualitative research allows us to think about ourselves in relation to others. In

The meaning and practice of trust

particular, within multicultural and diverse contexts, we want to be cautious about and actively learn about the communities and individuals we want to work with, whether in face-to-face or in socially distanced environments. (You can read more about online research in Chapter 6.) In this chapter, we discussed key ideas about building relationships and creating trust. Throughout, we included questions for you to consider to help guide your research study considering social capital, how data is gathered, and ways participants may be able to be incorporated into a participatory role.

As researchers, we occupy a privileged status in society, and such a position is central to relationship building, power dynamics, and cultivating trust and addressing vulnerability (Parson, 2019; Råheim et al., 2016). Therefore, when we enter into a community, regardless of our ethnic or religious standing in that community, our relationship is not solely based on actual status but also on *perceived* status. Our perceived status within society can enable us to gain access to people at times solely due to our "professional citizenship" (Association of Social Anthropologists, 2018; Connelly, 2016; Krefting, 1991). The fine art of establishing trust is magnified when working with traditional, conservative families, who do not easily participate in research or wish to put their private lives on display. Ultimately, trust is built on the researchers' perceived intentions, their project, and the process.

Ultimately, a deeper understanding can be forged if participants are given a chance to trust you as a researcher. Instead of seeing trust as a given, we can look at how to earn and construct it over time. Trust, for some cultures, takes time to build. It's not just about friendly connection but seeing an authentic person (Karlsen et al., 2008). The inclusion of local community members can offer ways to negotiate and provide entrance into the community as gatekeepers and community brokers. As we further reflect on potential issues of trust and ethics, we can create more robust and socially just qualitative research.

Reflective questions about trust

In this chapter, we explored what it means to develop trust in a research study and how it is negotiated and navigated throughout a research process. The complicated nature of working with others and listening deeply to others' experiences requires us to consider and critically self-reflect on the processes we're engaging in to hear others. We saw the centrality of such concepts as empathy, vulnerability, positionality, and ethics. While many directions were incorporated throughout the chapter, the following table provides additional topics and questions for you or a group to consider connected to trust and your current or future research.

Topic	Questions
Developing trust	• How are you building trust, and what type of trust are you developing? • Where could you expand your trustworthiness in concrete ways? • How can participants trust that the impact of our study will not affect them negatively? • How can we ethically create trust with communities whose linguistic, religious, ethnic, or cultural practices differ from the researchers?
Moving into partnership	• What are two or three specific ways you could move the relationship with participants beyond a scientific one, such as through bringing community together or addressing social issues at the community or individual level?
Social impact to build partnerships and trust	• Imagine you are on an ethics review board reviewing multiple proposals for community research. • What types of comments and descriptions could help signal that the research team is knowledgeable about building trust? • Is there anything that might stand out as a "red flag" that the team or individual has not properly thought about building trust with participants?

References

Allard, A. C. (2005). Capitalizing on Bourdieu: How useful are concepts of "social capital" and "social field" for researching "marginalized" young women? *Theory and Research in Education, 3*(1), 63–79.

Alvarez, R. A., Vasquez, E., Mayorga, C. C., Feaster, D. J., & Mitrani, V. B. (2006). Increasing minority research participation through community organization outreach. *Western Journal of Nursing Research, 28*(5), 541–560.

Amankwaa, L. (2016). Creating protocols for trustworthiness in qualitative research. *Journal of Cultural Diversity, 23*(3), 121–127.

Association of Social Anthropologists. (2018). Ethical guidelines for good research practice. Retrieved March 10, 2019, from https://www.theasa.org/ethics/guidelines.shtml

Bancroft, M. A. (2015). Community interpreting: A profession rooted in social justice. In *The Routledge Handbook of Interpreting* (pp. 229–247). London: Routledge.

Baser, B., & Toivanen, M. (2018). Politicized and depoliticized ethnicities, power relations and temporality: Insights to outsider research from comparative and transnational fieldwork. *Ethnic and Racial Studies, 41*(11), 2067–2084.

Berry, J. W. (2011). Intercultural relations in plural societies: Research derived from Canadian multiculturalism policy. *Canadian Ethnic Studies, 43*(3), 5–18.

Bhopal, K. (2009). Identity, empathy and "otherness": Asian women, education and dowries in the UK. *Race, Ethnicity and Education, Special Issue: Black Feminisms and Postcolonial Paradigms: Researching Educational Inequalities, 12*(1), 27–40.

Bhopal, K. (2010). Gender, identity and experience: Researching marginalised groups. *Women's Studies International Forum, 33*(3), 188–195.

Boivin, N. (2015). Peripheral ritualized practices: Threads connecting decorations to the cloak of identity. *Journal of Intercultural Communications Research, 44*(1), 44–63.

Boivin, N. (2018). Kazakh transnational multiliteracies: Building intergenerational communities of learning. In S. Brunn & R. Kehrein (Eds.), *Handbook of the Changing World Language Map*. Cham, Switzerland: Springer.

Boivin, N. (forthcoming). Foodscapes: Multisensory food discourse resources initiating reciprocal interactions. *Language, Culture and Society Journal*.

Botterill, K. (2015). "We don't see things as they are, we see things as we are": Questioning the "outsider" in Polish migration research. *Forum Qualitative Sozialforschung/Forum: Qualitative Social Research, 16*(2), Art. 4.

Bourdieu, P. (1993). *Sociology in Question*. London: Sage.

Campbell, R., & Wasco, S. (2000). Feminist approaches to social sciences: Epistemological and methodological tenets. *American Journal of Community Psychology, 28*(6), 773–791.

Carby, H. (1982). White women listen! Black feminism and the boundaries of sisterhood. In *Centre for Contemporary Cultural Studies, The Empire Strikes Back: Race and Racism in 70s Britain* (pp. 212–235). London: Hutchinson.

Clark, T. (2011). Gaining and maintaining access: Exploring the mechanisms that support and challenge the relationship between gatekeepers and researchers. *Qualitative Social Work, 10*(4), 485–502. https://doi.org/10.1177/1473325009358228

Clark, T., & Sinclair, R. (2008). The costs and benefits of acting as a research site. *Evidence & Policy: A Journal of Research, Debate and Practice, 4*(1), 105–119.

CohenMiller, A. S., & Saban, G. A. (forthcoming). Rigor in qualitative research in the Asian context. In S. Wa-Mbaleka & A. Rosario (Eds.), *The SAGE Handbook of Qualitative Research in the Asian Context*. London: Sage.

Collins, P. H. (1991). *Black Feminist Thought: Knowledge, Consciousness and the Politics of Empowerment* (Vol. 2). New York: Routledge.

Connelly, L. M. (2016). Trustworthiness in qualitative research. *Medsurg Nursing, 25*(6).

Culley, L. (2006). Transcending transculturalism? Race, ethnicity and health-care. *Nursing Inquiry, 13*(2), 144–153.

Durrani, N., Kataeva, Z., CohenMiller, A., Seitkhadyrova, A., & Badanova, A. (2020, April). *"Ann's Much _ (Beautiful) than Mary": Gendered Discourses in Secondary School Textbooks in Kazakhstan*. Miami, FL: Comparative International Education Society (CIES). Online.

Durrani, N., Kataeva, Z., CohenMiller, A., & Makhmetova, Z. (2021, April). *Teacher Agency for Gender Justice in Kazakhstan*. Miami, FL: Comparative International Education Society (CIES). Online.

Eide, P., & Allen, C. B. (2005). Recruiting transcultural qualitative research participants: A conceptual model. *International Journal of Qualitative Methods, 4*(2), 44–56.

Galam, R. G. (2015). Gender, reflexivity, and positionality in male research in one's own community with Filipino seafarers' wives. *Forum Qualitative Sozialforschung / Forum: Qualitative Social Research, 16*(3). https://doi.org/10.17169/fqs-16.3.2330

Geertz, C. (1973). *The Interpretation of Cultures*. New York: Basic Books.

Guba, E., & Lincoln, Y. (1981). *Effective Evaluation*. San Francisco, CA: Jossey-Bass.

Guillemin, M., Barnard, E., Allen, A., Stewart, P., Walker, H., Rosenthal, D., & Gillam, L. (2018). Do research participants trust researchers or their institution? *Journal of Empirical Research on Human Research Ethics, 13*(3), 285–294. https://doi.org/10.1177/1556264618763253

Hall, B. L., & Kulig, J. C. (2004). Kanadier Mennonites: A case study examining research challenges among religious groups. *Qualitative Health Research, 14*(3), 359–368.

Heath, C., Hindmarsh, J., & Luff, P. (2010). *Video in Qualitative Research: Analysing Social Interaction in Everyday Life*. London: Sage.

Hennink, M., Hutter, I., & Bailey, A. (2020). *Qualitative Research Methods*. London: Sage.

Horn, E. J., Edwards, K., & Terry, S. F. (2011). Engaging research participants and building trust. *Genetic Testing and Molecular Biomarkers, 15*(12), 839–840.

Hua, Z. (2018). *Exploring Intercultural Communication: Language in Action. Introductions to Applied Linguistics*. New York: Routledge.

Jacquemet, M. (2015). Asylum and superdiversity: The search for denotational accuracy during asylum hearings. *Language & Communication, 44*, 72–81.

Karlsen, J. T., Græe, K., & Massaoud, M. J. (2008). Building trust in project-stakeholder relationships. *Baltic Journal of Management, 3*(1), 7–22.

Katyal, K. R., & King, M. (2011). "Outsiderness" and "insiderness" in a Confucian society: Complexity of contexts. *Comparative Education, 47*(3), 327–341.

Kokanovic, R., Furler, J., May, C., Dowrick, C., Herrman, H., Evert, H., & Gunn, J. (2009). The politics of conducting research on depression in a cross-cultural context. *Qualitative Health Research, 19*(5), 708–717.

Kondowe, C., & Booyens, M. (2014). A student's experience of gaining access for qualitative research. *Social Work, 50*(1), 146–152.

Krefting, L. (1991). Rigor in qualitative research: The assessment of trustworthiness *The American Journal of Occupational Therapy, 45*(3), 214–222.

Levkoff, S., & Sanchez, H. (2003). Lessons learned about minority recruitment and retention from the centers on minority aging and health promotion. *The Gerontologist, 43*(1), 18–26.

Li, G. (Ed.). (2009). *Multicultural Families, Home Literacies, and Mainstream Schooling*. New York: Information Age Publishing.

Lin, N. (2002). *Social Capital: A Theory of Social Structure and Action* (Vol. 19). Cambridge, UK: Cambridge University Press.

Lincoln, Y., & Guba, E. G. (1985). *Naturalistic Inquiry*. Thousand Oaks, CA: Sage.

Lomas, J. (2018). Using "linkage and exchange" to move research into policy at a Canadian Foundation. *Health Affairs, 19*(2), 236–240. https://doi.org/10.1377/hlthaff.19.3.23

McAreavey, R., & Das, C. (2013). A delicate balancing act: Negotiating with gatekeepers for ethical research when researching minority communities. *International Journal of Qualitative Methods, 12*(1), 113–131.

McLean, C. A., & Campbell, C. M. (2003). Locating research informants in a multi-ethnic community: Ethnic identities, social networks and recruitment methods. *Ethnicity and Health, 8*(1), 41–61.

Mertens, D. M. (2020). *Research and Evaluation in Education and Psychology: Integrating Diversity with Quantitative, Qualitative, and Mixed Methods* (5th ed.). London: Sage.

Miranda, M. K. (2003). *Homegirls in the Public Sphere*. Austin: University of Texas Press.

Morosanu, L. (2015). Researching coethnic migrants: Privileges and puzzles of "insiderness." *Forum Qualitative Sozialforschung / Forum: Qualitative Social Research, 16*(2), Art. 15. https://doi.org/10.17169/fqs-16.2.2371

Nowell, L. S., Norris, J. M., White, D. E., & Moules, N. J. (2017). Thematic analysis: Striving to meet the trustworthiness criteria. *International Journal of Qualitative Methods, 16*(1), 1609406917733847.

Opsal, T., Wolgemuth, J., Cross, J., Kaanta, T., Dickmann, E., Colomer, S., & Erdil-Moody, Z. (2016). "There are no known benefits . . .": Considering the risk/Benefit ratio of qualitative research. *Qualitative Health Research, 26*(8), 1137–1150. https://doi.org/10.1177/1049732315580109

Parson, L. (2019). Considering positionality: The ethics of conducting research in marginalized groups. In K. K. Strunk & L. A. Locke (Eds.), *Research Methods for Social Justice and Equity in Education* (pp. 15–32). Cham, Switzerland: Palgrave Macmillan.

Phoenix, A. (1987). Theories of gender and black families. In G. Weiner & M. Arnot (Eds.), *Gender Under Scrutiny: New Inquiries in Education* (pp. 50a–61). London: Hutchinson.

Phoenix, A. (2001). Practising feminist research: The intersection of gender and "race" in the research process. In K. K. Bhavnani (Ed.), *Feminism and Race* (pp. 203–219). Oxford, UK: Oxford University Press.

Pink, S., & Morgan, J. (2013). Short-term ethnography: Intense routes to knowing. *Symbolic Interaction, 36*(3), 351–361.

Råheim, M., Magnussen, L. V., Sekse, R. J. T., Lunde, A., Jacobsen, T., & Blystad, A. (2016). Researcher-researched relationship in qualitative research: Shifts in positions and researcher vulnerability. *International Journal of Qualitative Studies in Health and Well-Being, 11*. https://doi.org/10.3402/qhw.v11.30996

Rugkåsa, J., & Canvin, K. (2011). Researching mental health in minority ethnic communities: Reflections on recruitment. *Qualitative Health Research, 21*(1), 132–143.

Sanghera, G. S., & Thapar-Björkert, S. (2008). Methodological dilemmas: Gatekeepers and positionality in Bradford. *Ethnic and Racial Studies, 31*(3), 543–562.

Stahl, N. A., & King, J. R. (2020). Expanding approaches for research: Understanding and using trustworthiness in qualitative research. *Journal of Developmental Education, 44*(1), 26–28.

Tracy, S. J. (2010). Qualitative quality: Eight "big-tent" criteria for excellent qualitative research. *Qualitative Inquiry, 16*, 837–851.

Whyte, W. F. (2012). *Street Corner Society: The Social Structure of an Italian Slum.* Chicago: University of Chicago Press.

Woodward, E., & Marrfurra McTaggart, P. (2016). Transforming cross-cultural water research through trust, participation and place. *Geographical Research, 54*(2), 129–142.

Yancey, A. K., Ortega, A. N., & Kumanyika, S. K. (2006). Effective recruitment and retention of minority research participants. *Annual Review of Public Health, 27*(1), 1–28.

Yu, J. (2009). Qualitative research on the attitudes toward teenage sexual behaviour of Chinese British families: Methodological issues. *Journal of Transcultural Nursing, 20*(2), 156–163.

Uncovering the spectrum of insider-outsiderness

How am I being viewed by my participants and other stakeholders? Am I an insider because I match my participants' characteristics, or an outsider because I'm not from the community? This chapter highlights the tension in qualitative multicultural research regarding the researcher's **membership roles** as insiders and outsiders. In a simplified manner, being considered an insider or outsider provides a way to connect or establish separation from a topic or community (Savvides et al., 2014). However, the traditional dichotomy of either being a part of the community or separate from it is a false one (Dwyer & Buckle, 2009; Paechter, 2013; Sherif, 2001). The concepts of in-group and out-group participation are central for qualitative researchers within any research project, but are especially relevant for those researching within and across multicultural contexts. Practicing critical self-reflection can provide a means to understand our shifting group membership. Moreover, such critical reflexivity can lead to more reliable and ethical research when conducting research with those from multicultural backgrounds (Zempi, 2016).

For researchers, understanding the various perspectives inside and outside of our field, or **identity markers**, can enable us to capture understanding when investigating contexts and communities where we are perceived to be outsiders (Paechter, 2013; Sherif, 2001). For example, Crenshaw (1991) argued that "contemporary feminist and anti-racist discourses have failed to consider intersectional identities such as women of color" (p. 1243). Therefore, for researchers who are fortunate enough to be born with White privilege, understanding intersectional feminism strengthens any truths we seek. Groups at the intersection of two or more identity categories are often left out of focus in both analysis and politics. Those who self-identify or

DOI: 10.4324/9780429285691-4

are identified as groups positioned at the intersection of gender and race/ethnicity become marginalized as a group, such as Black women, ethnic minority women, or – broadly – "women of color." As a marginalized group, such a group can then "face limited options of political communities formed either around ethnicity or around gender, rather than political action that engages with the particular difficulties at the intersection" (Walby et al., 2012, p. 226).

Dwyer and Buckle (2009) ask: "Should qualitative researchers be members of the population they are studying, or should they not?" (p. 54). Being an insider or outsider, or a combination of the two over time, can provide a way to hear participants' voices. The definitions of these binary roles, however, are being reconsidered, reevaluated, and applied. For instance, McNess et al. (2015) suggest recontextualizing insider and outsider roles away from an "essentialist definition":

> Earlier essentialist definitions of the outsider as detached and objective, and the insider as culturally embedded and subjective, are re-examined and set within an international research and teaching context that recognises the increased migration of people, ideas and educational policies. It is argued that, in the context of such change, it has become more difficult to categorise and label groups and individuals as being "inside" or "outside" systems, professional communities or research environments.
>
> (p. 295)

As a dynamic spectrum, insider-outsiderness provides one way to consider working within a global world. The concepts relate directly to positionality and thereby touch upon discussion of power and positionality from Chapter 1. Thus, we can think about the roles of being an insider or outsider as a spectrum, one that shifts over time and can vary within the research process. While an insider in a research study may be considered a part of the community, or an outsider as someone on the periphery of the community, these positions shift and can be considered "fluid" (Bhattacharya, 2007). For example, the roles can be considered as co-constructed identities (Razon & Ross, 2012) or instead as having "some plasticity and can be moved inward and outward" (Beals et al., 2020, p. 596). In this chapter, we discuss how membership roles as insiders and outsiders can vary within a research study and explore how scholars have negotiated these roles. We unpack the nature of understanding our insider/outsider roles, the changing aspects of these roles as performed, ethical issues related to such roles, along with *Reflections from the Field* and further questions to consider.

1. How can we understand our insider-outsider roles?

The multifaceted nature of being an insider one moment, an outsider another minute, and then something in between provides opportunities and challenges for research with diverse communities. For Milligan (2014), a participatory practice provided more dependable access to work with secondary school students in Kenya. As adults coming into a school setting, we are automatically positioned as different, often not matching the typical physical attributes of the children within the institution. Yet, for qualitative researchers, there are steps we can consider to bridge this divide:

> an enabling tool for an outsider to both gain insider perspectives and develop a more insider role in that community by privileging and legitimating participant-driven data. Conclusions put forward the concept of the "inbetweener" researcher, neither entirely inside or outside, and consider how using such methods allowed the formulation of authentic participative knowledge (co-)construction and construction of meaningful relationships in the field.
>
> (Milligan, 2014, p. 1005)

These roles are described in various ways and often include different terminology based upon disciplinary background or perspective. For example, Smith (2006), who developed essential practices of Indigenous and decolonizing research, describes such roles as *margins*:

> The metaphor of the margin has been very powerful in the social sciences and humanities for understanding social inequality, oppression, disadvantage and power. It is used alongside other similar concepts such as borders, boundaries, bridges, centre/periphery, and insider/outsider to demarcate people in spatial terms as well as in socio-economic, political and cultural terms.
>
> (p. 6)

Other researchers describe the "space between" of being an insider and outsider. Dwyer and Buckle (2009) move from the discussion of being either the insider or outsider to being both an insider and outsider within a study of parental status. The authors were later invited to reflect back on their article, which became one of the top downloaded for the journal:

> We challenged the dichotomous perspective of insider-outsider and argued instead for a third space that allows researchers to occupy the position of both insider and outsider. Researchers can only ever occupy the space between, as we cannot fully occupy one or the other of those positions.
>
> (Dwyer & Buckle, 2018, p. 18)

We can also explore what it means to be within the spectrum of insider-outsider through the eyes of returning from the field with a new perspective. For Anna, when she was a doctoral student mother, she conducted research with other doctoral student mothers, continuing research with them into their careers (CohenMiller, 2018; CohenMiller & Demers, 2019). These transitions provided a mirroring of experience in different institutions and countries, along with some feelings of liminality – being at times on the margins of mainstream academics. For Nettie, she examined multicultural families' experiences, focusing on those having encountered multigenerational learning and interaction, a process that she had experienced herself (Boivin, 2018). Similarly, as Nettie's roles changed, her experiences in returning to the field also shifted.

In other research studies, a background in a similar field may help provide access. For Law (2019), who interviewed professional footballers, getting access to top athletes could have proven challenging. The researcher noted that participants became more comfortable, opening up for discussion when they learned that Law (2019) had a similar athletic background as a semi-professional footballer. He leaned on this and shared about his experience, explaining "I deliberately started off by chatting about my own moderate successes as a player" (Law, 2019, p. 4), and noted how it aided research participants in sharing their experiences as well.

Assumed commonality, whether of athletic background or ethnic origin, might lead into a myriad of other positions, based on age, education, or gender of the researcher and participants. In conversation, then, some positions facilitate rapport, whereas others might hinder mutual trust, as Ryan (2009,

2015) shows in her comparative research with Irish and Polish migrants. At each of the research stages, both the researcher and her participants actively and in relation to each other negotiate "positions" (Nowicka & Ryan, 2015, p. 6). We can think about a *fluid* move through positions and roles (Bhattacharya, 2020). Papadopoulos and Lees (2002) advocate "ethnic matching" between researchers and participants, arguing that ethnic matching will produce more accurate details in the research process. An insider view can encourage "ethnic sensitivity" that individuals who are not members of the communities may be unable to bring into the research (Verma & Ashworth, 1986). Ethnic commonalities are not just seen as a way of addressing cultural differences, but also as reducing intersubjective distances between the interviewer and respondent (Bhopal, 2009). Therefore, it might not just be about coming from the same community but rather how the community views who you are.

At times, the insider may be viewed more harshly than an outsider. For example, in a multiyear research study of student well-being in Kazakhstan, Anna was part of a multidisciplinary team including local Kazakhstani researchers (CohenMiller et al., 2017). She conducted interviews and focus groups in Russian and Kazakh throughout the country. As a non-native speaker of those languages, Anna relied on translators and researchers on the team who were fluent in those languages. In construct, the researcher as an insider can be seen as threatening *because* of their insiderness. The use of translators plays an important role in research and the nature of these membership roles. There are major considerations when using interpreters, such as sociocultural, gender, age, and linguistic constraints (Aragrande, 2018; Jacquemet, 2015; Martínez-Acchini, 2017; Resch & Enzenhofer, 2018). The practice of interpreting is rooted in social justice (Bancroft, 2015). It can be considered as an interactional relationship (Wadensjo, 2014), involving practical steps when collecting data across languages (see Resch & Enzenhofer, 2018).

In contrast, based upon the context and various other factors, a researcher as an outsider can be seen as sympathetic and approachable. Those from within the country were frequently confronted with linguistic and cultural opposition. Participants from various regions were affronted by the researchers who spoke with an accent or language from another region. In this way, the insiders to the local content faced some pushback based upon the dialect used and concern about the privacy of shared information. In this way, the local researchers become more intricately associated with government bodies and the university, an association that was not applied to me, as a foreigner – an outsider. For those of us researchers considered to be "foreigners," the participants seemed to feel more comfortable openly sharing their experiences without opposition to the linguistic difference. So, you can ask yourself, **how does my insider-outsider role affect access to research?** *Is there someone else I need to reach out to as a bridge to better demonstrate my commitment to socially just research?*

2. What is the changing nature of being an insider-outsider?

At present, there is an increase in research from multilingual, multiethnic, and multicultural perspectives (Paechter, 2013). With a recognition of new positionalities applied to a previously monocultural approach, the term "insider-outsider" is shifting and even becoming obsolete in some disciplinary fields (Dwyer & Buckle, 2009). For example, in studying Nepalese families and community, having the same linguistic or ethnic identity has been shown to carry less of an in-group, insider position than the researcher having the same role as a mother of a second-language learner to those being interviewed (Boivin, 2015, 2016)

Being considered an insider to a community can mean participants feel connected to the researcher. Perhaps participants see the researcher as someone who can understand their experiences without explaining. In that same vein, there lies the issue. If a participant *thinks* the researcher understands them because they share a common characteristic or experience (e.g., being a person of color, losing a child, being a single parent, facing bullying in the workplace), the similarity can lead to fewer descriptions and explanations provided by the participant themselves. For example, in a study of graduate student mothers, Anna conducted a study with those who had experienced becoming a mother for the first time during their doctoral studies (CohenMiller, 2014). As a first-time mother and also a doctoral student, I (Anna) fit the key criteria for participants and was an insider in many ways. I recall interviewing one doctoral student mother who explained many answers at length and often turned to me to confirm her understanding of a common experience. Because my participant knew I had gone through a common experience – becoming a mother while in a doctoral program – she appeared to feel connected and shared extensively with me, assuming a common understanding of experience (CohenMiller, 2014).

As researchers, we can be insiders in some ways and outsiders in other ways (Leigh, 2014). While participants can assume the researcher understands their experience, the reverse can also occur with the researcher. At times, there can be a challenge not to jump to an assumption about a commonly experienced event. It remains challenging for more experienced researchers to uncover participants' experiences, especially when there are great similarities between the researcher and participant. In using interviews, many researchers have explored challenges with understanding our position as insiders or outsiders, and the spectrum that exists. For instance, Roulston (2014) and Carolyn Ellis with Chris Patti (2014) have looked into various challenges and approaches for interviews. Part of the issues faced by interviewers directly relates to how participants perceive us, how we interpret our participants' words, and how to negotiate the space. Finding the ways to connect within our research provides chances to critically self-reflect on our process. How are we trying to show ourselves as similar to those we work with? Or perhaps we are emphasizing our differences? Smith et al. (2002), when working with youth, talked about the ways of negotiating relationships with participants – what she calls *finding the join*: "An approach we would situate it between the idea of establishing 'rapport' which is an 'outsider' approach to making connections and that of being acknowledged as having some 'street credibility' that we would define as an 'insider' approach" (p. 174). The challenges faced lead to new questions for us to consider. **How do we move beyond assumed responses by participants? How do we get to the deeper stories?**

The way we understand our own insider-outsider roles can be problematized and reexamined throughout a study. For instance, as discussed in Chapter 1, understanding various identity markers and aspects, such as language or background, can be key to access or group membership as an insider. As Rasool (2017) explains, people in our communities have life experiences and cultural experiences that are important to consider when working with communities (p. 314). Depending on the context and factors, outsiders can come to be seen as sympathetic and approachable (Adu-Ampong & Adams, 2020). Creating understanding and inclusion for each participant role can empower communities as agents of change (Rasool, 2017; Piller, 2017). These varied perspectives on insider-outsiderness are discussed across disciplinary and interdisciplinary lines.

For example, from a cultural anthropological perspective, being an insider may mean greater access to participants. For example, joining a community within an ethnographic study can mean the researcher becomes associated with the community, allowed to participate and see aspects of life that would not be possible if solely an outsider. As explained by Pather (2004), in her ethnographic study of educational inclusion within a South African school community, she was both an insider and outsider. She entered the South African school community as a South African of Indian descent. Pather (2004) was broadly an insider as a South African, but an outsider to the school and an outsider to that particular school's cultural community. In another case, Alegra Ally, an applied anthropologist, immersed herself in an ongoing ethnographic study of birthing within nomadic tribes around the world (Wild Born Project, n.d.). She started as an outsider in many ways, not a part of the cultural community but as a White westerner. But as a mother, she could enter the space and be present for the rituals of birthing. She immersed herself in the community, learning characteristics of the communities, further establishing her insider role through her own birthing process. While these examples provide a sense of the varied way insider-outsider roles can be addressed and experienced, these concepts have also been shifting in conceptualization across and within disciplines.

In sociology, the concepts of in-group and out-group membership have been discussed as well. One such study examines insider and outsider roles through a study of Black men's experience of bullying in online gaming spaces (Ortiz, 2019). While the researcher, Stephanie Ortiz, is not a Black man, she notes how she negotiated her outsiderness as a woman, working to show her ability to delve into her participants' experiences. Other research drawing from feminist and masculine studies problematizes the insider-outsider debate in considering the changing dynamic of a once insider who has changed over time. An example of the changing nature of the researcher and their involvement in their home community can be seen in the work of Saeed and Griffin (2019) in Pakistan. The researchers' changed circumstances affected how they were able to gain access to participants and required a change in research approach, such as through indirect questions facilitated using vignettes (Saeed & Griffin, 2019). We can look at another disciplinary perspective as well, from that of health sciences and midwifery. Burns et al. (2012) explores the insider-outsider "debate" as a woman entering a familiar setting within a midwifery ward. In her study, she problematizes her role as both insider and outsider.

The spectrum of insider-outsiderness

In a study that sought to understand how to develop interactive theater for toddlers, Olaussen and Hovik (2019) describe her perspective as a director, researcher, and actor. As a director, she was an insider. Yet, she points to the fact that perspective in and of itself shifts: "my perspective in the project was still outside the performance as artwork, but my focus shifted constantly between all elements in play" (Olaussen & Hovik, 2019, p. 672). These shifting narratives of insider and outsider provide some insight into the importance of self-reflection. So, you can ask yourself, *in what ways might I be considered an insider? In what ways as an outsider? What do these roles suggest to those around me?*

3. Are we seeing and understanding our roles?

Without taking an additional step to discuss with participants the *reasoning* behind an action, for instance, the researcher and others reading the account can be left wondering and unsure of the insider-outsiderness of the researcher. For example, we can look at this example of being an outsider and potentially misunderstanding information within a diverse context. In being a researcher as an outsider to the ethnic community and age group, the researcher ended up making assumptions from their observations. During a presentation of migrant youth during an ethnographic research study in a vocational school, a researcher observed that during a school culture day, a Somali youth grabbed a scarf from an adjacent table at which information about Afghanistan was presented. The Somali youth proceeded to put on the scarf. One researcher concluded that the youth was "bullying" the other ethnic group by wearing the cultural object, the scarf, as making fun of the other's ethnicity (RECLAS Research Forum, 2017) Yet, there are other ways to unpack this interaction. How could we consider this interaction? Do we *know* the intent of the youth?

Yet, as researchers we may attempt to unpack an action observed and also encounter challenges such as with participants shying away from discussion, being unsure of how to articulate their actions, or identifying only partial rationales for them. Thus, it's important for qualitative researchers to continually critically self-reflect upon our work, asking ourselves questions along the way to best identify the significance, meaning and cultural context of artifacts, interactions, and discussions. Part of a negotiation of insider and outsider status can be seen in the work of Hill (2006). As a "teacher researcher in Hip-Hop Lit," Hill examined his role, which at times appeared straightforward as an insider to the school yet not fitting into that role, nor allowing the affordances of an outsider (p. 935). Ultimately, Hill (2006) suggests critically reflecting on "issues of identity, authority, and power" by asking ourselves questions about our work with our participants: "Who am I to them? Who am I for them? Who do I want to be to them? What stories do I tell? How do I want readers to see them? How do I want readers to see me?" (p. 947).

Another way the insider-outsider discussion can be framed is that of a type of performance. In all instances, as Goffman (1959) explains, as people we perform a role and adjust ourselves based upon the responses of others. In qualitative research, we can also consider the roles we undertake as performance, whether through our own reflective research (CohenMiller, 2020) or in relationships with others (Boivin, 2016). For instance, in research conducted by Bodi Hansen Blix, in researching within Indigenous communities, the researcher follows Denzin's (2001) conceptualization of an interview as a performance. Blix (2015) explains that "both the interviewee's and the interviewer's identities are framed and shaped, facilitated and inhibited by the broader stories and discourses that are available in a particular socio-historical context" (p. 177). For Blix, she identifies as ethnically Sami and conducted research about and with Sami self-identified individuals. Her interviews were then framed as a type of performance, one that was negotiated in relationship with others, "My affiliation as Sami was not for me to perform independently of the elderly woman and her niece. Rather, I was continuously negotiating this affiliation according to the elderly woman's and her niece's acceptance of it" (p. 181).

Membership roles continue to be explored and have the potential for us to understand experiences that would be challenging, or impossible, to research if we were separate from the community. The insights gained by survivors of illness, of mental health crisis (Johnston, 2019), provide an understanding of the experience that may have been impossible without the researcher having lived through similar aspects. This example of insiderness can provide unique and important insights. But the rationale for such studies of survivor-centered insiderness, the ethics, and the practicalities, still rests on the shoulders of the researcher to explain and argue. The nature of membership roles can guide us as thoughtful, socially aware researchers to confront issues of power, trust, vulnerability, and ethics. Such power struggles as insider/outsider can involve language, culture, gender identity, age, ethnicity, ability, religion, and exposure to sociopolitical issues, to name just a few. In considering our roles as insiders and outsiders as a performance, we can then question our interactions (see Acevedo-Gil, 2019; Ladson-Billings & Tate, 1995, for in-depth discussion of concepts of how our roles intersect with issues of power). So, what can you ask yourself at this point? Perhaps, you could ask, **in what ways am I enacting power as an in "insider-outsider"?** *In what ways does my "performance" shift with various stakeholders in my research?*

4. What ethical dilemmas should we be prepared for relating to the spectrum of insider-outsiderness?

For qualitative researchers, identifying our membership roles connects as well to ethical considerations, whether in face-to-face or in socially distanced and online research. Considering ethical dilemmas can connect to the ways in which we interact and see similarities or differences with our participants. For instance, **how can we study the experiences of someone undergoing great loss?** *Is it best to have gone through a similar loss or to be an outsider who is allowed to see and hear the lived experience?* Typically, for experiences of loss, the researcher has had some connection to a similar type of experience, yet this is not always the case. For Ellis and Bochner (2016), for instance, they were pivotal in developing autoethnographic practices and collaborative co-production of knowledge through the application of evocative autoethnography. Additionally, Ellis has expanded our understanding of how to interview compassionately through her explanations of working with those who survived the Holocaust. While Ellis did not have a history of survival from similar trauma, she found a way to connect to those who did. As an outsider to the experiences, she worked hand in hand with an insider – a survivor – from the concentration camps during World War II, Jerry Rawicki, to learn and write about the experiences together (see Ellis & Rawicki, 2018).

Another ethical consideration is in studying one's own family. For Foster (2009), she studied her own family; she was thus an insider in many ways. She examined the ethics, methods, and trustworthiness of her research of being someone who experienced a close family member become sick with a rare form of cancer. Although not embracing the terms "insider" and "outsider" as purely dichotomous, she uses them to explain how she was able to understand the phenomenology of experiencing a loved one going through a particular type of illness.

Other examples of ethical considerations for insider and outsider roles and everything between are in the production and ownership of knowledge. While we discuss this topic at length in Chapter 7, it's useful to consider here as well. Pollack and Eldridge (2015) explain how researchers can work collaboratively with participants to collect, analyze, write, and publish. In this way, the researchers note the "move beyond 'giving voice to marginalized populations' a qualitative convention that maintains the authority of the academic scholar as privileged toward a collaborative approach to knowledge production" (Pollack & Eldridge, 2015, p. 133).

We can also look at how ethical consideration of insider-outsiderness relate to how data is shared across cultural contexts. The work of Lincoln et al. (2016) addresses important social justice issues of "'translations,' whether of language, culture, heritage, or field relationships" and "more openness toward international students and their indigenous research" (p. 532). Across research studies, we have a chance to go deeper, to understand a community context more fully, whether the researcher has similar traits or not. An aim for qualitative researchers is then to be continually prepared for shifting globalized multicultural and superdiverse research contexts, critically self-reflecting on our roles. These examples provide ways to think about membership roles for ourselves in the spectrum of insider and outsider roles in working with diverse communities. We have a chance to consider how artifacts are associated with communities and what meaning we apply to them. Recognizing that everyone shifts their roles and constructs their identities over time as "a process of becoming, rather than acquisition" (Rogoff, 1993, p. 142), what can you ask yourself to better understand your participants and their words and actions? How can we connect ethical preparation to performing and awareness of our roles? Perhaps it can be something as simple as, *what do I think I'm understanding?* **How can I work with my participants to better understand?**

5. Reflections from the field: spectrum of insider-outsiderness

In the following *Reflections from the Field*, two researchers consider the fluid and challenging nature of being insiders and outsiders. First, we hear from Linda Tuhiwai Smith, an Indigenous education scholar at the University of Waikato in New Zealand, who delves into discussion of these roles through descriptions of borders, histories of colonizing research, and Indigenous knowledge as a Māori researcher. Through her reflection, we have the opportunity to hear about the development of decolonizing and Indigenous research approaches. Smith provides a chance for us to unpack the complexity of the insider-outsider spectrum while seeing the ways in which joy and love of research can emerge.

Inside the inside

Linda Tuhiwai Smith

There is nothing like building a wall or barbed wire fence to keep people in or out that tells a story about the visible and invisible territorial power of borders and boundaries. Escaping over or under or passing through these borders signifies some kind of transition, not just of the physical body but of the ontological process of changing identity and sense of being. Those visible borders are easy to identify. They are unambiguous in their existence and speak directly to a specifically constituted system of state power that actively constructs borders. However, there are many borders less obvious and more subtle in the way they appear. There are epistemic borders, disciplinary borders, institutional borders, and linguistic and psychological borders. They are borders between categories of reality and fantasy, truth and lies, spirit and body, all of which are socially constructed and reinforced through institutional power. Indigenous researchers often work along the edges of these kinds of borders, work that has marked my career.

I have written and taught graduate students about insider-outside research for decades as a broad but useful concept that covers some of the obvious challenges for researchers working across boundaries, or bridging the academic world with Indigenous community contexts or working across categories and groups of race, gender, and class, researching up, talking back, or speaking truth to power. The concept is a good entry point to a rich vein of critical thought, ethics and personal insight. Indeed there is a significant literature that talks about such constructs as borders and margins, living within and living outside these human-made constructs of power. For colonizing research approaches, the objective for knowing about these borders was mainly to find out how a Western-trained researcher from inside the settler colonial knowledge system could get through the borders to those outside the system as expediently as possible to carry out whatever research the researcher wanted to do. The insider was the researcher and the outsider was the researched. There were these images of the outside that evoked the savage unknown, the risks to one's life and sense of being, and the fears that a researcher might "go native." Establishing relationships was mostly transactional and exploitative. The decades of such practices gave researchers and the work they did a really bad reputation among Indigenous peoples and other excluded communities. They exploited hospitality and generosity, destroyed trust, and took important parts of a community, their material objects, their voices, and a part of their being. The researcher located inside power holds the power to research.

For decolonizing and Indigenous approaches, the objectives for navigating borders are both different and more challenging in terms of learning to become and to be a researcher. This can range from overcoming the anxieties of returning "home" to a traumatized history, people, and community; understanding how to be patient and wait for the invitation to cross a border; building or rekindling a relationship; explaining or negotiating a research topic and method to elders; and knowing how to co-design and share benefits and sustaining relationships over time. I have focused much of my work on educating Indigenous researchers to think critically about what it means to research as an Indigenous person within Indigenous contexts. There is a complexity to being a researcher within one's own community who has to navigate the spaces of power that come from the privilege of being a researcher (educated and employed) and the responsibilities of being a member of a community (many or some of whom will not have had the opportunities to be educated or have employment, housing, or security). The insider researcher in this paradigm is the Indigenous researcher who may not necessarily see themselves as coming directly from within an Indigenous community, and the Indigenous researcher who has lived their lives inside an Indigenous community. Each of these positions, and the multiple positions between them, speak to a set of identities constituted by our colonized experiences that land us in various degrees of insiderness or outsiderness. The outside is the system of nation-states founded in imperialism and colonialism and their institutions and knowledge hierarchies. The inside is the history of being Indigenous and the relational world that comes from an Indigenous world view.

My work as a Māori researcher constantly reminds me that the inside of our Indigenous world is vast and full. It can be wondrous, often traumatizing, and deeply sad, and yet inspiring and fulfilling. When I began my career as a researcher, I never thought I would talk about research as a work of love or joy, but researching with Indigenous communities and using Indigenous methodologies has brought me joy and reinforced a commitment to love my people. In that sense, being inside is fully accepting who we are now and who we aspire to be and knowing that research can be an act of love as well as a way of knowing.

Arceli Rosario, an educational scholar at the Adventist International Institute of Advanced Studies in the Philippines, speaks to her experience of traversing both insider and outsider roles within a family community. Through a reflection on her thesis research, she provides insight to how our membership roles can suddenly shift in unexpected ways. Rosario's reflection allows us to consider how to be reflective to the communities we enter – whether we are familiar with their practices or not – while also recognizing and honoring ourselves.

Insider-outsider experience

Arceli Rosario

For my thesis, I decided to retrieve and record the oral literature of my mother's home place. I asked my mom to come with me. For her, it would be the first time to visit since she left 34 years ago. For me, it would be the first time to see the place. But when we arrived, we got a warm welcome from almost everywhere, even from the municipal hall where I secured the permit to gather data.

I could speak my mother's language fluently, although every now and then I would be laughed at and told, "Your accent is adulterated." Even then, I felt accepted. I loved the food that they served, I ate the way they ate, I could follow some of the songs that they sang, I could recite some of their "jousts." The jousts are words we use for a literary genre, which is usually a four-line rhyme recited during the wake after someone dies. It happened that when I was there, there was a wake and I attended the nightly vigil. The village folks were amazed and delighted that I could recite some jousts. The jousts are like a conversation or a debate. One person says a joust and the next person gives a response either by agreeing or disagreeing. They were happy that I behaved like I was homegrown. I felt like an insider; they treated me like an insider. Old and young volunteered to share with me their stories, their songs, and their jousts. The sharing happened in various settings – while shelling corn from early to late evenings, during the wake of a dead person, by the sides of the rice paddies, or under shady trees.

There was one incident, however, where I discovered how quickly, in the fleet of a moment, a researcher could transition from being an insider to an outsider. For me, it was not my conscious doing nor of the people around me. In hindsight, I realized it was about who they were and who I was, that there was a part of me that did not perfectly fit. I was joining a group of village folks that was going house to house with a carved image of the patron saint. The group offered songs and prayers to each house. I tried to stay at the back, first because I did not know how to say the prayers and how to sing the songs, and second because of my religious orientation. Several of the young girls pulled me in, showed me the prayer book and the song book, and encouraged me to participate. They tried to embrace me in their circle, but I felt like a fake. I was not sure if they sensed the divide between us, but for me I felt like I was on the other side of a big, wide gulf. That night, I lay awake for a long time and asked myself several questions – who I was, why I was there, how I could be who I was and still be true to what I was doing.

The spectrum of insider-outsiderness

There were several things I was sure of. First, I am a researcher. Second, as a researcher I also have my set of beliefs and values – some negotiable, some non-negotiable. One of those I cannot fake just to blend with the community that I study are my spiritual beliefs and values. Third, as a researcher I want to behave ethically and fairly, that is, I do not impose my beliefs and values on the community. I also hope to be treated ethically and fairly; that is, the community cannot impose their beliefs and values upon me. Fourth, as a researcher I should not allow that one uncomfortable moment to frighten me, but rather I should seek for points where we can converge and celebrate. And I realize that our love for that literary legacy, which is theirs and which I also claim as mine, is strong and real, and that's the point we can converge and celebrate.

While I did not find all the answers I was seeking, in the morning I had peace. I resolved to be respectful to others for who they were and, at the same time, to honor who I was.

In spite of that incident, I considered myself an insider. Being one, I was able to easily gain access into the village, into my participants' homes, and into their hearts. I gathered a rich collection of the village oral literature, but my greatest takeaway was that I gained a better understanding of who I was and a deeper appreciation of my heritage. This heightened understanding and appreciation, I realized, came about because in the process of data collection and analysis, there were times I stepped back and took an outsider's role – to reflect, to ask questions, to engage in intentional wonderings, and to attempt to find answers.

6. Engaging more deeply: concluding thoughts on insider-outsiderness

How can we determine our role as an insider or outsider? *How can we determine how to move forward with our research and in which manner is most appropriate?* It may then come down to the centrality of an insider-outsider debate and how to best include and empower our participants. **How can we best hear their voices?** The chapter began with an overview

The spectrum of insider-outsiderness

of insider and outsider definitions, considering the spaces between these opposing extremes. Then the chapter illustrated new views regarding how to define these original terms. Within a multicultural research context, fitting in or belonging is less important than co-constructing and equal research relationship-building. Moving beyond trust and vulnerability (as examined in Chapter 2), this chapter detailed the distinguishing nature of insider-outsiderness with concepts of trust, power, and co-production of knowledge. It included a discussion as to the ethical considerations from the perspective of diverse and marginalized populations.

While insider-outsiderness can be intertwined with concepts of ethics, it's important to examine these ideas and positionalities separately, especially for marginalized groups who have historically been disadvantaged and/or affected by research in negative ways. To help distinguish the differences between insider-outsiderness, this chapter discussed examples from different fields showing how insider-outsider power struggles are faced and mediated to address language, culture, gender, identity, age, ethnicity, religion, and historical sociopolitical issues. In this way, the positive view of an insider can be flipped on its head, and a participant or community could view the researcher as threatening because of their insiderness; conversely, the outsider could be included more easily into research. But this is a very black-and-white description of the dichotomy of membership roles, terms, and concepts that we realize we need to move beyond as researchers. The ways in which we move beyond the roles of insider and outside can vary. For some, there is a "space between" (Dwyer & Buckle, 2009), gray areas, changing dynamic roles, or as we termed in this chapter, the spectrum of insider and outsiderness. These membership roles are not concrete and can vary throughout a research project. Our job is then to determine how we fit, how we are being seen, and how we can compassionately move through, as researcher, wherever we are in the spectrum of membership roles to best hear the voices within multicultural contexts.

Reflective questions about insider-outsiderness

The chapter raises several questions for researchers to critically reflect upon regarding your position along the spectrum of insider-outsiderness. We've discussed the false dichotomy of being either an insider or an outsider as a static position. This topic adds to our understanding of our power, positionality, and trust in relationships during a research study. We explored considerations of this topic throughout the chapter. Here are a few questions to guide you through thinking about these ideas as a whole in terms of your role and group membership as related to qualitative research in multicultural contexts and your own study.

Topics	Questions
Spectrum of insider-outsiderness	• How do you understand yourself as an insider, outsider, or along the spectrum of membership roles? • What knowledge or perspectives might you be missing by being associated in this role?
Topics of insider-outsiderness	• In what communities or with what topics would you consider yourself an insider? An outsider?
Research planning	• Are you an insider or an outsider, or fitting in a space between? How do you know? • What could you do to move yourself along the spectrum of insider-outsiderness, and why could this be helpful? • How might your membership role change during the course of your research, if at all?

References

Acevedo-Gil, N. (2019). Toward a critical race nepantlera methodology: Embracing liminality in anti-colonial research. *Cultural Studies ↔ Critical Methodologies, 19*(3), 231–239. https://doi.org/10.1177/1532708618819625

Adu-Ampong, E. A., & Adams, E. A. (2020). "But you are also Ghanaian, you should know": Negotiating the insider – outsider research positionality in the fieldwork encounter. *Qualitative Inquiry, 26*(6), 583–592. https://doi.org/10.1177/1077800419846532

Aragrande, G. (2018). Migrants in translation: A corpus-based approach to the representation of migrants by four news broadcasting channels. In I. Ranzato & S. Zannoti (Eds.), *Linguistic and Cultural Representation in Audiovisual Translation* (Ch. 7). London: Routledge.

Bancroft, M. A. (2015). Community interpreting: A profession rooted in social justice. In *The Routledge Handbook of Interpreting* (pp. 229–247). London: Routledge.

Beals, F., Kidman, J., & Funaki, H. (2020). Insider and outsider research: Negotiating self at the edge of the emic/etic divide. *Qualitative Inquiry, 26*(6), 593–601.

Bhattacharya, K. (2007). Consenting to the consent form: What are the fixed and fluid understandings between the researcher and the researched? *Qualitative Inquiry, 13*, 1095–1115.

Bhattacharya, K. (2020). Nonsense, play, and liminality: Putting postintentionality in dialogue with de/colonizing ontoepistemologies. *Qualitative Inquiry, 26*(5), 522–526. https://doi.org/10.1177/1077800418819624

Blix, B. H. (2015). "Something decent to wear": Performances of being an insider and an outsider in Indigenous research. *Qualitative Inquiry, 21*, 175–183.

Boivin, N. (2015). Peripheral ritualized practices: Threads connecting decorations to the cloak of identity. *Journal of Intercultural Communications Research, 44*(1), 44–63.

Boivin, N. (2016). Multiliteracy practices for trans-migrant children and youth: Intercultural access to the local domain. *Journal of Intercultural Communications Research, 45*(6), 470–486.

Boivin, N. (2018). The Kazakh trans-multiliteracy project – multigenerational communities of learning. In S. Brunn (Ed.), *Changing World Language Map* (Ch. 11). Cham, Switzerland: Springer.

Burns, E., Fenwick, J., Schmied, V., & Sheehan, A. (2012). Reflexivity in midwifery research: The insider/outsider debate. *Midwifery, 28*, 52–60. https://doi.org/10.1016/j.midw.2010.10.018

CohenMiller, A. S. (2014). The phenomenon of doctoral student motherhood/mothering in academia: Cultural construction, presentation of self, and situated learning [Doctoral dissertation]. University of Texas at San Antonio. ProQuest Dissertations Publishing.

CohenMiller, A. S. (2018). Creating a participatory arts-based online focus group: Highlighting the transition from DocMama to motherscholar. *The Qualitative Report, 23*(7), 1720–1735.

CohenMiller, A. S. (2020). Performing, passing, and covering motherhood in academia: A heartful autoethnography. *LEARNing Landscapes, 13*(1), 97–114. https://doi.org/10.36510/learnland.v13i1.1006

CohenMiller, A. S., & Demers, D. (2019). Conflicting roles of mother and academic?: Exploring the use of arts-based self-care activities to encourage wellbeing. *Art/Research International: A Transdisciplinary Journal.* https://journals.library.ualberta.ca/ari/index.php/ari/article/view/29391

CohenMiller, A. S., Faucher, C., Hernández-Torrano, D., & Brown Hajdukova, E. (2017). Practical steps for using interdisciplinary educational research to enhance cultural awareness. *International Journal of Research and Method in Education, 40*(3). https://doi.org/10.1080/1743727X.2017.1310834

Crenshaw, K. (1991). Race, gender, and sexual harassment. *Southern California Law Review, 65*.

Denzin, N. K. (2001). The reflexive interview and a performative social science. *Qualitative Research, 1*, 23–46.

Dwyer, S. C., & Buckle, J. L. (2009). The space between: On being an insider-outsider in qualitative research. *International Journal of Qualitative Methods*, 54–63. https://doi.org/10.1177/160940690900800105

Dwyer, S., C., & Buckle, J. L. (2018). Reflection/commentary on a past article: "The space between: On being an insider-outsider in qualitative research."

International Journal of Qualitative Methods, *17*, 1–2. https://journals.sagepub.com/doi/pdf/10.1177/1609406918788176

Ellis, C., & Bochner, A. (2016). *Evocative Autoethnography: Writing Lives and Telling Stories*. New York: Routledge.

Ellis, C., & Patti, C. (2014). With heart: Compassionate interviewing and storytelling with Holocaust survivors. *Storytelling Self Society: An Interdisciplinary Journal of Storytelling Studies*, *10*(1), Art. 8. https://digitalcommons.wayne.edu/storytelling/vol10/iss1/8

Ellis, C., & Rawicki, J. (2018). Remembering the past/anticipating the future: A professor from the white working class talks with a survivor of the Holocaust about our troubled world. *Qualitative Inquiry*, *24*(5), 323–337. https://doi.org/10.1177/1077800417741387

Foster, J. (2009). Insider research with family members who have a member living with rare cancer. *International Journal of Qualitative Methods*, *8*(4), 16–26. https://doi.org/10.1177/160940690900800404

Goffman, E. (1959). *The Presentation of Self in Everyday Life*. New York: Doubleday.

Hill, M. L. (2006). Representin(g): Negotiating multiple roles and identities in the field and behind the desk. *Qualitative Inquiry*, *12*, 926–949.

Jacquemet, M. (2015). Asylum and superdiversity: The search for denotational accuracy during asylum hearings. *Language & Communication*, *44*, 72–81.

Johnston, M. S. (2019). When madness meets madness: Insider reflections on doing mental health research. *International Journal of Qualitative Methods*, *18*. https://doi.org/10.1177/160940691983535

Ladson-Billings, G., & Tate, W. F. I. V. (1995). Toward a critical race theory. *Teachers College Record*, *97*(1), 47–68.

Law, G. (2019). Researching professional footballers: Reflections and lessons learned. *International Journal of Qualitative Methods*, *18*, 160940691984932. https://doi.org/10.1177/1609406919849328

Leigh, J. (2014). A tale of the unexpected: Managing an insider dilemma by adopting the role of outsider in another setting. *Qualitative Research*, *14*(4), 428–441.

Lincoln, Y. S., González y González, E. M., & Massera, A. C. (2016). "Spanish is a loving tongue . . ." Performing qualitative research across languages and cultures. *Qualitative Inquiry*, *22*, 531–540.

Martínez-Acchini, L. M. (2017). Hidden people, hidden identity: Socio-cultural and linguistic change among Quechua migrants in lowland Bolivia [Doctoral dissertation]. University of Florida, ProQuest Dissertations Publishing.

McNess, E., Arthur, L., & Crossley, M. (2015). "Ethnographic dazzle" and the construction of the "Other": Revisiting dimensions of insider and outsider research for international and comparative education. *Compare: A Journal of Comparative and International Education*, *45*(2), 295–316. https://doi.org/10.1080/03057925.2013.854616

Milligan, L. (2014). Conceptualising educational quality in Kenyan secondary education: Comparing local and national perspectives, *Compare: A Journal of*

Comparative and International Education, 44(6), 1005–1007. https://doi.org/10.1
080/03057925.2014.884355

Nowicka, M., & Ryan, L. (2015). Beyond insiders and outsiders in migration research: Rejecting a priori commonalities. Introduction to "researcher, migrant, woman: Methodological implications of multiple positionalities in migration studies." *Forum Qualitative Sozialforschung/Forum: Qualitative Social Research, 16*(2), Art. 18. http://nbn-resolving.de/urn:nbn:de:0114-fqs1502183

Olaussen, I. O., & Hovik, L. (2019). Artistic exploration of a storyteller's expressive repertoire in events with toddlers. In A. Østern & K. N. Knudsen (Eds.), *Performative Approaches in Arts Education* (pp. 71–80). Routledge. London.

Ortiz, S. M. (2019). "You can say I got desensitized to it": How men of color cope with everyday racism in online gaming. *Sociological Perspectives, 62*(4), 572–588. https://doi.org/10.1177/0731121419837588

Paechter, C. (2013). Researching sensitive issues online: Implications of a hybrid insider/outsider position in a retrospective ethnographic study. *Qualitative Research, 13*(1), 71–86. https://doi.org/10.1177/1468794112446107

Papadopoulos, I., & Lees, S., (2002). Developing culturally competent researchers. *Journal of Advanced Nursing, 37*(3), 258–264.

Pather, S. (2004). Attempts to achieve development in education through partnerships: Interrogating notions and methods of building local capacity from the inside. *The Development Education Journal, 10*(2), 15–17.

Piller, I. (2017). *Intercultural Communication: A Critical Introduction*. Edinburgh, Scotland: Edinburgh University Press.

Pollack, S., & Eldridge, T. (2015). Complicity and redemption: Beyond the insider/outsider research dichotomy. *Social Justice, 42*(2 [140]), 132–145.

Rasool, Z. (2017). Collaborative working practices: Imagining better research partnerships. *Research for All, 1*(2), 310–322. https://doi.org/10.18546/RFA.01.1.08

Razon, N. A., & Ross, K. (2012). Negotiating fluid identities: Alliance-building in qualitative interviews. *Qualitative Inquiry, 18*, 494–503.

Resch, K., & Enzenhofer, E. (2018). Collecting data in other languages – strategies for cross-language research in multilingual societies. In U. Flick (Ed.), *The SAGE Handbook of Qualitative Data Collection* (pp. 131–146). London: Sage.

Rogoff, B. (1993). Children's guided participation and participatory appropriation in sociocultural activity. In R. H. Wozniak & K. W. Fischer (Eds.), *Development in Context: Acting and Thinking in Specific Environments* (pp. 121–153). Mahwah, NJ: Lawrence Erlbaum Associates.

Roulston, K. (2014). Interactional problems in research interviews. *Qualitative Research, 14*(3), 277–293. https://ezproxy.nu.edu.kz:2364/10.1177/146879411 2473497

Ryan, L. (2009). How women use family networks to facilitate migration: A comparative study of Irish and Polish women in Britain. *The History of the Family, 14*(2), 217–231.

Ryan, L. (2015). "Inside" and "outside" of what or where? Researching migration through multipositionalities. *Forum Qualitative Sozialforschung/Forum: Qualitative Social Research, 16*(2). https://doi.org/10.17169/fqs-16.2.2333

Saeed, M., & Griffin, G. (2019). Researching a sensitive topic in an unstable environment, *Qualitative Research Journal, 19*(3), 248–258. https://doi.org/10.1108/QRJ-02-2019-0013

Savvides, N., Al-Youssef, J., Colin, M., & Garrido, C. (2014). Journeys into inner/outer space: Reflections on the methodological challenges of negotiating insider/outsider status in international educational research. *Research in Comparative and International Education, 9*(4), 412–425.

Sherif, B. (2001). The ambiguity of boundaries in the fieldwork experience: Establishing rapport and negotiating insider/outsider status. *Qualitative Inquiry, 7*(4), 436–447. https://doi.org/10.1177/107780040100700403

Smith, L. T. (2006). Researching in the margins issues for Māori researchers a discussion paper. *AlterNative: An International Journal of Indigenous Peoples, 2*(1), 4–27. https://doi.org/10.1177/117718010600200101

Smith, L. T., Smith, G. H., Boler, M., Kempton, M., Ormond, A., Chueh, H.-C., & Waetford, R. (2002). "Do you guys hate Aucklanders too?" Youth: Voicing difference from the rural heartland. *Journal of Rural Studies, 18*(2), 169–178. https://doi.org/10.1016/S0743-0167(01)00037-7

Verma, G., & Ashworth, B. (1986). *Ethnicity and Educational Achievement in British Schools*. London: Springer.

Wadensjo, C. (2014). *Interpreting as Interaction*. London: Routledge.

Walby, S., Armstrong, J., & Strid, S. (2012). Intersectionality: Multiple inequalities in social theory. *Sociology, 46*(2), 224–240.

Wild Born Project. (n.d.). Retrieved August 7, 2019, from www.wildbornproject.com/

Zempi, I. (2016). Negotiating constructions of insider and outsider status in research with veiled Muslim women victims of Islamophobic hate crime. *Sociological Research Online, 21*(4), 70–81. https://doi.org/10.5153/sro.4080

Awareness in social justice and transformative research

I care about social justice, but how do I create a project incorporating this as a central tenet? *I want to create transformative research that will create positive change, but how do I do this?* Social justice has become a catchall term across many disciplinary perspectives. It provides a way to think about being socially just or socially aware. In some directions, **social justice** emphasizes equity and inclusion, whereas in others the emphasis may be on transformative change. In this chapter, we are guided by Mertens (2020), who provided the origin story for transformative research, situating it deeply and integrally on social justice. (Later in the chapter, we will hear from Mertens as she critically self-reflects on the creation of this approach to research.)

As we continue on, let's look at a definition of social justice. Charmaz (2011) defines it in this way:

> When I speak of social justice inquiry, I mean studies that attend to inequities and equality, barriers and access, poverty and privilege, individual rights and the collective good, and their implications for suffering. Social justice inquiry also includes taking a critical stance toward social structures and processes that shape individual and collective life.
>
> (p. 359)

Let us consider how social justice can be framed within the changing sociocultural, socioeconomic, political, and historical landscape of multicultural research in general. For example, we can consider social justice a transformative approach, such as **decolonization**, as a way to make work across

DOI: 10.4324/9780429285691-5

multicultural contexts highlight the voices of those historically excluded (Mertens, 2020). We can also look to the foundational work from Māori researcher Smith (1999, 2012) to see how decolonizing methodologies can be implemented in practice and in education (McKinley & Smith, 2017). As explained in the introduction to *Decolonising the University* (Bhambra et al., 2018), "The emphasis on reflexivity reminds us that representations and knowledge of the world we live in are situated historically and geographically. The point is not simply to deconstruct such understandings, but to transform them" (p. 2). Overall, through the lens of social justice, as qualitative researchers we can aim to provide equity, inclusion, and voice for marginalized, underrepresented populations.

A relevant component within transformative research is the consideration of individuals, **how do we perceive one another?** And what are the meanings instilled in these perceptions? Therefore, it's important to consider the terminology used to refer to people working with in research. For example, *how has the term "immigrant" been used over time? And what does it mean for communities referred to in this way?* In this sense, *how does the alteration of terminology to transmigrants, migrants, refugees, asylum seekers, or settlers affect the identity of those within the community and others' perceptions?* Similar examples can show how definitions, as indicated on national surveys, can affect data and meaning-making. For example, in the United States, the census survey delivered throughout the country has changed the terminology for referring to ethnicity. At times the descriptions become more specific or broader (e.g., Latino, Mexican, Puerto Rican, Spanish heritage). Leavy (2017) offers a useful explanation of how our choice of language in methodological approaches suggests important differences:

> Just taking the first example of the words used to describe the people on whom our research is focused, different approach lead us to weight words differently . . . in qualitative research, we may see *participant*; in mixed methods research, we may see *respondent, subject, or participant*; in arts-based research, we typically see *participant, co-creator, or collaborator*; and in community-based participatory research we generally see *co-creator or collaborator*. These differences in language are not random but rather speak to deeper issues about the philosophical beliefs and research practices guiding inquiry.
>
> (p. ix)

The cultural and sociohistorical context creates baggage for the terms we use for ourselves and those who read/learn about our work. Like other definitions, social justice as a concept is not static, but instead changes with our disciplinary fields and sociocultural contexts as just a couple of directions. Depending on the multicultural context, such terms bring up feelings in ourselves and others. For instance, we can look at Anna's move from the United States to Central Asia and Nettie's international moves. Anna explains: "I moved from the United States to Kazakhstan and was considered by many to be an 'expat' (expatriate). By being referred to and welcomed into expat communities, I was immediately allowed into a privileged position instead of how I might have been treated if I was an *immigrant*." For Nettie, her research was affected as well. She explains: "I have been seen as a white *outsider* with knowledge, one who benefited from such a label and identity framing" (Boivin, 2020). Such experiences are not unique to any one country. Instead, depending on our backgrounds and social standing, we are treated differently. These differences in how others interact with us relate to researching with people from various backgrounds and experiences, especially when we're looking across multicultural, diverse, and **superdiverse** contexts. These various terms suggest different ideas and concepts about society, equity, and social justice.

Superdiversity as a concept was intended to move past the concept of multiculturalism to rectify racism (see Vertovec, 2007; Blommaert & Rampton, 2012). It was coined by European sociolinguists, who noticed that European colonizer countries were wrestling with an influx of immigrants (economic, colonial, and refugee). Yet, researchers and communities use different terminology, which fortunately doesn't impede our work. Instead, this is how social justice research opens a door for change. It's not specifically how we define the research (e.g., multicultural, superdiversity) but how we engage in the research, such as building trusting relationships with participants during the research process. As Campbell and Pahl (2018) state in her recent book about reimaging communities, "The same co-production and arts-based methodologies that engage communities, methodologies which we advocate for in this book, can also help communities build coping and resilience mechanisms to combat racism" (p. 12). Recognizing this perspective, we can promote research that investigates societal impact and looks to effect positive changes as articulated by the communities themselves. This is not a new research perspective or approach. There is a broad historical landscape of multicultural research relating to social justice.

98

Qualitative researchers, especially those involved in extensive research with multicultural and marginalized communities, enter a complicated realm to be cognizant of the subtle layers to any particular context. So, what do we do? **How can we move forward in our research in a socially just manner?** This is where we can return to critical self-reflection and examine the ways others have entered into such research. The other chapters in this book also delve into topics integrated with social justice, particularly issues of power. In this chapter, we focus on the steps others have taken to develop qualitative research studies that they see as socially just and transformative.

1. Where does social justice fit?

Social justice has become at times a catchall term across disciplinary perspectives. It can be examined through social justice theory, a framework providing an interpretation of the world highlighting an intersectional understanding of individual and collective experiences. For example, Breunig (2019), drawing from Maxine Green, states that "social justice theory embraces the idea that social identities do not exist independently. Rather, race, class, sexuality, skin color, and gender (among other identities) exist in intersectionality" (p. 9). In this way, social justice can be seen within teaching and learning centering on topics of privilege and power. But, *who has privilege? In what ways and how do these ideas intersect? And how can I ensure others have access to not just share their story but to effect change?* Breunig (2019) continues on, explaining that "the concept of privilege, special rights, advantages, or immunities granted or available to a particular person or group of people" is inherent to this framework and any discussion of social justice (p. 9).

Social justice in research is about making changes for the good of communities and the world at large. The imperative is to make the research relevant and accessible to effect systemic and systematic changes. At times we may research one aspect of equity, such as through a gender audit in higher education (see CohenMiller & Lewis, 2019; Kelly, 2017). At other times the emphasis is on the intersection of multiple intersecting categories. Within higher education institutions, often issues of social justice emerge based upon who has privileged knowledge. Aparna and Kramsch (2018) offer another way to conceptualize the traditional divide between academic knowledge and local knowledges, one they term "asylum university lens." From this perspective they consider practical issues, such as scheduling meetings, as ways to value everyone while ensuring confidentiality to those of precarious positions. Ultimately, they reflect on their work, noting that it's a

> call for rethinking everyday relations producing university life, both spatially (bridging town/gown tensions) and socially (activating relations of knowledge exchange instead of privilege and "distant gazing" towards marginalised groups, in this case refugees and those involved in their support).

> (p. 104)

We can now turn to a couple of other examples focusing on building relationships between local communities and newly arrived immigrants. For example, let's look at Nettie's two-year study in Finland with Building Bridges, from 2018–2020. In this study, Nettie worked to build community bridges between local Finnish and newly arrived or settled communities. The study utilized the universal topic of food to connect people. In it, a co-production was implemented where participants acted as co-researchers. Over the two years, an evolution of understanding was created between the divergent groups, including cognitive understanding and also emotional, intimate relationships created through reciprocal sharing of multisensory food discourse resources (Boivin, forthcoming). Here is an example from fieldnotes (please note all ethical guidelines were followed and the names have been anonymized):

> Another informal moment that highlighted the reciprocal interaction with the participants occurred at the refugee centre. Over several sessions, the participants from the initial dinner discussed their memories of learning to make certain foods. They all spoke openly of their memories of family members who were dead or displaced because of conflicts in their home regions (Iran, Iraq, Syria, and Afghanistan) and of the loss they felt. During the meals shared after the weekly cooking lesson, many of the refugee cooks mentioned this loss. Towards the last session, the loss was also reflected on by administrators at the community centre. Petu said, "I am surprised how hard leaving is for them"; in the eighth session, Mika observed, "I feel like I have learned about their life more than the food." (Conversations at the centre were

translated from Finnish to English.) The food connected to a memory of the participant's historical body, including the pain of loss as a refugee. These stories emerged slowly in the form of side remarks made during the preparation and sharing of a meal; thus, shared food gathered people to spend time together and to talk to each other.

(Boivin, forthcoming)

This session illustrated that simple conversations could be data and also can be moments of reflection that create small forms of societal impact.

In addressing inequities, socially just research can also focus on inclusive research practices. Nind (2017), who has specialized in working with people with learning disabilities, explains: "The concept of inclusive research epitomizes the transformation away from research *on* people, to research *with* them" (p. 278). She offers one way to conceptualize the overlap between inclusive research with emancipatory research, participatory research, and participatory action research. Nind (2014) suggests an image of a large circle and a Venn diagram within the larger circle. The Venn diagram includes three overlapping circles of equal size. While Nind (2014) explains there remains discussion about the equal representation of each approach, inclusive research is the overarching umbrella approach with the three others situated within:

This image [of the Venn diagram] is in keeping with the stance of Walmsley and Johnson (2003) and French and Swain (1997) that participatory and emancipatory research share certain characteristics, despite their different social and historical roots. While the overlap may not be great, these are at least complementary approaches to achieving meaningful social change through research.

(p. 10)

For others, such as those working with Deaf communities internationally, the emphasis on social justice is about inclusion and advocacy for community rights. The inclusion of Deaf researchers is essential for working with Deaf communities (Byun & Plumlee, 2021; Friedner & Kusters, 2015; Ladd, 2003; Mertens, 2009) and connects to extending the disciplinary field of Deaf studies (Kusters et al., 2017).

So, take a moment and think to yourself about your educational institution, **how many educators do you know from varied backgrounds?** *Where can you see the multicultural perspectives? Age? Ethnicity? Immigrant status?*

Language proficiency? If studying about those with disabilities, how many of the instructors have a disability themselves? If studying about Deaf communities, how many of the instructors are Deaf? If we aim to conduct socially just and transformative research, we can continue to consider whose voices are being heard and prioritized within academia and beyond. For example, collaborations across departments and with those historically excluded from conversations can lead to important solutions for inclusion and accessibility (Spires & CohenMiller, 2018). Yet in our attempts to be inclusive, we don't want to inadvertently colonize the stories and experiences of others. In this regard, it's important to be cognizant of these issues and to carefully reflect on how we position ourselves and others in representations of our research.

We can also consider how a social justice framework can connect to practices we may already be working with. For example, Janesick (2007) argues for using oral history as a purposeful approach to provide voices that are historically marginalized a space and place to be heard. Another example of building relationships in multicultural community contexts can be seen in the work of Tshimangadzo Selina Mudau in South Africa. Framed by Ubuntu philosophy, which centers on human respect and value, Mudau (2021) showed that "social constructs can create and perpetuate acceptance, integration, and formation of networks to enhance positive relationships between migrants and locals" (p. 261). Through her research, Mudau (2021) found that immigrant-local cohesion could be developed through community engagement strategies. Through such practices, we can move forward and work toward decolonizing our practices to uncover voices historically marginalized (Mertens et al., 2013; Smith, 1999, 2012).

2. Why transformative research?

Another research approach to social justice that emphasizes community engagement is the transformative approach. Working and researching *with* instead of *at* is central to socially just research, in particular transformative research. Transformation is possible when we reflect and take action (Freire, 2000 [1970]). The concepts of social justice can be incorporated into an exploration of **transformative research**.

> *Transformative research has a central purpose to uncover and improve issues of social justice and human rights.*

Awareness in social justice

This critical paradigm was developed by Mertens (2009), providing a framework to unpack issues of injustice and work with communities to undo historical inequity and power imbalance. As she explains, it's "an extension of a paradigm framework developed by Guba and Lincoln (1994, 2005) for social research that they based on a modified version of paradigm as they were described by Kuhn (1996)" (Mertens, 2016, p. 6).

Moving from an "emancipatory paradigm" to a transformative paradigm, Mertens (2009) further explains that "I changed the name of the emancipatory paradigm to *transformative* because of a desire to emphasize the agency role for the people involved in the research. Rather than being *emancipated*, we work together for personal and social transformation" (p. 2). (As we discuss the transformative paradigm and approaches within and across multicultural contexts, key concepts of power, privilege, trust, positionality, insider-outsiderness, and disciplinary boundaries can be deeply embedded and can be explored again in the other chapters of this book.)

At the heart of transformative research is a story about a researcher who realized too many people were being studied *at*, instead of worked *with* to assess their attitudes, experiences, and needs. In studying *at* other people, there is a concept of *othering* them (Dervin, 2016; Jensen, 2011; Said, 1978). By othering, people become associated with an inferior group in comparison to a dominant group and marginalized. Othering is the viewing of those different as "not us." It's a tool of division. In contrast, transformative research centers on social justice and uncovering the importance of everyone's lives. Mertens (2009, 2016) highlights that as an outsider to a community, we cannot know the relevant components of those within the community without including them in it.

Such recognition and incorporation of those traditionally excluded or marginalized not only offers a way to better understand communities but also opportunities for extending academic perspectives. In transformative research, a central focus is on uncovering and improving major social inequities. This involves not only within the research process, who we work with, but after the end of the study, in the ways dissemination of findings are employed with an emphasis on social justice and human rights (Mertens, 2009). So, you could ask yourself, **what are the preferred methods for disseminating findings, according to the participants/community?**

At the center of all these examples is the idea of respecting and valuing all individuals. As we continue exploring the transformative paradigm, we can see how it addresses "power structures that perpetuate social inequities," and as described can be integrated with any group or individual facing inequity (Mertens, 2009, p. 4). Mertens further explains the transformative paradigm as including vulnerable and oppressed communities, noting that it

> is applicable to people who experience discrimination and oppression on whatever basis, including (but not limited to) race/ethnicity, disability, immigrant status, political conflicts, sexual orientation, poverty, gender, age, or the multitude of other characteristics that are associated with less access to social justice.
>
> (Mertens, 2009, p. 4)

Studies integrating a transformative research paradigm would then focus on uncovering inequity and improving the lives of individuals *with* the people themselves. Some qualitative approaches include **participatory action research** (PAR; Chevalier & Buckles, 2019) and **community-based participatory research** (CBPR; Hacker, 2013), which incorporates social justice and transformation as a central component of research with communities. Or in another framework, such as suggested by Onwuegbuzie and Frels (2013), transformative research offers an extension of social justice through **critical dialectical pluralism 1.0**. They highlight four grounding ideas for those integrating this approach: "promotes and sustains an egalitarian society; aims to promote both universalistic theoretical knowledge and local practical knowledge; and promotes culturally progressive research" (Onwuegbuzie & Frels, 2013, p. 9). Often these approaches integrate an emancipatory focus, drawing from transformative educational paradigms (Freire, 2000 [1970]). As Leavy (2017) describes, "CBPR is an attempt by researchers to actively involve the communities they aim to serve in every aspect of the research process, from the identification of a problem to the distribution of research findings" (p. 10).

For example, Nnawulezi et al. (2018) explain the ways transformative research methods can be used to address gender-based violence. They explain that such violence "can affect men and women and is rooted in structural gender inequities, patriarchal belief systems, and power imbalances" (p. 507). They examine a central question about transformative research with vulnerable populations: "How does one create equitable research conditions and produce this type of evidence when working in communities and a broader culture marked by historical social inequities and oppression?" (Nnawulezi et al., 2018, p. 508). They explain that transformative CBPR approaches provide "tremendous potential" to address issues of power and liberation (Nnawulezi et al., 2018, p. 508). In using a transformative research approach, we have an opportunity, and many would argue too, a responsibility, for researchers to have a chance to work with others to directly address major issues of power, inequity, social justice, and human rights:

> The transformative paradigm emerged in response to individuals who have been pushed to the societal margins throughout history and who are finding a means to bring their voices into the world of research. Their voices, shared with scholars who work as their partners to support the increase of social justice and human rights, are reflected in the shift to transformative beliefs to guide researchers and evaluators.
>
> (Mertens, 2009, p. 3)

The transformative paradigm has been further extended to directly integrate an Indigenous lens incorporating "care, relationality, and accountability" (Adyanga, foreword in Romm, 2018, p. vii). For Romm (2018), the research approach is described as **responsible research practice** and encourages us to "to highlight more collaborative relationships in the research enterprise" (p. 5). One such way to approach this type of work is offered in a practical tip by Romm (2018) in the creation of a research study, such as by "using verbs that express an action intent" for the development of "research questions expressing transformative intent" (pp. 472–473). This transformative focus can also be seen in participatory action research, such as in a study of using the arts with trans youth (Asakura et al., 2020) or in a youth participatory action research to explore the hidden curriculum of schooling (Carl & Ravitch, 2018). (Additional descriptions of using the arts and co-production of research for social justice are discussed in Chapter 7.) So, you can ask yourself, **what research questions am I using to show a socially just intent?**

A final direction we can consider is the ways social justice and transformative approaches can be used as we move online. In some instances, these shifts online happen suddenly, such as during the COVID-19 crisis. While people around the world were faced with reduced social interaction, Deaf communities faced unique challenges. As Plumlee (2021) describes:

> Under the best of circumstances, due to communication barriers resulting from the inaccessibility of audio input, Deaf people have less access to information than hearing people. Under imposed COVID-19 quarantine regimes, movement restrictions created additional barriers to accessible information sources and reduced opportunities to meet with people sharing the same language who could provide missing information as well as social support.
>
> (p. 165)

Fortunately, technology in the form of texting groups can offer a useful means of learning and connection (Gimranova et al., 2018) and as noted by Plumlee (2021), afforded opportunities for interaction and reduced feelings of isolation during the global crisis.

We can also look to online spaces by considering access. For example, Lockley (2018), used a decolonizing lens as a way to address issues of access to learning and knowledge online. She explores the idea of open access and higher education: "If openness is linked to a form of social justice via access then it should focus on those under-served by existing institutions" (Lockley, 2018, p. 147). However, Lockley (2018) argues that open access knowledge "fails" in many ways (p. 149), is inherently political, and presents major issues to consider, such as the future of Indigenous knowledges and the potential for colonization of open sources (p. 161). So, you can ask yourself, **how might I be able to conduct studies in online spaces to support transformational research?** With the disruption during COVID-19, considerations for how to move forward methodologically is a process (see Nind et al. [2021] on their work with the Centre for Research Methods for resources and training).

3. What dilemmas of ethics can we consider related to social justice and transformative research?

Seeing the ways social justice and human rights are a foundation for transformative research can lead us to recognize the challenging nature of ethics in qualitative and mixed-methods research. As researchers seeking to become more socially aware and socially just, questions about ethics emerge around every corner. When researching across multicultural

Awareness in social justice

contexts, it's particularly important to critically self-reflect and delve into the ways of knowing for local community. For example, Chilisa (2005) and Chilisa with Gaelebale Tsheko (2014) describe the transformative research they conducted in Botswana to address the health crisis around HIV/AIDS. Clear issues of ethics can be seen from early interventions and research that focused on assumed needs of the community, such as the need for sex education and prevention (Chilisa, 2005). Instead, an ethical way forward in working with the community is to work with them instead of *at* them. In this way, Chilisa and Tsheko (2014) brought in a transformative paradigm that allowed the voices of individuals to be heard. They explained the need to use local processes including oral traditions and cultural knowledge in order to uncover the actual needs of the community and what steps to take (Chilisa & Tsheko, 2014). They incorporated a transformative paradigm with qualitative research, Indigenous research with mixed methods, in an interactive process to understand the needs and steps to work with the community (Chilisa & Tsheko, 2014). So, you can ask yourself, **might I be inadvertently hurting the community I'm trying to help?** *Who could I talk to in order to better understand my thinking process?*

For example, we can think about some of these ethical considerations around labeling participants, such as we started with at the beginning of the chapter. The term "immigrant," for instance, or the term "victim" – what do these imply for participants and the communities they are in? How can a change in terms help us to see and understand our work differently? Better? So, you can ask, **where am I using terms to label people (and myself)?** And *which terms are acceptable and welcomed in the community or with the individuals I'm working with?* The ways in which we use words come into play in further significant ways as we move into online spaces. In such virtual or socially distanced research, we may find ourselves using modes of data collection such as discussion forums or texting groups, and these provide deep considerations for our choice of terminology and the ethics around them. Such terms may relate to how we label an individual (and ourselves) as well as the cultural objects, traditions, or experiences related to working across multicultural contexts.

Those working in the UK with marginalized communities may not agree with the term immigrant. Some use the term "asylum seeker" whereas others may use "refugee," and still others may use "economic migrant," "newly arrived and local," "forced migrant," or even "transmigrant." **What are the**

ethical considerations when labeling participants? *Whose terms are acceptable?* In addition, *what are the ethical concerns, limitations, and procedures to researching Indigenous cultures if we come from colonizers in (White) settler groups?* And ultimately, *how does this all play out within a social justice framework seeking to effect transformation?*

Another ethical factor regarding transformative research connects to cultural and sociohistorical knowledges of the communities we work in. For instance, each community can have its own sets of priorities regarding ethics. We can then think about what type of ethics might exist, such as in working toward social justice and decolonization research with Indigenous communities (Jimmy et al., 2015). The *ways of knowing* for Indigenous communities, or in working across and within other multicultural contexts, requires us to think about ethics as extending to whose voices are heard and prioritized (Battiste, 2013; Ermine, 1995; Mertens et al., 2013; Smith, 1999). As Battiste (2013) explains in her work on decolonizing education in Canada, there are important conversations about "decolonization, moving beyond cultural awareness and inclusion" and to ask then, "How will we enter into those ethical conversations?" (p. 12). These conversations of ethics and voice are echoed in previous chapters of this book. In this way, similar questions you may ask about power and privilege, trust, and insider-outsiderness interrelate to create equitable, inclusive research.

4. Reflections from the field: social justice and transformative research

In the following *Reflections from the Field*, we sought to understand transformative research and how social justice research is practiced on the ground. We reached out to researchers from around the globe, including those living and working in the US, the UK, and India. In the first reflection, Donna M. Mertens, from Gallaudet University in the US, details how she developed the transformative approach in research. She explains her background, experiences, and research work, which led her to where the voices of individuals and full communities were missing from research and social change.

Expanding social justice through transformative research?

Donna M. Mertens

Many factors in my life led me to develop the transformative approach to research. In 1962, my family moved from Washington State to Kentucky. In Washington State, I only saw people who looked like me (White, middle class). In Kentucky, even though I was only in seventh grade, I was struck by the number of people of color who were living in poverty in the inner city. I asked my teacher why there were no Black people in my school, neighborhood, or swimming pool. She said that it was because they preferred to be with their own kind. Even at that tender age, I knew there was something wrong with that explanation. This transformative moment for me was fortunately aligned with the civil rights movement in the United States. I began to ask questions like: what effect are the marches for civil rights having on the lives of Black people? So, I had a researcher's way of thinking before I even knew there was such a profession.

My values led me to want to work to improve conditions for people who were poor or being marginalized for whatever reason. I tried to focus my research work on these communities, but I knew there was something missing: the opportunity to be close to or immersed in a community that experienced discrimination on a regular basis. I saw an advertisement to teach research at Gallaudet University in Washington, DC, the only university in the world that serves Deaf students as its mission. In my encounters with members of the Deaf community, I became aware of the damage done when researchers from outside a community conduct studies that are not responsive to the culture and lived experiences of members of that community. In this case, Deaf people were often portrayed as being inferior to hearing people; however, this research did not include Deaf people on the research team and rarely, if ever, used a visual language (e.g., American Sign Language) to insure accurate communications.

Members of the Deaf community challenged me to develop an approach to research that was culturally responsive and focused on providing a foundation for constructive action to transform a world in which they experienced discrimination and oppression on a regular basis. The other fact that was immediately apparent to me was that the Deaf community was a microcosm of the larger world and that issues of gender, economic status, religion, language, race/ethnicity, sexual identity, and presence of other disabilities were relevant for a research approach focused on social transformation.

I saw that what was needed was an umbrella for a research approach that could include the relevant dimensions of diversity that are used as a basis for discrimination and oppression. Hence, the transformative paradigm was born. It was not an easy birth, as what I proposed was a challenge to the dominant discourse in research methods. One reviewer of my first book proposal said his "hands were shaking with rage" because of the deliberate inclusion of political issues in framing research questions and methods. Another reviewer asked, "Why is this woman thing" included when he read that I found guidance in feminist theory. In one large research project, the project director asked me for a survey to gather the data they needed, with no critical reflection on whether that was an appropriate strategy given the context of the study. I told the project director that I would not provide a survey, but I was willing to discuss strategies that might lead to continued transformative actions after the research study ended. I asked him if he thought this particular research project that was ending had solved all the problems, in this case, related to the preparation of teachers for students who are Deaf and have disabilities. He acknowledged that there was still much to be done in that area, so we discussed and eventually implemented a transformative, mixed-methods study that engaged the broader educational community in identifying points for transformative action based on the study findings.

The transformative paradigm continues to evolve based on interactions with members of many marginalized communities. In this paradigm, the researcher starts with the ethical question: how does my research contribute to increased environmental, economic, and social justice and enhanced human rights? All methodological choices derive from an answer to that question. From the initial beginnings of the transformative paradigm in 1983, I have been invited to work with many different communities in many different countries that experience discrimination and oppression with the goal of providing a research base for social transformation. I am always pleased to work with members of communities who see a need to work toward this goal because it means that there are people from that country/community who care deeply about increasing social justice and enhancing human rights. A paraphrase from Franklin Delano Roosevelt sums up my thinking: world peace will not come as the result of the efforts of one person, one country, one nation. It takes all of us working together.

In the next reflection, Tineke A. Abma from the Amsterdam University Medical Centres in the Netherlands critically self-reflects on the concepts of reflexivity for researchers in multicultural contexts. In working on topics of health and social well-being, she describes how she employs tools of framing and emotion work to research with diverse communities.

Researcher's reflexivity in a multicultural context: the role of framing and emotion work

Tineke A. Abma

Qualitative researchers learn that they are their own instrument. Their ways of seeing, listening, and feeling are decisive for what is learned from a studied context but also influence the relationships with participants in the field. Certain frames may reestablish unequal power relationships and feelings of stigmatization. So, more than in any other context, being the instrument as a researcher in a multicultural context is definitely not a matter of being neutral and impartial. In my work I have committed myself to participatory research as a pathway to social justice. Such a commitment requires a serious effort from the researcher to realize underlying values such as respect, inclusion, democratic decision-making, mutual learning, collective action, and integrity. Over the years, I have learned this includes framing and emotion work.

Framing work

Can we see the cultural frames we use if we have invested in them? I noticed that in our studies on diversity with minority and majority medical students and doctors in hospitals, my research team often searched for the right words. All too easily, we felt we were reproducing the categories and labels that are part of a Dutch, White-innocence culture – categories and labels we sometimes initially did not even notice as being harmful, because we were fully part of that culture. We learned that words like *autochtoon* (Dutch person, with parents born in the Netherlands) versus *allochtoon* (non-Dutch person, with parents coming from abroad) were often felt as fueling the polarization. So, we searched for alternatives and asked participants. They came up with notions like bicultural or Dutch-Moroccan. These often felt strange and unnatural to us, but if participants could identify themselves instead of being identified by the labels used by others, this increased their sense of agency and control. The lesson we learned is that it is crucial to engage participants and be reflexive about the labels and categories one uses. I call this "framing work."

This framing work is at the heart of qualitative research in a multicultural context. It entails identifying and focusing on ethically remarkable features of a situation, understanding yourself and the situation within a political social context and negotiating frames and images with others, including colleagues and others whose lives or work are at stake. Framing stands for the ways in which people see themselves and understand their situations. So, it is about the perception of reality and the recognition that one's perception does not coincide with reality. As the famous biologist Bateson (2000 [1972]) said: "The map is not the territory." Images and frames are often unconscious and determine what we see and what we don't see, which facts and arguments are important or not. The moral perception of a situation and the framing of ethical issues have to do with what is considered a good life or good care (ethical issues), and relate to harm, benefits, rights, and responsibilities.

Framing work requires a willingness to see larger connections and structural inequalities that contribute to ethical issues; for example, to see a particular incident as an example of racism. In our research on diversity in Dutch hospitals, participants shared situations like a female Muslim who repeatedly met patients who did not want to be washed by her because of her headscarf; or a Black medical doctor who was more than once approached as a cleaner; or students who felt offended by the stereotypical cases as part of their curriculum ("They are all called Fatima or Mohammed"; "They never have a flu [like the Dutch patients], all [medical] cases are problematic"). The presented Dutch cases were more balanced and less one-sidedly focused on complex situations and implicitly generated positive associations. This all fueled reproduced stereotypical imagery. We saw a pattern in these incidents and deliberately framed these as "micro-aggressions" and acts of "everyday racism." We thereby named and emphasized the structural nature of disadvantage, exclusion, and othering of people with a minority background. Incidents were no longer framed as an individual problem but as an institutional and societal problem. Diversity became a shared responsibility in the hospital and medical school.

Emotion work

Doing research in a multicultural context makes you aware of your own cultural upbringing and your privileges – in my case, as a White, middle class female and professor in a medical university. It may create feelings of discomfort, shame, guilt, and pain when a "diverse" person tells about experiences of disadvantage and exclusion. It makes you feel very White, Dutch, and elitist. This requires "emotion work." Emotion work includes being caring, compassionate, and empathic, managing emotions, building trust, and responding to emotions of others. I learned how important emotions are in the multicultural context. Participants are not always nice to each other or other stakeholders. They may carry a lot of pain and despair; some may feel exploited and used by the institution. In such circumstances it can be very hard to respect and understand each other. Dealing with the emotions of participants who feel they are not acknowledged, who feel irrelevant, confronts us with their suffering, the losses in their lives, and the bereavement due to loss and sorrow.

Emotion work is grounded in the notion that good care requires embracing rather than glossing over emotions and feelings. In our research, we engaged an artist to work with us on the expression of feelings of minority students and workers to heighten the sense of empathy among participants not familiar with these themes. For example, I worked with minority students on a performance to give an insight in their feelings of anger, indignation, and sadness when faced with discriminatory remarks. This performance was presented at a conference organized by the medical school. Afterwards, we engaged in so-called courageous conversations with the audience composed of teachers, staff, and leaders in the hospital. It was not easy to engage with people who in different ways experienced, talked about, and dealt with disadvantage, exclusion, and othering, or to organize dialogue sessions with minority and majority students and workers, but it offered a great learning experience for us all.

Epilogue

In a multicultural context, the researcher-as-instrument is not neutral and carries an ethical and political responsibility when working toward social justice and inclusion. Yet, we do not find many texts that talk about the development and cultivation of this "instrument." How do we develop this instrument? How do we develop ourselves as qualitative and participatory researchers in a multicultural context? I have shown this entails more than a process of technical sophistication; it is more about personal development, becoming a reflexive person, becoming a person who is aware of the structural inequalities one is part of, and a person who is willing to engage in courageous conversations with and between people with a minority and majority background. This requires hard work, and entails both framing work and emotion work to become a good qualitative researcher. This can be acquired in the company of good friends and a safe context to share complex situations and moral dilemmas.

References

For further readings on participatory research, see:

Abma, T., Banks, S., Cook, T., Dias, S., Madsen, W., Springett, J., & Wright, M. T. (2019). *Participatory Research for Health and Social Well-Being*. Switzerland: Springer Nature. https://doi.org/10.1007/978-3-319-93191-3.

Bateson, G. 2000 (1972). *Steps to an Ecology of Mind: Collected Essays in Anthropology, Psychiatry, Evolution, and Epistemology*. Chicago: University of Chicago Press. ISBN 0-226-03905-6. Retrieved 19 March 2013.

In this final reflection, Nupur Samuel from O. P. Jindal University in India critically self-reflects on how power relates to her educational research. Using a feminist lens, she describes her struggles in teaching, and the purposeful steps and iterative process she engaged in to hear the voices of her students. Through such a practiced process, Samuel provides us with a way to see the connection between how we teach and the world we live in, as an entry point to addressing voice, social inclusion, and equity in society.

Reflections on teaching in English as a Second Language (ESL) classrooms: social inclusion and equity

Nupur Samuel

I can still see the books flying out of the window while I maintained a calm demeanor, though I was anxious and worried at the same time. This was more than ten years ago when I had started teaching eighth graders, those excited and excitable teenagers whose purpose in coming to school was to do anything but learn English. Oh, and those books were my own books on theories of language learning and educational psychology; they didn't literally fly, but if you paid enough attention, you could definitely see my confidence taking a nosedive. Nobody tells you in your pre-teacher-education days that most of all, you learn you will be tested and sorely tried, and that you will have to trust your own instincts gently peppered with all the theories you have picked up along the way.

I have come a long way since those early rookie days, but I have been at my wit's end many times. Such is the nature of this job, that we are constantly asking ourselves difficult questions or facing self-doubt. These types of questions are ones that connect to the teacher-education research I have conducted for years. For instance, in one study I found that materials mediate classroom discourse more favorably for the students when teachers allow for students' active participation (Samuel, forthcoming).

Growing up in the 1980s and '90s, we were not yet exposed to the more communicative approach to teaching and learning, so when as a teacher I was expected to follow the interactive approach, I only had my books to fall back on. Like many colleagues, I had no actual experience to recall and learn from. The classroom became my school, and reflecting on my own practice and behavior helped me revise my approach.

One of the challenges that I faced while teaching undergraduate students was to engage them in classroom discussions. Many of them were first-generation learners of English, belonged to socioeconomically disadvantaged backgrounds, and like most teenagers, were constantly afraid of tripping and falling face down in front of the whole world. Add to this their secondary school experience of being part of large classrooms with no opportunity to speak aloud in class, and you have with you a quiet class of students only waiting for the teacher's word to note down and memorize. These experiences led me to do some research in reflective practices that made my basic-level ESL students use reflection as a learning tool, helping them not only to become more proficient in English but also more developed critical thinkers (Samuel, 2019a).

When attempts to elicit response as a whole class and even as part of small groups failed, I asked each student to write their response to the day's topic in their notebooks. Then I randomly called out names for students to read aloud what they had written. And this time, I waited. I had been thinking of my approach earlier and had come to the conclusion that though it seemed to me that I had given my students enough time, they thought that if they didn't speak for 5–10 seconds, I would move to some other student and they wouldn't have to speak. By allowing the students some quiet time to think of their response and to note down what they wanted to say, then giving them enough time to read aloud, I implied that each voice mattered and that I was willing to wait for them because I thought they were worth listening to. By the end of the semester, I saw many of these reticent students become more confident, engaging in classroom discussions and not shying away from sharing their thoughts. It taught me that my earlier impressions that they did not have much to contribute were incorrect, and that equal opportunities also meant empathy and patience. (See Samuel, 2019b, for more thoughts on this topic.)

Overall, I have learned that reflection, self-assessment, and critical thinking are crucial to being a more enabling ESL teacher, and I hope that integrating diverse voices – especially those of the marginalized and women – in future research across multicultural contexts will lead to a more equitable and just society.

References

Samuel, N. (2019a, January). Adventures of a journal writer-teacher: Some reflections on writing. *FORTELL, 38.*
Samuel, N. (2019b). Social inclusion and the role of English language education: Making a transition from school to higher education in India. In S. Douglas (Ed.), *Creating an Inclusive School Environment,* British Council. www. teachingenglish.org.uk/article/creating-inclusive-school-environment
Samuel, N. (forthcoming). Mediating materials: Contextualizing language learning in English as a second language (ESL) classrooms in India. In *New Perspectives on Material Mediation in Language Learner Pedagogy.* Springer.
For further readings on teaching and social inclusion, see:
Samuel, N. (2016). *Developing Writing Skills through Mediated Interaction.* Workshop conducted for participants of TESOL 2016, Baltimore County, MD

5. Engaging more deeply: concluding thoughts on social justice and transformative research

How can we work with marginalized communities to hear their voices? How can we work with them to improve inequity facing the world? How can we fight injustice using qualitative research? These are just some of the

Awareness in social justice

ideas we touched upon in this chapter through discussion of social justice and transformative research. The complicated nature and multifaceted levels of consideration when working across multicultural contexts to address human rights is a major feat. Yet, we encourage you to continue in this work to engage with communities to hear *their* needs and their knowledges. As qualitative researchers focused on conducting socially just research and becoming more aware, it's our job then to continually critically self-reflect to see how to value and respect others.

Likely, most of you reading this are academics in higher education. By studying and working in higher education institutions, we are implicitly (or explicitly) part of systems of knowledge that have traditionally excluded and at times harmed others. So, our work to undo harm and uncover and prioritize other voices will . . . take work. Yet, what we can see from hearing from others' research, approaches, and efforts to decolonize knowledge and highlight the contributions of others is that new ways of being and researching are possible. Through such approaches in working with others and critical self-reflection, we can see problems being uncovered and solutions unfolding. Donna M. Mertens (2018, 2020), along with Amy Wilson (Mertens & Wilson, 2019) identify processes for transformative research and ways in which we, as socially aware researchers, can aim to emulate and co-create participatory research for the benefit of society.

Reflective questions about social justice and transformative research

In this chapter, we discussed the ways in which social justice and transformative research are fundamental for uncovering the voices of those historically marginalized. Approaches such as decolonizing methodologies allow for and encourage communities including Indigenous knowledges to be heard and amplified. In this type of socially just work, it takes critical self-reflection and working with others to see how we are working with others during and after the research process. While we have included questions embedded throughout to consider reflexivity, the following table provides a few more to consider individually or in groups about knowledge production, voices, and risks.

118

Topics	Questions
Beyond academia with transformative research	• How can transformative research open up new ways of knowing that move beyond "purely" academic knowledge?
Voices	• In social justice or transformative research, what kinds of experiences are we letting in? • Whose voices are we prioritizing, why, and in what context? What are the benefits and detriments to these decisions?
Varied risks	• What steps are you taking to attend to the needs of the community? • What are the potential risks for your populations? For the stakeholders? Are there any risks to the research team? How can these risks be minimized? • What resources might you need to minimize the risks?

References

Adyanga, A. (2018). Foreword. In *Responsible Research Practice: Revisiting Transformative Paradigm in Social Research* (pp. vii–ix). Cham, Switzerland: Springer.

Aparna, K., & Kramsch, O. (2018). Asylum University: Re-situating knowledge exchange along cross-border positionalities. In G. K. Bhambra & K. Nişancıoğlu (Eds.), *Decolonising the University* (pp. 93–107). London: Pluto Press.

Asakura, K., Lundy, J., Black, D., & Tierney, C. (2020). Art as a transformative practice: A participatory action research project with trans* youth. *Qualitative Social Work, 19*(5–6), 1061–1077. https://doi.org/10.1177/1473325019881226

Battiste, M. (2013). *Decolonizing Education: Nourishing the Learning Spirit*. Vancouver, Canada: Purich Publishing.

Bhambra, G. K., Gebrial, D., & Nişancıoğlu, K. (2018). *Decolonising the University*. London: Pluto Press.

Blommaert, J., & Rampton, B. (2012). *Language and Superdiversity*. Max Plank Institute for the Study of Religious and Ethnic Diversity, MMG Working Paper, 12–05. www.unesco.org/new/en/social-and-human-sciences/resources/periodicals/diversities/past-issues/vol-13-no-2-2011/language-and-superdiversity/

Boivin, N. (2020). Multisensory discourse resources: Ethnographic evidence of transnational identity framing, *Journal of Multilingual and Multicultural Development*. https://doi.org/10.1080/01434632.2020.1841215

Boivin, N. (forthcoming). Foodscapes: Multisensory food discourse resources initiating reciprocal interactions. *Language, Culture and Society*.

Breunig, M. (2019). Beings who are becoming: Enhancing social justice literacy. *Journal of Experiential Education*, *42*(1), 7–21. https://doi.org/10.1177/1053825918820694

Byun, K. S., & Plumlee, M. (2021). *From Oblivion to Hosts to the World in 20 Years: Korean Sign Language and its Speakers*. International Conference on Language Documentation & Conservation (ICLDC), University of Hawai'i at Mānoa.

Campbell, E., & Pahl, K. (Eds.). (2018). *Re-Imagining Contested Communities: Connecting Rotherham through Research*. Bristol, UK: Policy Press.

Carl, N. M., & Ravitch, S. M. (2018). Addressing inequity through youth participatory action research: Toward a critically hopeful approach to more equitable schools. *Action Research*. https://doi.org/10.1177/1476750318804623

Charmaz, K. (2011). Grounded theory methods in social justice research. In N. K. Denzin & Y. S. Lincoln (Eds.), *The SAGE Handbook of Qualitative Methods* (4th ed., pp. 359–380). Thousand Oaks, CA: Sage.

Chevalier, J. M., & Buckles, D. J. (2019). *Participatory Action Research: Theory and Methods for Engaged Inquiry*. London: Routledge.

Chilisa, B. (2005). Education research with postcolonial Africa: A critique of HIV/AIDS research in Botswana. *International Journal of Qualitative Studies*, *18*, 659–684.

Chilisa, B., & Tsheko, G. N. (2014). Mixed methods in indigenous research: Building relationships for sustainable intervention outcomes. *Journal of Mixed Methods Research*, *8*(3), 222–233.

CohenMiller, A., & Lewis, J. (2019). Gender audit as research method for organizational learning and change in higher education. In V. Demos, M. Segal, & K. Kelly (Eds.) *Gender and Practice: Insights from the Field* (*Advances in Gender Research* (Vol. 27, pp. 39–55). Emerald Publishing Limited. www.emerald.com/insight/content/doi/10.1108/S1529-212620190000027003/full/html

Dervin, F. (2012). Cultural identity, representation and Othering. In J. Jackson (Ed.), *The Routledge Handbook of Language and Intercultural Communication* (pp. 181–194). Abingdon, UK: Routledge.

Dervin, F. (2016). Discourses of othering. In F. Dervin (Ed.), *Interculturality in Education: A Theoretical and Methodological Toolbox* (pp. 43–55). London: Palgrave Pivot.

Ermine, W. J. (1995). Aboriginal epistemology. In M. Battiste & J. Barman (Eds.), *First Nations Education in Canada: The Circle Unfolds* (pp. 101–112). Vancouver: University of British Columbia Press.

Freire, P. (2000 [1970]). *Pedagogy of the Oppressed* (30th anniversary ed.). London: Bloomsbury.

French, S., Gillman, M., & Swain, J. (1997). *Working with Visually Disabled People: Bridging Theory and Practice*. Birmingham: Venture Press.

Friedner, M., & Kusters, A. (Eds.). (2015). *It's a Small World: International Deaf Spaces and Encounters*. Washington, DC: Gallaudet University Press.

Gimranova, A., Nurmanova, M., & CohenMiller, A. S. (2018). Texting and language learning: WhatsApp group chats and near peer role modeling (NPRM).

LEARNing Landscapes: *Special Issue: Teaching with Technology: Pedagogical Possibilities and Practicalities, 11*(1), 121–135. www.learninglandscapes.ca/index.php/learnland/article/view/927

Guba, E. G., & Lincoln, Y. S. (2017). Paradigmatic controversies, contradictions, and emerging confluences. In N. K. Denzin & Y. S. Lincoln (Eds.), *The SAGE Handbook of Qualitative Research* (5th ed.). Thousand Oaks, CA: Sage.

Hacker, K. (2013). *Community-Based Participatory Research*. Thousand Oaks, CA: Sage.

Janesick, V. J. (2007). Oral history as a social justice project: Issues for the qualitative researcher. *The Qualitative Report, 12*(1), 111–121. https://nsuworks.nova.edu/tqr/vol12/iss1/8

Jensen, S. Q. (2011). Othering, identity formation and agency. *Qualitative Studies, 2*(2), 63–78.

Jimmy, R., Allen, W., & Anderson, V. (2015). Kindred practice: Experiences of a research group working towards decolonization and Indigenization in the everyday. *Education Matters: The Journal of Teaching and Learning, 3*(1).

Kelly, K. (2017). *Gender Audit: A Tool for Organizational Learning. A Five-Year Review of Student Led Gender Audits of the School of International and Public Affairs*. New York: Columbia University.

Kuhn, T. (1996, [1962]). *The Structure of Scientific Revolution*. Chicago: University of Chicago Press.

Kusters, A., De Meulder, M., & O'Brien, D. (2017). *Innovations in Deaf Studies: The Role of Deaf Scholars*. Oxford, UK: Oxford University Press.

Ladd, P. (2003). *Understanding Deaf Culture: In Search of Deafhood*. Bristol, UK: Multilingual Matters.

Leavy, P. (2017). *Research Design: Quantitative, Qualitative, Mixed Methods, Arts-Based, and Community-Based Participatory Research Approaches*. New York: Guilford Press.

Lockley, P. (2018). Open initiatives for decolonising the curriculum. In G. K. Bhambra, D. Gebrial, & K. Nişancıoğlu (Eds.), *Decolonising the University* (pp. 145–172). London: Pluto Press.

McKinley, E. A., & Smith, L. T. (Eds.). (2017). *Handbook on Indigenous Education*. Singapore: Springer.

Mertens, D. (2009). *Transformative Research and Evaluation*. New York: Guilford Press.

Mertens, D., Cram, F., & Chilisa, B. (2013). *Indigenous Pathways into Social Research: Voices of a New Generation*. Walnut Creek, CA: Left Coast Press.

Mertens, D. M. (2016). Advancing social change in South Africa through transformative research. *South African Review of Sociology, 47*(1), 5–17. https://doi.org/10.1080/21528586.2015.1131622

Mertens, D. M. (2018). *Mixed Methods Design in Evaluation*. Thousand Oaks, CA: Sage.

Mertens, D. M. (2020). *Research and Evaluation in Education and Psychology: Integrating Diversity with Quantitative, Qualitative, and Mixed Methods* (5th ed.). Thousand Oaks, CA: Sage.

Mertens, D. M., & Wilson, A. T. (2019). *Program Evaluation Theory and Practice* (2nd ed.). New York: Guilford Press.

Mudau, T. S. (2021). Community engagement as a strategy to facilitate the immigrant-local cohesion. In *Impact of Immigration and Xenophobia on Development in Africa* (Ch. 15). Hershey, PA: IGI Global. https://doi.org/10.4018/978-1-7998-7099-9.ch015

Nind, M. (2014). *What is Inclusive Research?* London: Bloomsbury.

Nind, M. (2017). The practical wisdom of inclusive research. *Qualitative Research, 17*(30), 278–288. https://doi.org/10.1177/1468794117708123

Nind, M., Meckin, R., & Coverdale, A. (2021). Changing research practice: Undertaking social science research in the context of Covid-19. *National Centre for Research Methods*. Retrieved January 25, 2021, from www.ncrm.ac.uk/research/socscicovid19/

Nnawulezi, N., Lippy, C., Serrata, J., & Rodriguez, R. (2018). Doing equitable work in inequitable conditions: An introduction to a special issue on transformative research methods in gender-based violence. *Journal of Family Violence, 33*(8), 507–513. https://doi.org/10.1007/s10896-018-9998-8

Onwuegbuzie, A. J., & Frels, R. K. (2013). Introduction: Toward a new research philosophy for addressing social justice issues: Critical dialectical pluralism 1.0. *International Journal of Multiple Research Approaches, 7*(1), 9–26. https://doi.org/10.5172/mra.2013.7.1.9

Plumlee, M. (2021). Sites of silence: Deaf online communication in the time of corona. In J. M. Ryan (Ed.), *COVID-19: Social Consequences and Cultural Adaptations* (pp. 165–178). London: Routledge.

Romm, N. R. A. (2018). *Responsible Research Practice: Revisiting Transformative Paradigm in Social Research*. Cham, Switzerland: Springer.

Said, E. W. (1978). *Orientalism: Western Conceptions of the Orient*. New York: Vintage Books.

Smith, L. T. (1999). *Decolonizing Methodologies: Research and Indigenous Peoples*. London: Zed Books.

Smith, L. T. (2012). *Decolonizing Methodologies: Research and Indigenous Peoples* (2nd ed.). London: Zed Books.

Spires, K., & CohenMiller, A. S. (2018). Accessibility in Central Asia: Collaboration between graduate school and library. *IFLA Journal, 44*(1), 35–43. https://doi.org/10.1177/0340035217751960

Vertovec, S. (2007). Super-diversity and its implications. *Ethnic and Racial Studies, 30*(6), 1024–1054.

Walmsley, J., & Johnson, K. (2003). *Inclusive Research with People with Learning Disabilities: Past, Present and Futures*. London: Jessica Kingsley Publishers.

Crossing disciplinary boundaries within the research team

Is it important to work outside my discipline? How do I best work with others from different fields? The concept of crossing disciplinary boundaries is straightforward in many ways – just work with another person in another field, right? However, the ways in which this is accomplished are varied and provide interesting and important insights for qualitative researchers, particularly when considering multicultural contexts and academic and non-academic knowledge sets. Working with others also brings up questions about who is part of the research team and how best to incorporate them within the qualitative inquiry.

Qualitative researchers are approaching diverse teams to better understand their work with and across multicultural teams and contexts. When we discuss crossing disciplinary boundaries, we refer to researchers joining together in teams beyond one viewpoint. As encouraged by many funding bodies and departments, working across disciplines can open up the potential for having a broad reach, impact, and enhanced understanding. When working in multicultural contexts, the importance of critical self-reflexivity stands out as particularly important.

Global topics that touch people's lives worldwide challenge researchers and practitioners to come together to find solutions. Some examples of complex topics include issues such as climate change, poverty, disease, women's rights, and innovations to maintain relevance for technological changes, such as those that affect the future of higher education and beyond. The complexity inherent within the topics has led to global issues being referred to as "wicked" (Mertens, 2014, 2016; Rittel & Webber, 1973). Such major societal issues require viewing and addressing topics from multiple lenses and "diverse approaches" (Mertens, 2015, p. 3). Some refer to these

DOI: 10.4324/9780429285691-6

solutions as "radical innovations" (Brown, 2018) and innovative solutions to "support positive social change" (Reich & Reich, p. 51).

Across disciplinary fields, universities and funding agencies are encouraging the integration of multiple viewpoints. Many academic degrees include cross-disciplinary, multidisciplinary, interdisciplinary, and most recently transdisciplinary perspectives. These are just four terms that discuss the varied ways of crossing disciplinary boundaries, all concepts that can facilitate participant voice and socially just qualitative research. At times you'll find that some researchers will discuss other terms, or move between or even integrate disciplines without using one of these three terms. For example, in Hindley and Wall's (2018) research on climate literacy, they look to "an innovative unifying, boundary-crossing approach" (p. 263) instead of centering their work on one of the other terms. And as you've seen across these chapters, there are always multiple ways to define terms depending on your school of thought and training.

For example, back in her PhD program, Anna studied interdisciplinarity. The program explored how intentionally integrating disciplinary perspectives can enhance an understanding of a topic:

> I learned this from studying such key people in the field as Klein's (1990) or Moran's (2010) books on the topic. I remember in the first semester being invited to take part in a curriculum redesign project. I found myself surrounded by others, including peers in the doctoral program, faculty teaching in the program and in other departments, and representatives from a local school. The entire goal was to incorporate voices of diverse cross-section educational stakeholders. At first, it was uncomfortable bringing everyone together and trying to find a common way forward. The experience then becomes a demonstration of integrating voices and perspectives to better adapt the curriculum. I see now how our research was interdisciplinary and even transdisciplinary and action-based, connecting with local collaborators.

The generalist approach that begins teaching schoolchildren about the basics of social sciences, mathematics, and the arts then narrows and deepens. In this way, we can see how the purpose of degree programs is to become a specialist in a particular topic. But the particular emphasis on deepening a topic in higher education requires that other topics are left aside. While this is an important step in knowledge development, it's also important for us to know how to bring together diverse perspectives and understanding. As Klein (1990) warns, academics can become mired in "tunnel vision" of a particular disciplinary focus. Thus, one such way forward is to work with others, to intentionally recognize that solving large-scale problems across multicultural contexts requires multiple viewpoints and specializations to gain a holistic understanding. Through such a holistic perspective, there's potential for "transformative ideas and products to address it."

(Wada et al., 2020, para. 61)

In this chapter, we discuss ideas of researching within and outside our own disciplinary fields to develop, conduct, and promote socially just research. We explore how connecting additional disciplinary perspectives can help enhance socially just research, connect, and uncover solutions. We explore how qualitative research can be conducted across a diverse research team, including providing perspectives and approaches in crossing disciplinary boundaries. **How can we move forward in diverse research teams to be effective and ethical research collaborations?**

1. Where are the disciplinary boundaries?

So, **how can we understand working across disciplinary boundaries to enhance working in multicultural contexts?** Frequently, disciplines are considered fields or subjects that have become ingrained within academic institutions. At times disciplines further evolve and develop specializations, whereas at other times they dissolve. For example, many gender or women's studies programs have been defunded or consolidated within other programs. In contrast, funding has expanded for disciplines in robotics and mining. Within each field or discipline, the ways students and researchers are trained and think about research, participants, and social justice varies. One such way to refer to these differences is as varied "scientific cultures" in which different disciplines would need to learn to work together (Tobi & Kampen, 2018).

Another way to consider disciplines takes scientific cultures a step further, to consider disciplines as a form of "cultural group" (Reich & Reich, 2006). From this perspective, crossing disciplinary boundaries would require *becoming aware and accepting of others' cultural context*. Using this perspective, as socially aware qualitative researchers, we can become prepared for working with multicultural contexts both within the academy and beyond. So, consider for yourself, **what is the culture of your discipline?**

Now, let's unpack a few other terms: cross-disciplinary, multidisciplinary, interdisciplinary, and transdisciplinary. While there are varied definitions, here is one way to consider the differences in these terms related to qualitative research. As you determine which term best applies to your research, you can simultaneously consider how these concepts integrate with conducting socially aware research. So, what is **cross-disciplinary research?**

Cross-disciplinary research uses multiple disciplines side by side.

In cross-disciplinary research, the research team members will hold different perspectives from disciplinary backgrounds. For instance, maybe one researcher is from education and another from political science. While they are part of a larger team, they may work independently and discretely conduct parts of the study without necessarily seeking to integrate their perspectives from the beginning. In **multidisciplinary research**, however, the definition shifts:

Multidisciplinary research tends to connect disciplinary perspectives at some point within a research study.

Multiple perspectives or disciplines can be brought together in iterative ways. For example, one discipline may be at the center of the research and led from that perspective. The lead researcher could then pass on information to the next discipline to further the work at hand. The European Commission notes this sequential method as typical for Horizon2020 grants, which focus on science and technology, a method that fits within a concept of cross-disciplinary or multidisciplinary research:

In the well-established configurations the collaboration is one of a transaction: one discipline does its thing and hands over to the other one (a new material is synthesised, another group characterises it, and a third group works on the theoretical model).

(2014, para. 4)

Crossing disciplinary boundaries

Continuing with our example of the educational scientist and political scientist, the team members in multidisciplinary research would likely integrate their research further than the cross-disciplinary team. Perhaps, for instance, they will discuss their findings and collectively determine a common understanding of the results. **Interdisciplinary research** moves a step further than multidisciplinary research:

Interdisciplinary research seeks to purposefully integrate disciplinary perspectives throughout the research.

In interdisciplinary research, then, researchers can sit down together to talk through each step of their work, to intentionally consider the overlaps and connections: "Unlike research incorporating components of disciplinary knowledge from other disciplines or absorbs one type of work, IDR [interdisciplinary research] focuses on the intentionality of integrating knowledge" (CohenMiller & Pate, 2019, p. 1212). Thus, the educational scientist and political scientist would talk through and plan their study from the beginning, figuring how and where their disciplinary perspectives could "talk" to one another. Within diverse research teams, the members would then touch base throughout the study to further understand and enhance their data collection, analysis, results, and extension of their work to the community. In this way, interdisciplinary research focuses on intentionality, facilitating work within diverse teams, including community members who are part of the research team (CohenMiller & Pate, 2016, 2019). Bringing in other perspectives can also be incorporated from different research practices, such as using the arts to promote interdisciplinarity (Jones, 2006). So, you can think for yourself, **what steps can you take to intentionally work in other perspectives in your research?**

For example, Reich and Reich (2006) provide a framework for facilitating interdisciplinary research and practice. By considering disciplines as separate cultural groups, they explain how individuals can work together to "support positive social change" (Reich & Reich, 2006, p. 51). The authors describe that

each participant in interdisciplinary collaborations must value diversity, develop the capacity for self-assessment, work towards understanding one's own disciplinary culture, and be sensitive to the dynamics inherent when cultures interact. Additionally, members of

Crossing disciplinary boundaries

any interdisciplinary endeavor must be cognizant of power dynamics at play and avoid such things as tokenism, informal hierarchies, and disciplinary policing. Through awareness of one's own disciplinary culture and sensitivity to others, interdisciplinary research and practice may provide creative solutions to important problems.

(Reich & Reich, 2006, p. 51)

While the first three terms examine crossing disciplinary boundaries, which tends to center in academia, the last term, **transdisciplinary research**, moves yet one step further in the process of working with others:

Transdisciplinary research purposefully integrates disciplinary perspectives and knowledges throughout the research, including in application with/for communities outside academia.

In this way, the shift in perspectives and paradigms toward co-production of knowledge can be seen in transdisciplinary sustainability research projects. The research requires sharing rights and responsibilities between scientists and practice partners (Talwar et al., 2011; Lang et al., et al., 2012, p. 39). In other words, transdisciplinary research emphasizes socially aware research that recognizes the importance of partnerships throughout the research. So, you can think to yourself, **how could bringing in a transdisciplinary lens enhance my research?**

We can then consider transdisciplinary research as "most closely linked to expectations for science to be useful and socially relevant" (Rodela & Alašević, 2017, p. 1495). Another example can be seen from Toomey et al. (2015), who examined sustainable development, articulating the importance of using a transdisciplinary approach. They note that

trans-disciplinary work moves beyond the bridging of divides within academia to engaging directly with the production and use of knowledge outside of the academy.

In this approach, societal impact is laid out as a central aim of the research at hand.

(Toomey et al., 2015, p. 1)

Research on complex problems requires input from various communities to ensure the essential knowledge from all relevant disciplines and groups

Crossing disciplinary boundaries

related are incorporated (Lang et al., 2012, p. 26). Collaboration with stakeholders in transdisciplinary research situates the full research teams as working together to identify and describe real-world problems, negotiating agreed-upon outcomes, and empowering all to contribute actively to bridge different communities (Lang et al., 2012, pp. 28–34). Studying our own culture (Spivak, 2012) across disciplinary teams both within and outside academia can be deepened through reflexive practice (Alvesson & Sköldberg, 2017).

We can then think about how working with others across disciplinary fields and multicultural contexts can offer opportunities to better understand ourselves and the issues we are looking to address. One way to move forward is to consider how to create the space and opportunity to think about each discipline's potential in a research project. So, you can ask yourself, **how can I incorporate other disciplinary perspectives to enhance socially just research, voices of the community?** *Which disciplinary perspectives and/or researchers can I involve? Who outside the academic institution needs to be heard?*

2. Do we understand the implications of funding?

Across academic institutions, there is a strong push to apply for funding. We can think now about how these ideas of crossing disciplinary boundaries connect to higher education in general and to the sustenance of research. As Klein (2018) states, "Calls for interdisciplinarity abound. They appear across science and technology, social sciences, humanities, and arts. They also populate reports from professional societies, educational organizations, and funding agencies" (p. 14). The allocation of these funds tends to be determined by individual universities, organizations, and governmental bodies. Many of the calls for funding are increasingly highlighting cross-disciplinary research, supporting those researchers who work across disciplinary fields as well as those who address pressing issues of globalization. In recognizing the need to work across fields, there's also been an increase in recognition of connecting with local communities and organizations. Thus, in applying for large-scale funding, we see the call to work across disciplinary boundaries and recognize community stakeholders' unique contributions. In this way, the multicultural contexts of the communities we work with provide the key to socially aware research and financial support.

Crossing disciplinary boundaries

Internationally, we can see the ways funding bodies promote working across disciplinary fields and with multicultural contexts. One of the largest funding bodies in the United States is the National Science Foundation (NSF). They note their emphasis on interdisciplinary research by explaining the utility and need for it:

> NSF has long recognized the value of interdisciplinary research in pushing fields forward and accelerating scientific discovery. Important research ideas often transcend the scope of a single discipline or program. NSF also understands that the integration of research and education through interdisciplinary training prepares a workforce that undertakes scientific challenges in innovative ways. Thus, NSF gives high priority to promoting interdisciplinary research and supports it through a number of specific solicitations. NSF also encourages researchers to submit unsolicited interdisciplinary proposals for ideas that are in novel or emerging areas extending beyond any particular current NSF program.
>
> (n.d., para. 1)

The emphasis on interdisciplinary research can also be seen in major funding bodies in Europe, such as the European Commission. They encourage cross-disciplinary and interdisciplinary research to address large scale problems:

> Science needs to come up with quicker and effective solutions for complex grand challenges and analyses of complex systems that call for crossing departmental boundaries and inter-disciplinarity to generate new knowledge of transformative power.
>
> (European Commission, 2015, p. 4)

For other large-scale organizations, such as the United Nations Development Programme (UNDP), interdisciplinarity is seen as a solution for working in multicultural contexts. One such example is discussed by UNDP Turkey, which highlighted the interdisciplinary work bringing together collective experiences of the Yoruk nomads with technological solutions (2018). Across these examples from major funding sources, working with others in fields beyond our own is not only prioritized but recognized as the preferred way forward for research. So, you can think to yourself, **which fields might be able to expand my research?**

The ways disciplines and team members interact provide different approaches and outcomes for research. When a research team intentionally and purposefully joins together to collaborate and work with local members, there is a greater potential for understanding diverse communities. The integration of purposefully working across disciplinary fields can lead to valuable insights: "Without this final step of *intentionally* working to integrate our knowledge, we would have had a multidisciplinary study, and likely would have missed nuances uncovered through purposefully sharing of disciplinary perspectives, knowledge, and tools" (CohenMiller et al., 2017, p. 9, emphasis in original). In academic institutions, such an approach has become fairly common, but there is also a need to continue to extend our work. Also, we can see other descriptions such as described by Blassnigg and Punt (2013):

> More sophisticated strategies are required in order to facilitate and build future trajectories for world-class research in terms of scholarly quality and also in term of their inclusivity of integral, ethically viable and creatively innovative concerns that transcend cultural, economic, geographical and social boundaries.
>
> (pp. 2–3)

Thus, as socially aware academics, we can aim to integrate insights from both within and outside academic institutions to cultivate innovative solutions at the intersection of perspectives, experiences, and knowledge.

3. Can we further extend our perspectives?

We can see then that bringing together disciplinary perspectives can extend our understanding of a particular topic. Whether in large-scale or smaller studies, integrating multiple disciplinary perspectives and/or community researchers can promote valuable understanding as well as marginalized voices. There have been recent shifts in various fields to be more collaborative and inclusive by utilizing an interdisciplinary and transdisciplinary approach, such as in health care, sociology, humanities, education, and migration studies. Across these fields, recent texts highlight the importance of crossing disciplinary boundaries. We can take a look at some of these studies as examples. In developmental psychology, for example, the work of

Sperry et al. (2020) directly discuss the importance of crossing disciplinary lines. They mention the transition in their field to include a cultural perspective and highlight the important linkages discovered when incorporating ethnographic approaches to understand the cultural context. In a study of well-being, White and Jha (2018) emphasize the interdisciplinary nature of understanding the topic. In their study in Zambia, they used a cross-cultural, interdisciplinary approach to uncover how well-being is thought of and implemented in a mixed-methods study integrating a traditional quantitative approach for understanding well-being with interviews and narrative analysis.

Other studies specifically examine the concept of crossing disciplinary fields. For example, in a study conducted at the intersection of aging and technology, Wada et al. (2020) researched perspectives and experiences with transdisciplinary research. Their findings speak to the relevance of crossing disciplinary boundaries to recognize benefits and promising practice for transdisciplinary research. Participants in Wada et al.'s (2020) study noted that transdisciplinary research could provide "Mutual learning and growth, Improved capacity to understand and solve issues, Community engagement and empowerment for older adults" (para. 12). Moreover, the researchers also found common concerns and challenges with integrating multiple disciplinary across diverse teams. Their participants noted, for instance, "Contradictions between TDR [transdisciplinary research] principles and participants' understanding" and challenges including "Communication and conflicting priorities among team members, Systemic and cultural barriers: Academic and organizational expectations, Identifying partners and developing partnerships" (Wada et al., 2020, para. 12). So, you can think for yourself, how can I work with others from different disciplines? How can I help facilitate a common framework for working together?

Other examples from various fields incorporate disciplinary insights. For example, to address "complex health-related problems," Lakhani et al. (2012) examined the attributes of successful interdisciplinary research teams. They found "seven attributes important to effective interdisciplinary research teams: team purpose, goals, leadership, communication, cohesion, mutual respect and reflection" (p. E260). Lakhani et al. (2012) point to the need to emphasize "relational aspects of the team, rather than individual expertise and contributions" (p. E264). Such research working across disciplinary teams can provide insights to improve relationships and effectiveness of research in other health contexts. Urquhart et al. (2013) explain how cancer

Crossing disciplinary boundaries

care can be improved by integrating disciplinary perspectives, including a multidisciplinary, interdisciplinary, and transdisciplinary approach. They explain that to address the complicated nature of cancer detection and care, disciplinary perspectives and expertise need to be incorporated:

> Many innovations implemented in cancer care settings are complex and require both engagement from clinicians and adoption, acceptance, and support (for example, resource support, infrastructure, changes in processes and policies) from organizations and the broader health system.
>
> (Urquhart et al., 2013, p. e518)

The importance of collaboration within the medical system and between practitioners, academics, and the public shows how transdisciplinary research can benefit and address health care issues. In working across teams, critical self-reflection is useful for all team members (Pajalic, 2015). Ideally, this process would occur throughout the study, which can help determine a purposeful integration of perspectives (CohenMiller et al., 2017). As Janesick (2015) explains, such reflective practices can become "good habits of mind" and a regular process, including developing a "habit of writing in multiple forms" (p. xiv).

Another approach to developing a research team and considering extending equity and inclusion concepts is to consider how participants can become active research team members through "eco-production." In this way, participant researchers have the opportunity to share, negotiate, and co construct the knowledge produced in the research project. Often, shared practices can occur through multimodal mediums (e.g., video, text, writing, dance). For example, participant researchers can create data through filming their participation within a study. In such a case, they may choose to share this information with friends and family, creating a wider circle of research beyond the typical boundaries of qualitative research (Boivin & CohenMiller, 2018). The idea of co-researching is essential for a participatory approach: the knowledge is produced together with the various stakeholders (local residents, but also local service providers, representatives of local elderly, activists, and invited artists) as co-researchers and co-actors (Lavrinec, 2014, p. 54). The research team can recognize everyone's importance, moving co-researchers to become more than just collaborators within data (Pahl, 2014). In this way, participant researchers in a research team are encouraged to share multiple voices and identities, offering more nuanced results and solutions. For your own research, then, you can think about the ways you can further include community members. For instance, you can ask yourself, **how can I demonstrate my appreciation and inclusion of members from outside my workplace/university as equal contributors to the research?**

4. What ethical dilemmas should we be prepared for relating to working across disciplines?

Both challenges and ethical concerns are found within all research projects, especially noticeable when seeking to conduct socially just research. These considerations are essential for working in face-to-face or online environments. Working across disciplinary fields provides impressive opportunities, insights, and considerations with diverse and vulnerable populations, such as to consider relational ethics (Ellis, 2007). Yet, there are also challenges in these approaches, both within the research team and in working with the broader community.

For example, problems can emerge at any stage in the research process, especially when working across diverse fields and communities. Musa (2018) points to potential challenges of crossing disciplinary boundaries in research teams, including "conflicting standards of research philosophies, methodologies, and methods shapes empirical inquiries" (p. 149). And other researchers, such as in education, discuss the complexities of working across race, gender, and ethnicity in research teams (Oikonomidoy & Wiest, 2017), addressing risks (Lillard, 2018), and navigating methodological barriers (K. K. & Al-Maskari, 2018). Ethical concerns can then relate to how a team of researchers or an individual considers the place of and prevalence of knowledge. A central question then comes back to the idea of participant and researcher voice: **whose disciplinary knowledges are being privileged?**

Beyond individual studies, large-scale funding and research centers also point to challenges of collaboration within and across disciplinary teams. For instance, the European Commission (2015) highlights the importance of "collaborative interdisciplinarity" (p. 4) and points out the potential obstacles of such an approach:

Crossing disciplinary boundaries

> Communities of IDR-practice [interdisciplinary research–practice] have to embrace trust in the expertise, skills, curiosity, motivation and capabilities of colleagues from other fields in order to trigger social and cognitive dynamics that may help generate a blooming group flow and find a common ground of shared interests and level playing field. Interdisciplinarity begins with exposing bachelor students to different disciplines, familiarizing them with different perspectives, perspective-taking and "reading" different scientific vernaculars.
>
> (p. 5)

Thus, while there's a growing body of research explaining how researching across disciplinary fields can bring about a broader understanding of complex problems, the challenges of such collaborative research need attention. Even just coming to a common choice of terms and language used in a study can be problematic (Urquhart et al., 2013). Moreover, bringing together those from within and outside academic environments or from different disciplinary backgrounds can mean a lack of understanding or awareness of the work environment for each team member (Urquhart et al., 2011). One potential challenge regarding ethics is how institutional review boards view working with different disciplines and the concept of researching vulnerable populations (Opsal et al., 2016).

Some obstacles to consider relate to issues of cultural competence, such as awareness of others' needs and values within the research team and within the community. Communication can act as an essential step for bridging divides between team members. We can see how communicative competence is useful for enhancing interdisciplinary learning even within the classroom setting (Taylor, 2018). In Chapter 2 we discussed building and managing trust in research with diverse and multicultural communities, but it's useful to point this concept out again. Developing trust and confidence across a team is an important component of developing and maintaining an ethical research project in the field. At times this could mean providing equity of knowledge across disciplines (Aagaard-Hansen & Ouma, 2002) or among individuals. Using "cycles of action and reflection," Eriksen and Heimestøl (2017) explored how collaboration can improve interdisciplinary research in health fields, finding that determining set processes and responsibilities are particularly noteworthy (p. 1). Irrespective of the disciplinary field, the concepts of identifying and communicating about roles

Crossing disciplinary boundaries

and responsibilities affect all teams. And while working within and across multicultural groups who may be recognized as "vulnerable populations," the ways we proceed need to be considered carefully.

What becomes clear across the discussion of working across disciplinary teams is the range of ways describing the potential collaboration, process, and design. So, if the dynamic of the research process can shift, and definitions are varied for working across disciplinary teams, then what does this mean for conducting research within and outside academia? Broadly, you are offered a chance to critically self-reflect on your research process and outputs in ways to enhance social justice in working with others. So, you can ask yourself, **what does my disciplinary knowledge suggest for working with others?** *How can I expand my understanding of who has knowledge?*

The integration of disciplinary perspectives can then be elicited in different ways. For instance, the research team could be associated or have backgrounds in different disciplinary perspectives, even if under a larger disciplinary umbrella. An example of this approach was used in the study of secondary school well-being conducted in Kazakhstan. The research team included those from educational psychology, anthropology, and specialists in qualitative, quantitative and arts-based research, and incorporated local stakeholders in various ways (see CohenMiller et al., 2017). At other times, the research team may be interdisciplinary, drawing from community or government stakeholders to engage in the research steps themselves, co-producing knowledge and research from the project's onset (Banks et al., 2019). In this way, communities of knowledge are addressed in recognizing their experience and capacity.

Crossing disciplinary boundaries then can be seen in the formal disciplinary border crossing and with stakeholders in communities. Likewise, understanding large-scale, complex issues can also be approached through sustainable research projects. These types of projects allow for sharing of rights and responsibilities between academics, more practice-based partners, and others in the community. In further considering ethical considerations in this topic, many questions emerge. You can think about such topics as, **how can I fully explain to ethical review boards the interdisciplinary approach that may not fit neatly into one approach?** *Or, how can my incorporation of partnerships for research help overcome structural inequality (e.g., socioeconomic, status, colonial)?* The integration of voices in a research project is an opportunity to develop an ethically just and socially

136

aware project. You have a chance to promote voices of those historically marginalized both in the study results and within the research team itself.

5. Reflections from the field: crossing disciplinary boundaries

To provide additional insight into crossing disciplinary perspectives, we have asked multiple scholars and practitioners worldwide to critically reflect on integrating ideas, knowledge, and tools. These ideas connect to concepts of decolonizing knowledges (Mertens, 2020; Smith, 1999, 2013). Agnes Atia Apusigah, from the Regentropfen College of Applied Sciences in Kansoe, Bolgatanga, Ghana, delves into how cross-cultural considerations can be combined into cross-disciplinary research teams. She highlights the issues of complexity and social justice, emphasizing the hopefulness for greater understanding through integration of multiple disciplinary perspectives by finding a common ideology.

"It doesn't have to be hard work": finding common ideology and learning as an insider and outsider in cross-disciplinary research teams

Agnes Atia Apusigah

Cross-disciplinary research teams have become critical to cross-cultural and cultural studies due to the multiplier effects on shaping meaning. Cross-disciplinary teams draw and build on the strengths of researchers from diverse disciplines to tackle complex problems. The challenge of complexity drives cross-disciplinary studies, especially in the context of cultural studies where innovative problem-solving and critical meaning-making underpin research. I share this reflection as a professor of development sociology and vice president of a college in northern Ghana, near the border with Burkina Faso. From my work as a scholar-activist, a member of the women's movement of Ghana, and one active in civil society governance, I have worked in many cross-disciplinary research teams. In particular, my work has emphasized women's empowerment and access to knowledge and resources.

In the context of development and human well-being, cross-disciplinary studies provide the framework for tackling hydra-headed life problems on the environment, human rights, social inclusion/justice, socioeconomic progress, and more. For instance, in one study, I worked with a team to understand the inequities in funding for women's organizations in Ghana. The team included many different people, bringing together disciplinary backgrounds such as law and African studies. We had to come together to understand the unique context of women's organizations across the country and try to understand how women were losing out on national funding.

Against the backdrop of community development, where integrated human development strategies are called into play, working in cross-disciplinary teams allows for the complex analysis necessary for the multidimensional nature of living. Yet, cross-disciplinary teams have to be guarded in their manner of working to avoid slips to the traditional silos that limit the cross-fertilization of analysis for complex meanings. It was important for the team to be kept abreast and comment on the study's aims and objectives from the beginning. We met constantly to remind ourselves of these, which had all been outlined in the proposal and methodological steps. There was also a team leader who was very focused, measured in moderating views and learnings, and provided constant support.

Yet, there were challenges, in particular when we reached the analysis and interpretation stage. *What gets glossed over and what gets emphasized?* This is where people's disciplines came across strongly. Rooted in the agenda of integration, cross-disciplinary teams can draw from and nurture diverse researchers' strengths. However, dwelling on strengths tends to neglect the essence of cross-disciplinary teams: the weaknesses that accompany the strengths. The challenge then is for the researchers to conclude the exercise by gaining improved tools from their learning from other disciplines.

As a team, we recognized that some voices were getting priority while others were more silenced. We came together and discussed our views and analyses and came to an agreement that our perspectives complemented one another. We were writing together, too. For instance, if someone was pushing the legality of issues or on human rights, it was seen as enriching the data and viewed as part of the analysis instead of *the* analysis. We asked of ourselves and our data, what other directions can we bring to help the issues be understood better? What could help someone from another field look and understand the Ghanaian context? What are culturally safe and sound solutions for this context, which can enable us to reflect on the issues? In this way, there was no need to defend a discipline or viewpoint. Definitely, each of us has our own viewpoints and preferences, but to manage multiple perspectives meant that we saw our coming together as making data richer and the analysis even stronger.

The object of sharing and learning across disciplines is not just about producing an integrated research product but also for the researchers to enhance their traditional tools of research. The research site becomes one of transforming meaning and skills. The experience of sharing and learning can then become particularly fulfilling for all *willing* researchers. In a cross-disciplinary team, we can move from traditional boundaries as insiders in the discipline into new territories where we can develop new meaning, learn from the process of how to blend in, and learn as both a disciplinary insider and outsider. Disciplinary outsiders are not necessarily naïve of the new territory encountered but may be limited in appreciating the complexities of that discipline in the way that an insider might.

When social scientists and physical scientists work together in a cross-disciplinary research context, it is not expected that one becomes the other. Rather, it is the case that the expertise (skills and knowledge) of one lends itself to that of the other to enrich and deepen meaning. The individual disciplines are expected to be influenced and thus reshaped in ways that enhance and enrich not just the product but also the processes and mechanisms of the research. That transformative process will ideally result in a better version of the existing one rather than the same version of it.

For those looking to bring together a cross-disciplinary team, I have found it useful to understand and find a common ideological or philosophical background of the team. For instance, much of the research

Crossing disciplinary boundaries

in Ghana is very positivistic, so to try to introduce a critical analysis or perspective to a team of positivists would push against the research culture and the ideological basis of the group. Instead, bringing together a cross-disciplinary team doesn't have to be hard work. If you have this understanding, if you want to have positivist research, then you bring together positivists. If you want to conduct a study from a critical lens, bring together those with that underlying interest in power and inequity. The ideology that drives people's research is important to consider. If the same ideology drives you, it is easier to work together because you come to the table with some common ground to reach a product.

In the next reflection, Akmaral Sman reflects on her work with a United Nations organization in Kazakhstan. She discusses how she and a cross-disciplinary team worked together with local communities to identify key issues of livelihood integral to the area. Sman critically self-reflects on the development of trust through working with academic, governmental, and community members.

Reflecting on crossing disciplinary divides with academics and communities

Akmaral Sman

In August 2019, I worked with one of the UN agencies in a rural area of East Kazakhstan. I have a background in public administration focused on international funding and empowerment for women and girls. My team included those also from agricultural and environmental fields. Working with the local municipality in this vulnerable area, we conducted a three-day workshop in the forestry industry to identify the local needs and raise awareness of gender issues.

The local institution provided a sense of trust for the rural community, acting as gatekeepers for us to enter. Over time, the community began to trust us. The workshop was based on a previously developed handbook and gender analysis framework. Ultimately, about 50 people joined the workshop, across all job positions, all interested in learning and sharing their concerns.

In talking with the women in the groups, I found that they were open to sharing their daily challenges. For example, they explained that getting basic medications was problematic. There weren't very many drug stores, and the distance between them was too great for those who had young children or were unemployed. The efforts to find medications for themselves or their children if someone became ill were tremendous.

These on-the-ground discussions helped us see the experiences of those living in the area. Once they felt comfortable, community members provided the key insights to problems faced instead of the academic researchers. For instance, we heard about an overabundance of pubs and small shopping centers compared to a lack of kindergartens and spaces for women to spend time.

While the city has one of the biggest ironworks, with over half of the male population employed in mining, the women participating in the workshop explained that many of their small businesses had been shut down due to a lack of funding and support from the area. As a result, the women shared how they actively participated in the forestry industry (e.g., tourism, wood handcrafting, pickling products, forest guards). But as the women shared, to get the job in that industry, they had to compete with men and the related stereotypes, discrimination, and lack of infrastructure (e.g., domestic care work), which continue to be main challenges for those living in that area.

From working in a cross-disciplinary team and building trusting relationships with local community members, we actively listened and worked to address the challenges the community faces. Afterward, we went to other places throughout Kazakhstan and conducted a similar workshop with the same analysis. We then connected to an international business school to offer training to ten women interested in small business development in their area. For example, if one of the women wanted to launch a project, then we might propose training on project management and leadership. It varied based upon the needs of the interested women and their focus. In total, ten women were educated and returned back to their community.

Crossing disciplinary boundaries

> The work with the local community then led to trainings based upon the needs of individuals and led to the first-ever national conference on gender and forestry. People were invited from across sectors and areas, including those from the workshop and public servants. In this way, the women who had been trained first at the workshop and then through the business training were provided with a platform to share their work in front of an important audience.
>
> While all issues have not been resolved in the area, the potential for continued connections and opportunities remain and suggest the continued evolution of long-term connections to promote human rights.

Then we heard from a cross-disciplinary team from the United States, India, and South Africa. Roxanne Henkin from the University of Texas at San Antonio, Gopal Krishna Sharma and Purva Gopal Sharma from Dev Sanskriti Vishwavidyalya, and Mashaba Mashala from the University of Mpumalanga, critically reflect on their multiyear work incorporating co-production of workshops and research. Their work highlights how coming together across disciplines and international boundaries can promote the voices of those from historically marginalized spaces and multicultural contexts.

> ## Working across disciplinary and multicultural contexts
>
> Roxanne Henkin, Gopal Krishna Sharma, Purva Gopal Sharma, and Mashaba Mashala
>
> **What are the benefits and challenges of working across disciplinary and multicultural contexts?** We recently talked about this question in two online discussions on two different occasions. Gopal Sharma and Purva Sharma shared their insights on their experiences in the Haridwar, India Writing Project (2015) and then in San Antonio for the Texas Writing Project (2016). Mashaba Mashala discussed her reflections on the Limpopo, South Africa Writing Project (2009), her academic work, and her stay with Roxanne Henkin and Mary Lou Daugherty in San Antonio during the winter break of the first year.

Henkin led these workshops, along with other teacher consultants, as the director (2006–2016) of the San Antonio Texas Writing Project (SAWP) and as the director of the international writing workshops that SAWP has offered. Daugherty was one of the team of co-directors for both of these workshops.

Crossing disciplinary boundaries through lived experiences

We began by talking about the highlights of participating in the workshops and living in and/or visiting the United States and what the participants learned about themselves. "I think living in a different culture teaches you about yourself," said Mashaba. "In my culture, a lot of things go unsaid. I don't need to tell my friends to come to my home because they are automatically invited. In the US, you have to say what you want."

Purva and Gopal discussed the many learning opportunities they had in San Antonio, including learning for the first time about the Holocaust. "We even were introduced to Anna Rado, a Holocaust survivor." Crossing disciplinary boundaries included seeing commonalities in religion and spirituality:

> We also had mutual interfaith dialogues where we discussed the idea, the philosophy and the practices of the world *gayatri pariwar* mother institution of *dev sanskriti vishwavidyalya*, the founder Acharya Shriram Sharma ji, and various socio-spiritual activities. We came with no expectations – we were open.

Cross-disciplinary writing process and learning

Focusing on the writing process was another highlight and surprise. Mashaba explained:

> The workshop changed how I teach writing. Now I start by having my students write from something familiar. I learned about journaling and I use journaling in my classes now. Then the students can build on what they've written and add to it. This is a very powerful tool.

Mashaba also highlighted the role of personal writing for her. "Having people from different perspectives sharing our personal writing and seeing how other people think was great. I was able to think about ideas from a number of different angles."

Gopal and Purva also discussed the power of personal writing. Gopal's field is computer science and Purva's is psychology. Gopal said:

> Even before we entered the workshop, Roxanne gave a speech in which she talked about the importance of writing to heal and to know yourself. She told us to just put the pen on the paper and keep on writing. We could also write in Hindi. The thing was to go on writing and fix it later. . . . This personal writing also helped us afterwards while we were writing our PhD dissertations.

Purva shared that listening to her peers and sharing her own personal stories in a safe space was powerful. "Before the workshop we knew and worked with our colleagues," she said. "During the workshop they became our friends."

Challenges of working across disciplinary and multicultural contexts

There were three major challenges: availability of funding, paperwork with each university, including visas, language, and technology. Many of the expenses were personally paid for by the co-directors in Limpopo and in the United States when participants came to visit. Since the workshops were conducted in English, which was not the home language for the participants, at times individuals struggled in the learning process or in understanding that could be challenging for non-natives to understand easily.

Another challenge at that time, which has now improved, is access to technology. Mashaba reminded us that in the 2009 Limpopo workshop, Mary Lou Dougherty helped participants get their first emails. Now Mashaba imagines working with Roxanne in classrooms across South Africa through Zoom or other platforms.

Crossing disciplinary boundaries

Suggestions for participatory workshops across multicultural contexts

In these discussions, we agreed that a key aspect for success was for all involved to be open to new ideas and changing perspectives. Also, the workshops provided opportunities, but without attending them for the full time, there were large gaps in knowledge and community building. Participants who were called away to teach or complete other work responsibilities were not fully able to benefit from the experience.

In spite of the challenges, we all agreed that working internationally with people in diverse fields, different countries and cultures, and with multiple languages is well worth working through the challenges. Gopal shared:

> As human beings we are so connected – it's not about nationality or religion – we are all one. When we came back to India from the US, we were like the experts and we told people that when you try to put everyone in a box, you can't. . . . when we came back to our country, we had shifted, and we had new insights.

Mashaba concluded that her most important insight is what she learned about other cultures:

> When you live in another culture, it teaches you that there are different ways of doing things. You learn to see things from other peoples' perspectives. It would go a long way to have peace around the world, if more people traveled to different parts of the world and/or participated in interdisciplinary workshops and learning experiences.

In these participatory workshops and by working hand in hand with the local communities, participants can establish friendships that can effect positive change. Friendships that began in 2009 and 2015 have now become lifetime friendships that include both life-cycle celebration and academic scholarship (see Dippenaar et al., 2016; Henkin

Crossing disciplinary boundaries

et al., 2016; Iyengar & Henkin, 2015). Roxanne said that "by sharing our life stories, we became so close that we moved from acquaintances to friends and from friends to family." She continued:

> We are recognizing all that we have in common both with each other and with others around the world. That's the beauty of these interdisciplinary, multicultural writing projects, we have created an international community that transcends borders and provides hope for the future.

References

Dippenaar, H., Henkin, R., Logan, C., Ralfe, L., & Benn, M. (2016). Exploring writing institutes for teachers in South Africa. *Journal for Language Teaching, 50*(1).

Henkin, R., Wilson, T., Paloma, R., Bippert, K., & Cataldo, R. (2016). Reflections and insights on the teaching of writing. *Dev Sanskriti International Journal, 7*, 80–95. https://doi.org/10.36018/dsiij.v7i0.79

Iyengar, K., & Henkin, R. (2015). Topic choice and attitude towards writing in an invitational summer institute professional development writing project. *European Journal of Research and Reflection in the Arts and Humanities, 3*(2), 1–25.

6. Engaging more deeply: concluding thoughts on crossing disciplinary boundaries

Which knowledge is centered in the research study, and whose voices does this privilege in working across multicultural contexts? Working across disciplinary fields and knowledges will ideally focus on building collaboration and socially aware approaches. Such work could emphasize reflexivity or integrative approaches; detail methods as a driving force or a socially pressing issue; aim to enable learning, action and advocacy, or products; and/or address another process or outcome bringing together varied perspectives and insights. Locating team members' common aims and roles remains a key issue in working across disciplinary fields within and across multicultural contexts. Fortunately, as the emphasis on more research within and across disciplinary teams is growing, the solutions are becoming clearer. There are

Crossing disciplinary boundaries

often challenges encountered in working across disciplinary teams, yet the benefits outweigh the potential problems.

In this chapter, we explored working across disciplinary fields and becoming aware of knowledges within and outside academia. Varied definitions of such approaches range, yet at the heart of this work is the idea of moving beyond one field to incorporate knowledge from another. We focused in particular on the intentional move to integrate knowledge, methods, and tools across disciplines and knowledge from within and beyond academic institutions. As qualitative researchers concerned with social justice and seeking to improve equity and inclusion, we can become more aware of our own practices and embedded ways of knowing. Through the continual self-reflection of our processes, our disciplinary views, and uncovering our unconscious ways of being, we can develop more ethical and socially just research across contexts.

Reflective questions about crossing disciplinary boundaries

This chapter raises several ideas and questions about the ways in which as socially just qualitative researchers we can work with others. We've discussed ways of purposefully integrating disciplinary and non-academic insights to enhance research and promote equity and inclusion. We had a chance to consider questions embedded throughout the chapter and consider how research memberships can evolve. Now, here are a few questions to guide you through thinking about these ideas as related to crossing disciplinary boundaries for working with and across multicultural contexts.

Topic	Questions
Research project members	• Consider your research project: how can you expand who is part of your research? • What other voices are not yet being heard? • What steps would you need to include to incorporate them in a meaningful way into your research? • What extra tools or resources might you need?
Collaboration and investment	• Consider a team research project. What is your role and what are the roles of others? How can you help everyone feel valued equally? • What steps are important for your research to help all stakeholders feel invested throughout the research project and upon completion of the work?

147

Topic	Questions
Considering collaboration and crossing disciplinary and knowledge boundaries	• What shared values does your team have? Are they the same as your participants? Same as the stakeholders? Where do you deviate from one another? Is it important to bridge this gap? Why or why not?

References

Aagaard-Hansen, J., & Henry Ouma, J. (2002). Managing interdisciplinary health research – theoretical and practical aspects. *The International Journal of Health Planning and Management, 17*(3), 195–212. https://doi.org/10.1002/hpm.671

Alvesson, M., & Sköldberg, K. (2017). *Reflexive Methodology: New Vistas for Qualitative Research*. Thousand Oaks, CA: Sage.

Banks, S., Hart, A., Pahl, K., & Ward, P. (Eds.). (2019). *Co-Producing Research: A Community Development Approach*. Bristol, UK: Policy Press.

Blassnigg, M., & Punt, M. (2013). *Transdisciplinarity: Challenges, Approaches and Opportunities at the Cusp of History*. Plymouth, UK: Transtechnology Research.

Boivin, N., & CohenMiller, A. S. (2018). Breaking the "fourth wall" in qualitative research: Participant-led digital data construction. *The Qualitative Report, 23*(3), 581–592.

Brown, B. (2018). Interdisciplinary research. *European Review, 26*(S2), S21–S29. https://doi.org/10.1017/S1062798718000248

CohenMiller, A. S., Faucher, C., Hernández-Torrano, D., & Brown Hajdukova, E. (2017). Practical steps for using interdisciplinary educational research to enhance cultural awareness. *International Journal of Research and Method in Education, 40*(3). https://doi.org/10.1080/1743727X.2017.1310834

CohenMiller, A. S., & Pate, E. (2016). *Promoting New Knowledge Making Across Disciplines: A Model for Developing an Interdisciplinary Theoretical Framework for Teaching and Learning*. International Union of Anthropological and Ethnological Sciences (IUAES) Inter-Congress, Dubrovnik, Croatia.

CohenMiller, A. S., & Pate, E. (2019). *A Model for Developing Interdisciplinary Research Theoretical Frameworks, 24*(6), 1211–1226. https://nsuworks.nova.edu/tqr/vol24/iss6/2

Ellis, C. (2007). Telling secrets, revealing lives: Relational ethics in research with intimate others. *Qualitative Inquiry, 13*(1), 3–29.

Eriksen, K. Å., & Heimestøl, S. (2017). Developing a culture of pride, confidence and trust: Enhanced collaboration in an interdisciplinary team. *International Practice Development Journal, 7*, 1–14.

European Commission. (2014). Living interdisciplinarity. Retrieved January 3, 2021, from https://ec.europa.eu/programmes/horizon2020/en/news/fet-living-interdisciplinarity

European Commission. (2015). *Directorate General for Research and Innovation & Research, Innovation, and Science Policy Experts (RISE)*. Quests for interdisciplinarity: A challenge for the ERA and HORIZON 2020. https://data.europa.eu/doi/10.2777/499518

Hindley, A., & Wall, T. (2018). A unifying, boundary-crossing approach to developing climate literacy. In W. Leal Filho (Ed.), *Implementing Sustainability in the Curriculum of Universities: Approaches, Methods and Projects* (pp. 263–278). Cham, Switzerland: Springer. https://doi.org/10.1007/978-3-319-70281-0_16

Janesick, V. J. (2015). *"Stretching" Exercises for Qualitative Researchers* (4th ed.). Thousand Oaks, CA: Sage.

Jones, K. (2012). Connecting research with communities through performative social science. *The Qualitative Report, 17* (Rev. 18), 1–8. http://www.nova.edu/ssss/QR/QR17/jones.pdf

K. K., S., & Al-Maskari, A. (2018). Issues and challenges in interdisciplinary: Methodological barriers. In M. N. Al-Suqri, A. K. Al-Kindi, S. S. AlKindi, & N. E. Saleem (Eds.), *Promoting Interdisciplinarity in Knowledge Generation and Problem Solving* (pp. 181–207). Hershey, PA: IGI Global. https://doi.org/10.4018/978-1-5225-3878-3

Klein, J. T. (1990). *Interdisciplinarity: History, Theory, and Practice*. Detroit, MI: Wayne State University Press.

Klein, J. T. (2004). Prospects for transdisciplinarity. *Futures, 36*, 515–526.

Klein, J. T. (2018). Current drivers of interdisciplinarity: The what and the why. In M. N. Al-Suqri, A. K. Al-Kindi, S. S. AlKindi, & N. E. Saleem (Eds.), *Promoting Interdisciplinarity in Knowledge Generation and Problem Solving* (pp. 14–28). Hershey, PA: IGI Global. https://doi.org/10.4018/978-1-5225-3878-3

Lakhani, J., Benzies, K., & Hayden, K. A. (2012). Attributes of interdisciplinary research teams: A comprehensive review of the literature. *Clinical & Investigative Medicine, 35*(5), E260. https://doi.org/10.25011/cim.v35i5.18698

Lang, D. J., Wiek, A., Bergmann, M., Stauffacher, M., Swilling, M., & Thomas, C. J. (2012). Transdisciplinary research in sustainability science: Practice, principles, and challenges. *Sustain Science, 7*(1), 25–43. Cham, Switzerland: Springer.

Lavrinec, J. (2014). Community art initiatives as a form of participatory research: The case of street mosaic workshop. *Creativity Studies, 7*(1), 55–68.

Lillard, L. (2018). Is interdisciplinary collaboration in academia an elusive dream? Can the institutional barriers be broken down? A review of the literature and the case of library science. In M. N. Al-Suqri, A. K. Al-Kindi, S. S. AlKindi, & N. E. Saleem (Eds.), *Promoting Interdisciplinarity in Knowledge Generation and Problem Solving* (pp. 139–147). Hershey, PA: IGI Global. https://doi.org/10.4018/978-1-5225-3878-3

Mertens, D. M. (2014). Mixed methods and wicked problems. *Journal of Mixed Methods Research, 9*(1), 3–6. https://doi.org/10.1177/1558689814562944

Mertens, D. M. (2016). Advancing social change in South Africa through transformative research. *South African Review of Sociology, 47*(1), 5–17. https://doi.org/10.1080/21528586.2015.1131622

Mertens, D. M. (2020). *Research and Evaluation in Education and Psychology: Integrating Diversity with Quantitative, Qualitative, and Mixed Methods* (5th ed.). Los Angeles, CA: Sage.

Moran, J. (2010). *Interdisciplinarity* (2nd ed.). Abingdon: Routledge.

Musa, A. I. (2018). Cultural and communication barriers to interdisciplinary research: Implication for global health information programs – Philosophical, disciplinary epistemological, and methodological discourses. In M. N. Al-Suqri, A. K. Al-Kindi, S. S. AlKindi, & N. E. Saleem (Eds.), *Promoting Interdisciplinarity in Knowledge Generation and Problem Solving* (pp. 148–180). Hershey, PA: IGI Global https://doi.org/10.4018/978-1-5225-3878-3.ch011

National Science Foundation (NSF). (n.d.). Introduction to interdisciplinary research. Retrieved January 3, 2021, from www.nsf.gov/od/oia/additional_resources/interdisciplinary_research/

Oikonomidoy, E., & Wiest, L. R. (2017). Navigating cross-boundary connections in educational research. *International Journal of Research & Method in Education, 40*(1), 53–65. https://doi.org/10.1080/1743727X.2015.1036851

Opsal, T., Wolgemuth, J., Cross, J., Kaanta, T., Dickmann, E., Colomer, S., & Erdil-Moody, Z. (2016). "There are no known benefits . . .": Considering the risk/benefit ratio of qualitative research. *Qualitative Health Research, 26*(8), 1137–1150. https://doi.org/10.1177/1049732315580109

Pahl, K. (2014). The aesthetics of everyday literacies: Home writing practices in a British Asian household. *Anthropology and Education Quarterly, 45*(3), 293–311.

Pajalic, Z. (2015). A researcher's self-reflection of the facilitation and evaluation of an action research project within the Swedish social and care context. *Global Journal of Health Science, 7*(3), 6. http://dx.doi.org/10.5539/gjhs.v7n3p105

Reich, S. M., & Reich, J. A. (2006). Cultural competence in interdisciplinary collaborations: A method for respecting diversity in research partnerships. *American Journal of Community Psychology, 38*(1–2), 1–7. https://doi.org/10.1007/s10464-006-9064-1

Rittel, H. W. J., & Webber, M. M. (1973). Dilemmas in a general theory of planning. *Policy Sciences, 4*, 155–169.

Rodela, R., & Alašević, D. (2017). Crossing disciplinary boundaries in environmental research: Interdisciplinary engagement across the Slovene research community. *Science of The Total Environment, 574*, 1492–1501. https://doi.org/10.1016/j.scitotenv.2016.08.144

Smith, L. T. (1999). *Decolonizing Methodologies: Research and Indigenous Peoples*. London: Zed Books.

Smith, L. T. (2013). *Decolonizing Methodologies: Research and Indigenous Peoples* (2nd ed.). London: Zed Books.

Sperry, D. E., Miller, P. J., & Sperry, L. L. (2020). Hazardous intersections: Crossing disciplinary lines in developmental psychology. *European Journal of Social Theory*, *23*(1), 93–112. https://doi.org/10.1177/1368431018812465

Spivak, G. C. (2012). *In Other Worlds: Essays in Cultural politics*. Abingdon-on-Thames, UK: Routledge.

Talwar, S., Wiek, A., & Robinson, J. (2011). User engagement in sustainability research. *Science and Public Policy*, *38*(5), 379–390.

Taylor, S. (2018). To understand and be understood: Facilitating interdisciplinary learning through the promotion of communicative competence. *Journal of Geography in Higher Education*, *42*(1), 126–142.

Tobi, H., & Kampen, J. K. (2018). Research design: The methodology for interdisciplinary research framework. *Quality & Quantity*, *52*(3), 1209–1225. https://doi.org/10.1007/s11135-017-0513-8

Toomey, A. H., Markusson, N., Adama, E., & Brockett, B. (2015). *Inter- and Trans-Disciplinary Research: A Critical Perspective*. GSDR Brief. Retrieved January 3, 2021, from https://sustainabledevelopment.un.org/content/documents/612558-Inter-%20and%20Trans-disciplinary%20Research%20-%20A%20Critical%20Perspective.pdf

United National Development Program (UNDP). (2018). Interdisciplinary and innovative: Innovation at its best. Retrieved January 3, 2021, from www.tr.undp.org/content/turkey/en/home/presscenter/articles/2018/02/disiplinleraras_-ve-yenilikci – en-guezel-eklyle-novasyon.html

Urquhart, R., Grunfeld, E., Jackson, L., Sargeant, J., & Porter, G. A. (2013). Cross-disciplinary research in cancer: An opportunity to narrow the knowledge – practice gap. *Current Oncology*, *20*(6), 512. https://doi.org/10.3747/co.20.1487

Urquhart, R., Porter, G. A., & Grunfeld, E. (2011). Reflections on knowledge brokering within a multidisciplinary research team. *Journal of Continuing Education in the Health Professions*, *31*(4), 283–290. https://doi.org/10.1002/chp.20128

Wada, M., Grigorovich, A., Fang, M. L., Sixsmith, J., & Kontos, P. (2020). An exploration of experiences of transdisciplinary research in aging and technology. *Forum Qualitative Sozialforschung / Forum: Qualitative Social Research*, *21*(1). https://doi.org/10.17169/fqs-21.1.3332

White, S. C., & Jha, S. (2018). Towards an interdisciplinary approach to wellbeing: Life histories and self-determination theory in rural Zambia. *Social Science & Medicine*, *212*, 153–160. https://doi.org/10.1016/j.socscimed.2018.07.026

6 Moving between face-to-face and online engagement

How can I conduct my research online when I had planned to work face-to-face? What do I need to be aware of when conducting socially distanced research? As we start this chapter, a starting point is to recognize many people around the globe don't have home access to online resources for various reasons. These constraints can vary, and may be based upon the socioeconomic digital divide restricting access, a generational divide, or national and political regulations, to name a few. Therefore, when we discuss moving online, we're assuming the researcher's and community's privileges from the start by talking about conducting research online. With such benefit also comes essential topics related to power, trust, and ethics in multicultural research.

In this chapter, we discuss conducting research using various modalities and platforms and the specific issues related to such approaches. We describe the idea of moving *between* face-to-face to online environments as way to emphasize how these two worlds, while potentially disparate, also can be used in tandem, or as a path from one to the other. Terms such as *online research, technology-driven research, virtual research*, and *digital research* can refer to how we conduct research with participants using technology. Researchers may conduct such research entirely online. For example, participants and researchers could post to a shared online document (e.g., Bröer et al., 2016; CohenMiller, 2018; Legewie & Nassauer, 2018) or use technology to share lived experiences (e.g., Boivin, forthcoming; Boivin & Amantay, forthcoming; Salmons, 2015).

During times of socially distanced research, moving to online spaces can be important for continuing the momentum of collaborations. These online spaces offer chances to interact and to understand lives and experiences.

However, we can also think about how people are often locally based, interacting in local lives that may not connect with global or online cultures. In this way, for some researchers, their research is locally based, with organizations working on the ground. During the COVID-19 pandemic, working locally often took on different meaning. The same organizations that pre-pandemic communities used through face-to-face interactions often had to shift their processes, adapt their focus, or close their doors.

Being online can allow for a rich source for data collection, as it reaches a large number of people. For example, in the UK, an estimated 82 percent of adults aged 16 and older use the internet, and 53 percent use social media websites (Kelly et al., 2018; Ofcom, 2013). We can see an increasing amount of information available for research about individuals becoming publicly and readily available online (Beninger et al., 2014, p. 4; Marchant et al., 2017). However, with the access and global reach shrinking and saving money on interviewing large groups of participants, other issues arise.

How people communicate has shifted with technology, particularly through social networking (e.g., Facebook, WhatsApp; Kelly et al., 2018; Susilo, 2014). Moving online has been more acutely highlighted during the COVID-19 pandemic, which forced business, education, and social interaction online. Even qualitative researchers situated in ethnography were forced to grapple with restrictions. In the past, researchers may have used email with participants. Such an approach creates a time lag between question and participant response, which can be useful and challenging. Today, with an extension of internet speeds, interaction can be *assumed* synchronous, occurring almost immediately, as in a face-to-face conversation. Yet, we've seen this is not the case. For instance, the recent pandemic has made it particularly clear that not everyone has stable internet access to allow for quick communication (Boivin & Kozhabayeva, forthcoming). With increased internet speeds, there is a growing global creation, discussion, communication, culture, and knowledge production. However, there aren't consistent policies and procedures to protect users, whether in using social media or posting on a blog. Depending on which cultural, national, or geographical contexts we are researching, the policies, regulations, and availability of the internet and digital media will vary significantly (e.g., the General Data Protection Regulations [GDPR] in Europe).

While we have discussed the importance of ethics for each of the topics in this book, special considerations build upon all the other issues and add additional constraints and considerations in working online. The speed at which technology changes means that as researchers, we need to become aware of these changes and how they could affect our research and communities. For example, while technology is not new for research, mobile digital technology is a relatively new tool for collecting data and communicating with participants. Thus, for those interested in socially just research and working with vulnerable populations, technology can lead to great insights or significant harm. We want to be aware of how data is treated, individuals' privacy, and how individual rights protection is adhered to.

So, **how do we research online with participants while appropriately addressing concepts of ethics and socially aware research?** As you read, you can learn about concepts of privacy, consent, data ownership confidentiality, anonymity, and identity protection for researching in online spaces. Amid these discussions, we can think about how these topics shift along with the policies, laws, and ethical guidelines requiring researchers to become more self-reflective and engaged. We explore and discuss various multimodal approaches for moving between face-to-face interactions with participants to a virtual world. The chapter highlights current changes, starting with definitions and explanations of various types of online engagement, social media interaction, and texting formats. Social media's uniqueness is a digital application that builds on earlier technology's ideological and technological foundations, allowing and involving researchers in communication, creation, and exchange of user-generated content and social interaction. As we move into the rest of the chapter, we can think about how research in online forms affects power and vulnerability issues.

1. How can we understand the changing nature of face-to-face and online engagement?

When we started writing this book, it was before the COVID-19 pandemic hit the world. Moving from face-to-face research to an online format was useful in some contexts. To reach specific populations or to extend their research, using technology could be helpful. However, with COVID-19, many qualitative researchers were faced with a sudden and drastic change in their research. With over a year in some cases of socially distanced work and research, it's become clear that becoming familiar with various types and ways to engage online is no longer a possibility but a requirement.

The affordances of online research provide abilities to easily access international locations but can present challenges in themselves to how we consider and approach multicultural contexts. As we move to online communication, a valuable consideration is becoming aware of *why* you want or *have to* move online and of the differences between online data versus using digital technology and modes to collect data. For instance, online data could come from social media sites, texting platforms, internet platforms, or discussion boards. In contrast, using digital technology could include online interviews, surveys, or commentary (e.g., Deng et al., 2017; Fielding et al., 2017). So, you can ask yourself, **why am I moving my study online?**

The term "online research" can be used broadly to refer to using the internet for conducting studies (Hesse-Biber & Leavy, 2006; Hooley et al., 2012). Online research can include a wide array of data gathered or generated from sources, such as social media, instant messaging via internet applications, virtual gaming worlds, forums, chatrooms, and online learning spaces. In conducting research in online spaces, how we interact and the ways in which participants interact can shift. As online communication and engagement shifts rapidly, so too do the terms used to refer to the research. For example, a useful text by Hewson et al. (2016) provides an overview of internet research. They use the term "internet mediated research" (IMR) to broadly describe online and offline data generation and analysis. This term was defined prior to the Cambridge Analytics data scandal and the 2018 European implementation of GDPR. However, research is not just about privacy and protection, which are inherently important, but also about creating relationships with participants through communication. Digital and online communication widens the types of communication that can occur with participants.

2. Do we understand online communication in multicultural contexts?

When we conduct research online, the ways people interact and what they share can change. You can think for yourself, *how comfortable are you sharing information online? Where do you feel most comfortable sharing and with whom?* The level of candor that participants feel changes based upon being in an online space (Hewson et al., 2016). Participants may either feel more exposed online or potentially more private and anonymous (Dawson, 2014). However, the feeling of protection and anonymity in online spaces presents unique challenges to the qualitative researcher in considering how to elicit and manage participant information. For instance, participants may feel that their information is private but may inadvertently publicly share when intended to share privately (Ahmed et al., 2020). Therefore, with the rapid changes in technology, technical accidents could occur. As researchers, we must become more diligent in ethically communicating and protecting our participants. Online research practices can be intimidating, but as Hewson et al. (2016) further discuss, internet research methods point to considerations for depth and reflexivity in qualitative studies online.

Hull et al. (2010) explain the importance of "making and sharing meaning across modes and media," particularly related to working across multicultural contexts. They describe this as "across divergent cultural, linguistic, geographic, and ideological landscapes both on- and offline" (Hull et al., 2010, p. 86). **Social media** is one means of online communication researchers can use. These networks can allow for a quick spread of ideas allowing for communication, even transnationally (Cooper, 2014; Kavoura, 2014). The use of new media can transmit cultural capital and build intercultural community (Sobré-Denton, 2016, p. 1716). Electronic media can be considered part of transnational and global cultural flows (Appadurai, 1990). This concept of shifting and crisscrossing global and local boundaries allows for a production and dissemination of images and knowledges, which Appadurai (1990) termed "mediascape." Thus, when we gather data from online platforms and social media sites, we can work to understand ethical research practices, decisions, and dilemmas involved in using these sites as part of the research process, such as in educational contexts when engaging with children and young people.

Another way we can think of online communication is as a relationship. The internet itself can be considered as a symbiotic relationship between consumer and producer. It enables marginalized groups to connect, create, and provide voice and agency. With these great affordances come challenges of exclusion, bullying, aggression, and responsibility that qualitative researchers must consider. For those of us from a Western, privileged position, we can keep this in mind when using online digital technology to communicate and research with diverse and marginalized communities. Consequently, we must view online research for instant messaging

Face-to-face and online engagement

communication, social media, content creation, information, discussion boards, chatrooms, forums, online content, and potential challenges and ethical issues. So, you can think for yourself, **in what formats am I considering communicating online for research? Or, in what formats am I looking to collect online data?**

Depending on the cultural context, some tools used to collect data and interact with participants are acceptable and reasonable, while they wouldn't be allowed in other contexts. For instance, messaging apps on social media can allow for quick discussion and reactions and communication in research. Yet, there are issues related to privacy and ethics. For example, Gaiser and Schreiner (2009) explain a process and the steps in developing and conducting online research, providing a useful tool for examining particular challenges in conducting research online and communicating with participants. As we critically self-reflect about researching online, we can consider such questions as:

- Can participant security be guaranteed? Anonymity? Protection of data?
- Can someone ever really be anonymous online? And if not, how might this impact the overall study design?
- Can someone "see" a participant's information when they participate?
- Can someone unassociated with the study access data on a hard drive?
- Should there be an informed consent to participate? If so, how might online security issues impact the informed consent?
- If a study design calls for participant observation, is it okay to "lurk"? Is it always okay? If not, then when? What are the determining factors?
- Is it okay to deceive online? What constitutes online deception? (Gaiser & Schreiner, 2009, p. 14)

Another format of communicating online involves video interviews. These applications offer a way to work with people across the world (Cserzö, 2020) and can be used to develop rapport over time (Weller, 2017). Yet as we know, along with the benefits, there are also considerations. For instance, you can ask yourself, **do I understand the cultural context in which I'm asking people to participate?** *What is expected of conversations prior to starting the research? What is the stability of the internet for my potential participants?*

3. What do we need to consider when collecting data online?

The variety of online communication is vast, including various modalities, platforms, and environments for communication, knowledge sharing, and expression. Each mode can be viewed ethically differently and lead to different forms of expression and identity. Each setting can allow us to see a different perspective on identity (Appiah, 2010). As a researcher, whether online or face-to-face, we hold a certain power. From this position, it's useful for us to continually consider how this affects our relationships with participants, especially those who are vulnerable or have been historically marginalized or oppressed, and where and how we collect data and disseminate it. One consideration is access and knowledge of technology. For example, as recently as 2014, Skype was recognized as a primary method for collecting online interviews (Janghorban et al., 2014). In contrast, in 2020, Zoom is used in many research contexts (Lobe et al., 2020). So, you can ask yourself, **which technology am I most comfortable with?** *Which technology is accessible and comfortable for my potential participants?*

The ethical nature, or lack thereof, is emphasized as a key component of online data collection. For example, social media companies often collect user data without the user being aware (i.e., location data). The uniqueness of social media users and the content they create provides opportunities and challenges in gaining ethical insight into lived experiences (e.g., social, sociotechnical, cultural, psychological, political, professional, economic, communicative, linguistic, semiotic). Despite the potential lack of direct interaction with online users/participants, the same ethical conditions exist. Social media users are defined as human participants, whether you observe them or use their data for research purposes.

We can consider there is an invisible vulnerability when researching on social media that is often overlooked. For example, some researchers assume that because social media and websites provide consumer terms of use before entering, this is enough to provide consent. As Beninger and colleagues (2014) reveal, terms and conditions were described as a source of information. However, participants reported difficulty staying up to date with constantly changing terms and conditions, such as on Twitter and Facebook. The frequency of website updating and the density of content, terms, and conditions were viewed as barriers to participants' understanding of how the site works (Beninger et al., 2014, p. 14). Therefore, a constraint on

Face-to-face and online engagement

social media is the assumption that people are aware of the reality of the space they inhabit online. This concern leads to understanding the fluidity and changes from face-to-face research to online digital space.

So, what happens when we start researching with children or other vulnerable populations? For instance, what do we do if we recognize illicit or reportable activities online? In a face-to-face environment, while it is still challenging to know when, if, and how to report issues, there are often in-depth discussions with participants to explain the potential for this outcome, or lack thereof. But what happens when such questions unfold online? What *is* an illicit activity that requires intervention online? For example, a project that evaluates how many times a 12-year-old "likes" different topics could easily be considered low risk. In contrast, a project that observes an online group discussion of adolescent HIV patients to see which ones report noncompliance with medications has a high-risk level (Moreno et al., 2013, p. 712). Therefore, we must understand who our participants are and critically self-reflect on this direction. For instance, you can ask yourself, **how could my participants be adversely affected in the future by participating in an online forum, group, or chat designed to gather qualitative data?**

Another consideration for online research is how interviews, surveys, and online comments have been raised by researchers, such as how individuals identify and share information. Suler (2004) found that people say and do things in cyberspace that they wouldn't ordinarily say and do in the face-to-face world. They loosen up, feel less restrained, and express themselves more openly. So pervasive is the phenomenon that a term has surfaced for it: the *online disinhibition effect*. Yet this is not always a positive result. Instead, there has also been a rise of hate speech, and online trolls are evidence of this: rude language, harsh criticisms, anger, hatred, even threats (Suler, 2004, p. 321). Suler (2004) states that under the influence of anonymity, a person may attempt an invisible non-identity, resulting in reducing, simplifying, or compartmentalizing self-expression (p. 324). This sense of invisibility can give people the courage to go places and do things they otherwise wouldn't. Yet during the pandemic, online isolation also left some people feeling inadequate and uncomfortable (Boivin & CohenMiller, forthcoming; Islam et al., 2020).

As we research across cultures, how people write and share can be affected by social and cultural norms just as offline in face-to-face research. For instance, depending on participants' ages, the use of texts with final punctuation has varied meanings (Riordan et al., 2018), while some cultures may have cultural expectations of either informality or formality in written forms. Texting may not work with some communities. With others, it can offer ease of communication (CohenMiller et al., 2019, 2020) or help establish a sense of community, such as through supporting student learning (CohenMiller, 2019; Gimranova et al., 2017). Some online videos may function in some contexts but be inaccessible in others. In another example, in the study of Kazakhstani teachers in COVID-19 lockdown, they used WhatsApp groups to communicate with students, families and other teachers. In this way, they created community to facilitate finding new teacher resources (Boivin & Kozhabayeva, forthcoming). So, you can ask yourself, **how might my age or culture be reflected in written form, and how might my potential participants see these responses?** If using online written responses, *which is the preferred mode of interacting with participants (e.g., text message, email)?*

4. What (other) ethical dilemmas should we consider regarding online research?

While we have discussed the integrated nature of ethics to online research, there are additional aspects we can expand upon here. Such topics as ownership of data are essential for further exploration and critical self-reflection to ensure our work does not inadvertently harm those we want to help. The nature of being online could be useful in democratizing power relations and act as a tool of decolonization, or it could further enact power differentials in a new digital platform (Lockley, 2018).

Social media is an interesting and tricky platform for research. There are particular affordances and related consequences, unlike other research contexts (Henderson et al., 2013, p. 546). While this research allows for conducting studies with populations that may be hard to reach in traditional research (Moreno et al., 2013, p. 708), one such issue is whether posts and texts are open for the public to use in research. Is such data considered the same as that from participants with corresponding ethical concerns of consent and privacy? (Henderson et al., 2013, p. 547). A direction researchers use to understand what counts as publicly available is to reflect on the purpose of the initial post and who it was intended for. For instance, if someone comments on a newspaper article online, it can generally be assumed that the person knew they were making a public comment. Taking that in mind,

Face-to-face and online engagement

as a researcher, you might want to study how people respond to online texts and could consider the use of the responses. There has been useful research helping uncover inequity, harassment, bullying online, and coping mechanisms (e.g., Barlett et al., 2020; Parris et al., 2011; Peebles, 2014). In some cultural contexts, online interactions and bullying have garnered nationwide attention. For example, in New Zealand, NetSafe (2021) provides guidance and free confidential support for "harmful content online" including bullying and harassment, image-based abuse, self-harm or suicide, child sexual abuse material, hate speech, violent extremism, stalking and spyware, privacy or data breach, and scams.

However, if someone posts on a personal page, the public nature of such posts become more complicated. For instance, does the person know if their page is publicly viewable? This has come into question in such studies examining profile pictures posted on Facebook (e.g., Emmons & Mocarski, 2014). Did all the people who posted their profile picture know they were allowing anyone to view them? This is a question for the socially aware researcher. So, perhaps we can ask ourselves when looking to social media for data, **how do I know this data was intended for anyone to view?** *What type of consent do I need to collect, analyze, and disseminate in online research? How can I confirm I won't do any harm in this process? If you are hesitant about the response*, that's an important awareness to look further at and an opportunity to talk with colleagues and mentors about their insights on ethics online.

For social media users, it's incumbent upon the consumer/user to read the terms of use when using these sites. Yet, have you read all of them? Do you understand their consequences? Maybe you have and do, and that's great – yet most people haven't. Therefore, agreeing to allow one's data (photo, email, name, etc.) to be reused and sold to other large corporations was recently occurring. Therefore, the question remains, **whose data is it?** Some researchers argue it's public data, and that people know this concept when they register. So, I can use that data, right? According to boyd and Crawford (2012), "it is problematic for researchers to justify their actions as ethical simply because the data are accessible. The process of evaluating the research ethics cannot be ignored simply because the data are seemingly public" (p. 672). So, you can ask yourself, **which data is actually *intended* for public use or intended for a researcher?**

Another issue that arises, which has become apparent with Facebook data leaks, is how data is stored and kept, even when it is thought to be deleted.

This raises the question: what is the difference between public domain and open access? Can we reuse and disseminate data from such sources as Facebook? What are the ethics of confidentiality? There is a permanent record of any information posted (Roberts, 2015), and direct quotations from participants can be traced back to the source (BPS, 2007) through search engines like Google. In this case, anonymity cannot be protected. This is related to the issue of copyright. For example, in the attempt of anonymizing participant data, researchers may exclude the participant's name, yet some users may feel that they should be given credit for their information being used (see Roberts, 2015; Beninger et al., 2014). Additionally, SMS and Facebook Messenger can be hacked and data can be stolen. Therefore, confidentiality and trust regarding data protection and storage are more difficult with online digital research, which can become challenging when working across geographic and cultural regions.

General Data Protection Regulation (GDPR). The GDPR is a regulation in European Union (EU) law on data protection and privacy for all individual citizens of the EU and the European Economic Area (EEA). These aspects continue to extend and become questioned, such as the shift in countries included within the EU. For instance, what happens for those UK academics following GDPR on research grants, with EU's separation, which ethical procedures will they follow? The GDPR also addresses the export of personal data outside the EU and EEA areas. These regulations were implemented on May 25, 2018. Therefore, many articles investigating digital and online ethics will need continual reviewing to stay up to date on the latest developments.

We can consider three categories as researchers when working with social media data related to legality, risk and privacy, and reuse and publication. These questions can help lead you through understanding the ethics around social media data irrespective of cultural context. So, you can ask yourself questions around legality, such as **what are the terms and conditions of the specific platform?** *What are the relevant disciplinary, funding, legal, or institutional guidelines?* Then, related to ethics around social media data in risk and privacy, you can ask yourself, **what type of expectation might my participant reasonably expect in terms of observation?** *How vulnerable are my potential participants? How sensitive is the subject matter?* Then, you can ask yourself, **how might you reuse and publish the data?** (Additional questions and answers relating to ethics and country regulations issues can be found on the GDPR website and other country-specific sites.) The process of

Face-to-face and online engagement

discovering the regulations and what feels right ethically is an undertaking that can take time but is worthwhile overall.

Video and social media. Let's explore a bit about videos posted online. You might want to conduct an observational study of YouTube videos using publicly posted and available content. In this case, the information is not private, and it does not require any interaction with the subject to access it (Moreno et al., 2013 p. 709). However, with the recent GDPR rules, in many European countries any form of participant identification is a breach. Thus, a reasonable expectation of privacy for an online user is a combination of the website's intent and the website's explicit statement of privacy rules. Yet, this changes if children or marginalized groups are involved. Thus, as research-ers, we can recognize this data comes from people regardless of modality. It's useful that we examine ethical rules explicitly stated in some parts of the world and our internal compass on what is appropriate.

For researchers, whether online postings are public or private is deter-mined to some extent by the online setting itself and whether there is a reasonable expectation of privacy on behalf of the social media user (British Psychological Association, 2017). For example, a password-protected "pri-vate" Facebook group can be considered private, whereas an open discus-sion on Twitter in which people broadcast their opinions can be considered public. In many cases, a social media user's data is accessed and analyzed without informed consent having first been sought. "Participants" in such research are rarely aware of their participation. Acquiring informed consent becomes more problematic the larger the data set and can seem virtually impossible in aggregate data containing thousands or even hundreds of thousands of data units (Townsend & Wallace, 2016, p. 5). However, new researchers must be aware that there are different rules, regulations, and policies from various countries.

For some researchers, the fact that you have to be a member (registered user) to access the data might suggest that the data are not public. For exam-ple, you can ask yourself, **how can I deal with, report, or interpret the different media such as photos, audio, video, "apps," game histories, and records of interaction with other people?** *How do we ethically work with children and young people in such a context to ensure they understand the implications of their real and virtual actions for people they do and do not know, especially when as researchers we are still learning?*

Thus, anonymization issues become more critical in cases where data sets or individual units of data are published; for example, online, in journal papers, and at academic conferences. Protecting unwitting participants' identities becomes even more crucial when the data accessed refers to the sensitive subject matter, particularly when exposing such data in new contexts and to new audiences may place the social media users at potential risk.

During socially distanced research, moving to online spaces can be important for continuing the momentum of collaborations. Modes of communication can be seen in many ways, such as *translanguaging* (e.g., Goodman et al., 2021), and in shifts with digital technologies (e.g., Kleifgen, 2006). Yet, while digital technology can provide agency and connection around space and time, the technology can also highlight a digital divide between those who have access and those who don't. Wright (2018) reflected on the use of digital technology across the various international projects: "Digital technologies demonstrate particular benefits in relation to efficiency, productivity, connectivity and access, but are also associated with alienation, privacy issues and the homogenization of individual experience" (p. 4).

These online spaces offer chances to interact, to understand lives and experiences. However, we can also think about how people are often locally based, interacting in local lives that may not connect with global or online cultures. In this way, their research is locally based for some researchers, with organizations working on the ground (see Wright, 2018). During the COVID-19 pandemic, working locally often took on a different meaning. The same organizations with pre-pandemic communities in face-to-face interactions often had to shift their processes, adapt their focus, or close their doors.

5. Reflections from the field: moving between face-to-face and online engagement

In the following *Reflections from the Field*, we asked two researchers to consider what online research meant for them as qualitative researchers. We wanted to better understand the challenges and insights they have found in their work. In the first reflection, Carolyn Ellis from the University of South Florida, USA, known for her foundational role in the development of autoethnography (Ellis, 2004), unpacks what it means for her to conduct meaningful interviews online. She touches upon the many years she had worked with a friend and research partner to understand lived experiences, first experiences during the Holocaust, and then those during COVID-19.

164

Is it possible to do meaningful interviewing online?

Carolyn Ellis

Jerry Rawicki, a survivor of the Holocaust, and I have been friends and research partners for a dozen years. We have written nine articles together, primarily about his Holocaust experiences, from video recorded interviews and conversations we do frequently. But due to COVID-19, I had not visited him for several months, and we both missed our time together. In addition to the shelter-in-place mandates and concerns about my own health, I was doubly concerned about protecting Jerry, who has lung and heart conditions in addition to being 93 years old. Wanting to understand his experience of the pandemic and how it compared to what happened to him during the Holocaust, I asked if I might interview him online. "Let's do it," he said enthusiastically.

I knew this would be tricky since, though Jerry is proficient on email and surfing the internet, he had not had experience with other social media platforms. Part of our interaction over the years had been my coaching Jerry in using Microsoft Word and helping him with his computer problems. But this time I wouldn't be there to help him. How were we going to cope with new technology?

Jerry tries to set up a Skype account, but he is unable to input his information successfully, especially deciphering the scrambled letters and numbers that prove he is not a robot. "I have put in what I see 50 times, for two hours," he says.

His frustration and anxiety are palpable and I worry about his heart. "Jerry, I also have trouble identifying those scrambled characters. Really, we can drop it. This interview is not that important."

"Yes it is," he replies. "I want to do it."

Next we connect through Zoom, but Jerry's computer is old, the picture is fuzzy, and it doesn't have a built-in microphone.

We turn to Messenger. Though our interaction can't be video recorded there, we can see each other as we talk, and I can audio record our conversation on a portable voice recorder close to my phone.

Face-to-face and online engagement

"I think we're set to go then if you're ready," I say to Jerry, when his bottom jaw fills up the messenger frame. It is April 13, 2020, two months into COVID-19.

"I'm ready."

"Can you hold your phone up higher so I can see your whole face?"

"It hurts my hand to hold up my arms. I get tired."

"Try to rest your elbows on the chair."

"Okay, just try to talk slow and loud, but don't yell at me."

I laugh. "You tell me if I'm not talking slowly or loud enough."

"Right now, it's fine. Go ahead."

Messenger works well for us and the conversation is lively and engaging. Days later, I write our story from the 70-minute interview and from the clarification emails that Jerry and I pass back and forth. Finally I send him a rough draft. Understanding that I have pushed Jerry about as far as I can on learning new technology, I resist suggesting tracking changes in Microsoft Word or in Google Docs editor. Instead, he sends me suggested changes by email and we then discuss the draft during a phone call.

"Do you think we have come up with something worthwhile here?" Jerry asks, when we are close to done.

"Yes I do," I say. "Readers will want to know how someone your age and with your experience of trauma is coping with the pandemic."

"I always like to talk to you and be interviewed by you. It keeps my mind working."

"Being able to experience each other, to see expressions and faces in addition to voices, to be aware of the nonverbal, that made me feel we had a significant visit. Our connection was deeper than we would have had on a phone conversation. What about you?"

"It was the difference between day and night. I can't even compare it," Jerry replies. "And I could hear every word, I'm comfortable with my arms resting on the arm chair, and I'm not even tired. Maybe we can do it again. It helps me to talk with you."

"It helps me too. I feel connected to you and like we're doing something meaningful together. Connecting and finding a way to engage in meaningful activity – two important ways to cope with our anxieties, fears, and sense of isolation during the pandemic. Perhaps that is as

Face-to-face and online engagement

meaningful as a project can be, especially now," I conclude, and Jerry agrees.

Note: Our article "A Researcher and Survivor of the Holocaust Connect and Make Meaning during the COVID-19 Pandemic" was published in the June 2020 issue of *Journal of Loss and Trauma*.

In the following reflection, Tamsin Hinton-Smith from the University of Sussex in the UK critically self-reflects on how communication has shifted online in her research. She shares past challenges when working with vulnerable populations through online video and connects this to current negotiations needed today in research with an international team. Hinton-Smith highlights how equity and issues of ethics are emerging with online research, which is no longer a new potential but one that is facing us all.

An equalities perspective applied to researching online

Tamsin Hinton-Smith

When communicating online by video camera rather than in a physical room with others, I cannot be read as easily by others and neither can I read others as easily. The room around me and the room around my research participant fall away, even our bodies fall away, aside from the often carefully sculpted image of head and upper torso, often against a video conferencing background, designed to shield the professional context from the intimacy of our own and others' wider lives.

This is important from the equalities perspective that I am committed to, this potential to shield participants at least partially from the vulnerabilities of the unequal research process and unwelcome public exposure of personal lives. And yet as a qualitative, feminist sociologist, it is some connection with the intimate, personal, embodied dimension of interaction that I seek. I grew up on the methodological reflections of Oakley (1974) researching the experiences of housewives, through interviewing in their homes, physically swamped in

167

the very subject matter of the research, including real-life messy, noisy children. Attracted to gender issues from the outset, my own early research as a student involved the same home interviews, often complete with children. By the early 2000s I had moved to my own first online research, learning as I went, and justifying how this could still unearth meaningful narratives despite the absence of in-person contact. My first online research was carried out over a year by ongoing individual email communication with 79 participants. In these narratives, domestic lives, children, and personal relationships remained very present in the stories that research participants chose to tell (Hinton-Smith, 2012, 2016).

Over time I joined collaborative projects. As the research relationships multiply, so multiply the complexities of hearing and understanding each other, power dynamics, communication challenges, and the need to tread softly among all these while always mindful that we will inevitably fall short of creating the ideal research encounter that we set out on. Complexities and opportunities for contrasting understandings multiply across distances of cultures, communities, languages, experiences, and assumptions that may be so taken for granted they remain unspoken.

One international project I was part of focused on experiences of international higher education mobility for Roma students in European countries. Roma are one of the most marginalized minorities in Europe (United Nations Development Programme, World Bank and European Commission, 2013), often living alongside but outside mainstream culture throughout European countries. The project included intersecting layers of complexity: Roma and non-Roma researchers and participants; academic and non-academic (from non-governmental organizations) partners; junior and senior researchers; and international partners (including Central and Eastern European [CEE], Spain, Sweden, and the UK). As a feminist researcher committed to acknowledging power and privilege including my own, the research generated messy, sometimes uncomfortable experiences to be navigated individually and as a team, which we wrote about (Hinton-Smith et al., 2017). This related to discomforts of process, alongside challenges of translation across cultural

Face-to-face and online engagement

contexts. For example, in the UK, Roma people are included within the policy category of Gypsy, Roma, and Travellers (GRT), while in Spain they identify by the translation *Gitano* (Hinton-Smith & Padilla, 2021). For Roma in CEE countries, this is a racial slur comparative to others that should never be spoken. These disjunctures posed challenges for achieving our equally important research commitments to produce internationally comparative and translated research reports, and to conduct the research in ethical, equitable ways without harm to participants, researchers, or others. Greatly facilitative of negotiating this research journey together as an international team was the opportunity to spend time together, within different international research contexts, developing understanding of tension points as they emerged, and addressing these together.

Six years later, in the midst of a global pandemic, remembering this looks like halcyon days for research. I am in the early stages of a new international project with partners in India, Kazakhstan, Morocco, and Nigeria. I submitted the proposal to the funder after the pandemic had commenced. We had by this point been briefed in my institution that research proposals should be *pandemic proof*, built around online data collection rather than requirements for international travel or in-person contact between researchers and participants. Hence this project will involve no physical visits between the research country leads, but only our fortnightly zoom meeting. This has been carefully scheduled in a feminist way for the optimal time at which children in the UK (including mine) have left for school in the morning and before Kazakhstan's children return home at the end of their school day.

We have learned in the last year through a forced rapid collective acceleration into conducting our work lives online, the positive opportunities that this can open up in terms of research. However we are learning at the same time how this new world creates new challenges. The discourse has necessarily shifted from online as an "innovative" resource to enrich research processes where appropriate, to online as often the only way, at least for now. This opens a Pandora's box for carrying out research in ethical, equitable, culturally sensitive ways, acknowledging with sensitivity the diversity of humans' experiences, and that none of us can ever hope to be accurately versed in all of these, we can only be open and humble to not knowing. Challenges relate to issues including but not restricted to time zones, internet, software, and hardware. Perhaps more importantly, though, is the reduction in non-verbal cues and wider opportunities to support "reading" and learning about contexts that may be unfamiliar. No colleague will be inviting me home to visit their family, and opportunities are greatly reduced for anyone to quietly take myself or another aside to explain what may have gone wrong in the research process, what may be culturally insensitive, and what needs to happen differently to remedy this. This is a brave new research world in which we find ourselves, with new challenges and responsibilities to navigate. Our greatest tools in handling this will be individual and collective inquisitiveness, openness, and collaboration as we move forward, willing to reflect on and share experiences, learning from each other in this new journey.

References

Hinton-Smith, T. (2012). *Lone Parents' Experiences as Higher Education Students: Learning to Juggle*. Leicester: Niace.

Hinton-Smith, T. (2016). Negotiating the risk of debt-financed higher education: The experience of lone parent students. *British Educational Research Journal*, *42*(2), 207–222.

Hinton-Smith, T., Danvers, E., & Jovanovic, T. (2017). Roma women's higher education participation: Whose responsibility? *Gender and Education*, 1–18.

Hinton-Smith, T., & Padilla-Carmona, M. T. (2021). "Roma university students in Spain and Central and Eastern Europe: Negotiating participation and identity in contrasting international contexts." *European Journal of Education*, 00: 1–14. https://doi.org/10.1111/ejed.12459

Oakley, A. (1974). *Housewife*. London: Penguin.

United Nations Development Programme, World Bank and European Commission (2013). The situation of Roma in 11 EU member states. Retrieved January 20, 2021, from https://op.europa.eu/en/publication-detail/-/publication/8711b498-ca9a-462b-99a5-70153df38fa1/language-en

6. Engaging more deeply: concluding thoughts on moving from face-to-face to online

How can I hear my participants' voices whether I'm working face-to-face with them or in online spaces? Moving from face-to-face research into online spaces provides both challenges and opportunities. The hardest times will likely be those when forced to move online, those times where you had planned sitting in a room with others. We can consider our work in online research as situated within cultural contexts. The benefits are immense in allowing and facilitating connections between people who may never meet face-to-face. However, in moving across national and international borders, the context of the location can be challenging to grasp, if not lost altogether.

There are tools at our disposal for conducting online research, including online video and online observations. These opportunities afford ways to maintain research, connections, and understand community experiences such as during socially distanced times. And each of our steps of moving online involves deep considerations of ethics. Working across multicultural contexts as socially just qualitative researchers, we can consider where to explore and find answers to the practical questions of ethics (e.g., regulations) versus what feels right. Both of these directions are essential as we move forward to conduct research to promote equity, inclusion, and social justice. With online research, we have a chance to reach disparate communities, seek to uncover voices missed, and highlight who still needs access. For instance, *who are we when interacting in online spaces?* We can also ask, *what do our relationships and how we present ourselves in these spaces mean for the power, privilege, and trust established, maintained, and lost in such research spaces?*

Ultimately, through learning about different studies, approaches, and ways to connect as we move from face-to-face to online engagement, we have chances to enhance our work and potentially move toward decolonizing online spaces. What that means for each person, each researcher, and each participant will vary. Technology is rapidly shifting, and so are the ways we interact and recognize cultural borders. Requirements for ethics will continue to adapt, so that at the heart of it, we can consider who we are as qualitative researchers committed to promoting social justice across in and beyond academic institutions.

Face-to-face and online engagement

Reflective questions about moving from face-to-face to online research

In this chapter, we had a chance to see the ways working online can offer ways to interact across multicultural contexts. In online spaces, people can become connected across geographic regions through various forms and modalities. In texting, video conferencing, and discussion forums, for instance, participants can interact and share experiences. However, we also heard of challenges and risks of moving to online platforms and the use of technology. Considerations of ability, accessibility, and access to such technologies are important to address, as well as integral issues of ethical regulations and moral considerations for these online interactions. The following continues the discussion a bit further with questions to consider individually or in groups about the move from face-to-face to online research.

Topic	Questions
Online engagement	• What considerations might you need to address to move your research study online? • How does this affect what data you can access, and with whom? • In what ways can it enhance your work? In what ways could it compromise your research?
Ethics in online engagement	• In conducting research in an online environment, how might you be able to address issues of confidentiality, copyright, and credit for information posted online (e.g., community forums that are no longer updated)? • How might working online be useful, and potentially risky, for your participants?
Online engagement in "the field"	• How can you describe where the *field* is when you are researching online or using different types of technology? • How might you explain this for an ethical review board about the dynamic nature of such a field? • How might you explain this for a lay audience?

References

Ahmed, W., Jagsi, R., Gutheil, T. G., & Katz, M. S. (2020). Public disclosure on social media of identifiable patient information by health professionals: Content analysis of Twitter data. *Journal of Medical Internet Research, 22*(9), e19746.

Appadurai, A. (1990). Disjuncture and difference in the global cultural economy. *Theory, Culture & Society, 7*(2–3), 295–310.

Appiah, K. A. (2010). *The Ethics of Identity*. Princeton, NJ: Princeton University Press.

Barlett, C. P., Heath, J. B., Madison, C. S., DeWitt, C. C., & Kirkpatrick, S. M. (2020). You're not anonymous online: The development and validation of a new cyberbullying intervention curriculum. *Psychology of Popular Media*, *9*(2), 135–144. https://doi.org/10.1037/ppm0000226

Beninger, K., Fry, A., Jago, N., Lepps, H., Nass, L., & Silvester, H. (2014). *Research Using Social Media; Users' Views*. NatCen Social Research, pp. 1–40. https://www.natcen.ac.uk/media/282288/p0639-research-using-social-media-report-fi nal-190214.pdf

Boivin, N. (forthcoming). Transmodalities: Co-constructing agency for transmigrant children, (new) materialist approaches in language education. In J. Ensser-Kananen & T. Saarinen (Eds.), *Towards Socio-Material Research Approaches in Language Education*. Cham, Switzerland: Springer.

Boivin, N., & Amantay, A. (forthcoming). Transmultimodality in post-Soviet Kazakhstan-transformative teaching approach for multilingual early learning. In C. Lütge & M. Stannard (Eds.), *Foreign Language Learning in the Digital Age: Theory and Pedagogy for Developing Literacies* (Ch. 17). Routledge.

Boivin, N., & CohenMiller, A. S. (forthcoming). Inclusion and equity through multi-modality during COVID-19. In D. Vyortkina, N. Collins, & T. Reagan (Eds.), *Keep Calm, Teach On: Education Responding to a Pandemic*, Series: *International Perspectives on Educational Policy, Research and Practice*. Hershey, PA: IGI Global.

Boivin, N., & Kozhabayeva, K. (forthcoming, Spring). Kazakhstan emergency remote teaching context: "Deprofessionalization" of teacher identity. In J. Chen (Ed.), *Emergency Remote Teaching: Voices from World Language Teachers and Researchers*. Cham, Switzerland: Springer.

boyd, d., & Crawford, K. (2012). Critical questions for big data. *Information, Communication and Society*, *15*(5). 662–679.

British Psychological Association. (2017). Ethics guidelines for Internet-mediated research. Retrieved January 27, 2021, from www.bps.org.uk/news-and-policy/ethics-guidelines-internet-mediated-research-2017

Bröer, C., Moerman, G., Wester, J. C., Rubinstein, L., Schmidt, L., Stoopendaal, A., Kruiderink, N., Hansen, C., & Sjølie, H. (2016). Open online research: Developing software and method for collaborative interpretation. *Forum Qualitative Sozialforschung / Forum: Qualitative Social Research, 17*(3). https://doi.org/10.17169/fqs-17.3.2388

CohenMiller, A. S. (2018). Creating a participatory arts-based online focus group: Highlighting the transition from DocMama to motherscholar. *The Qualitative Report*, *23*(7), 1720–1735. https://nsuworks.nova.edu/tqr/vol23/iss7/17

CohenMiller, A. S. (2019). Texting with students: Facilitating learning in higher education. In *Preparing the Higher Education Space for Gen Z* (pp. 167–186). Hershey, PA: IGI Global. https://doi.org/10.4018/978-1-5225-7763-8.ch009

CohenMiller, A. S., Demers, D., & Schnackenberg, H. (2019). *The Importance of Flexibility in Research: A Grounded Theory Study of Skyping, Zooming and Texting with Motherscholars Around the World*. Qual-World Interactive

Virtual Conference, University of Alberta, International Institute for Qualitative Methodology.

CohenMiller, A. S., Demers, D., & Schnackenberg, H. (2020). Rigid flexibility in research: Seeing the opportunities in "failed" qualitative research. *Special Issue: Failures in Qualitative and Mixed Methods Research, Sousa and Clark (Eds). International Journal of Qualitative Methods.* https://journals.sagepub.com/doi/10.1177/1609406920963782

Cooper, A. (2014). The use of online strategies and social media for research dissemination in education. *Education Policy Analysis Archives/Archivos Analíticos de Políticas Educativas, 22*, 1–24.

Cserzö, D. (2020). Intimacy at a distance: Multimodal meaning making in video chat tours. In C. Thurlow, C. Dürscheid, & F. Diémoz (Eds.), *Visualizing Digital Discourse: Interactional, Institutional, and Ideological.* Boston, MA: Mouton De Gruyter. https://doi.org/10.1515/9781501510113-008

Dawson, P. (2014). Our anonymous online research participants are not always anonymous: Is this a problem? *British Journal of Educational Technology, 45*(3), 428–437.

Deng, L., Chen, Y. H., & Li, S. C. (2017). Supporting cross-cultural online discussion with formal and informal platforms: A case between Hong Kong and Taiwan. *Research and Practice in Technology Enhanced Learning, 12*(5). https://doi.org/10.1186/s41039-017-0050-z

Ellis, C. (2004). *The Ethnographic I: A Methodological Novel about Autoethnography.* Walnut Creek, CA: AltaMira Press.

Emmons, B., & Mocarski, R. (2014). She poses, he performs: A visual content analysis of male and female professional athlete Facebook profile photos. *Visual Communication Quarterly, 21*(3), 125–137. https://doi.org/10.1080/15551393.2014.893752

Fielding, N. G., Lee, R. M., & Blank, G. (Eds.). (2017). *The SAGE Handbook of Online Research Methods* (2nd ed.). Thousand Oaks, CA: Sage.

General Data Protection Regulation (GDPR). Retrieved January 26, 2021, from https://gdpr-info.eu/

Gimranova, A., Nurmanova, M., & CohenMiller, A. S. (2017). Texting to motivate language learning: WhatsApp group chats and near peer role modeling (NPRM). *LEARNing Landscapes, 11*(1), 121–136. https://doi.org/10.36510/learnland.v11i1.927

Goodman, B. A., Kerimkulova, S. I., & Montgomery, D. P. (2021). Transfer of academic skills: Views of Kazakhstani students in an English-medium university (Ch. 10). In B. Paulsrud, Z. Tian, & J. Toth (Eds.), *English-Medium Instruction and Translanguaging.* Bristol, UK: Multilingual Matters.

Henderson, M., Johnson, N. F., & Auld, G. (2013). Silences of ethical practice: Dilemmas for researchers using social media. *Educational Research and Evaluation, 19*(6), 546–560.

Hesse-Biber, S., & Leavy, P. (2006). *Emergent Methods in Social Research.* Los Angeles, CA: Sage.

Hewson, C., Vogel, C., & Laurent, D. (2016). *Internet Research Methods* (2nd ed). London: Sage.

Hooley, T., Marriot, J., & Wellens, J. (2012). *What is Online Research? Using the Internet for Social Science Research*. London: Bloomsbury.

Hull, G. A., Stornaiuolo, A., & Sahni, U. (2010). Cultural citizenship and cosmopolitan practice: Global youth communicate online. *English Education, 42*(4), 331–367.

Islam, M. A., Barna, S. D., Raihan, H., Khan, M. N. A., & Hossain, M. T. (2020). Depression and anxiety among university students during the COVID-19 pandemic in Bangladesh: A web-based cross-sectional survey. *PLoS One, 15*(8), e0238162.

Janghorban, R., Roudsari, R. L., & Taghipour, A. (2014). Skype interviewing: The new generation of online synchronous interview in qualitative research. *International Journal of Qualitative Studies on Health and Well-Being, 9*(1), 24152. https://doi.org/10.3402/qhw.v9.24152

Gaiser, T. J., & Schreiner, T (2009). *A Guide to Conducting Internet Research*. Thousand Oaks, CA: Sage.

Kavoura, A. (2014). Social media, online imagined communities and communication research. *Library Review, 63*(6/7), 490–504. http://doi.org/10.1108/LR-06-2014-0076

Kelly, Y., Zilanawala, A., Booker, C., & Sacker, A. (2018). Social media use and adolescent mental health: Findings from the UK Millennium Cohort Study. *EClinicalMedicine, 6*, 59–68.

Kleifgen, J. A. (2006). Variation in multimodal literacies: How new technologies can expand or constrain modes of communication. *WORD, 57*(2–3), 303–324. https://doi.org/10.1080/00437956.2006.11432568

Legewie, N., & Nassauer, A. (2018). YouTube, Google, Facebook: 21st century online video research and research ethics. *19*(32). *Forum Qualitative Sozialforschung / Forum: Qualitative Social Research, 19*(3), Art. 32. http://dx.doi.org/10.17169/fqs 19.3.3130

Lobe, B., Morgan, D., & Hoffman, K. A. (2020). Qualitative data collection in an era of social distancing. *International Journal of Qualitative Methods, 19*, 160940692093787. https://doi.org/10.1177/1609406920937875

Lockley, P. (2018). Open initiatives for decolonising the curriculum. In G. K. Bhambra, D. Gebrial, & K. Nişancıoğlu (Eds.), *Decolonising the University* (pp. 145–172). London: Pluto Press.

Marchant, A., Hawton, K., Stewart, A., Montgomery, P., Singaravelu, V., Lloyd, K., Purdy, N., Daine, K., & John, A. (2017). A systematic review of the relationship between internet use, self-harm and suicidal behaviour in young people: The good, the bad and the unknown. *PLoS One, 12*(8), e0181722.

Moreno, M. A., Goniu, N., Moreno, P. S., & Diekema, D. (2013). Ethics of social media research: Common concerns and practical considerations. *Cyberpsychology, Behavior, and Social Networking, 16*(9), 708–713.

NetSafe. (2021). Report harmful content. Retrieved January 27, 2021, from https://report.netsafe.org.nz/hc/en-au/requests/new

Ofcom. (2013). Internet citizens 2013. Retrieved January 13, 2021, from https://www.ofcom.org.uk/research-and-data/internet-and-on-demand-research/internet-use-and-attitudes/internet-citizens-2013

Parris, L., Varjas, K., Meyers, J., & Cutts, H. (2011). High school students' perceptions of coping with cyberbullying. *Youth & Society*, *44*(2), 284–306. https://doi.org/10.1177/0044118X11398881

Peebles, E. (2014). Cyberbullying: Hiding behind the screen. *Paediatrics & Child Health*, *19*(10), 527–528. https://doi.org/10.1093/pch/19.10.527

Riordan, M. A., Kreuz, R. J., & Blair, A. N. (2018). The digital divide: Conveying subtlety in online communication. *Journal of Computers in Education*, *5*(1), 49–66.

Roberts, L. D. (2015). Ethical issues in conducting qualitative research in online communities. *Qualitative Research in Psychology*, *12*(3), 314–325.

Salmons, J. E. (2015). *Doing Qualitative Research Online*. London: Sage.

Sobré-Denton, M. (2016). Virtual intercultural bridgework: Social media, virtual cosmopolitanism, and activist community-building. *New Media & Society*, *18*(8), 1715–1731.

Suler, J. (2004). The online disinhibition effect. *Cyberpsychology & Behavior*, *7*(3), 321–326.

Susilo, A. (2014, June). *Exploring Facebook and WhatsApp as Supporting Social Network Applications for English Learning in Higher Education*. Conference on Professional Development in Education (PDE2014), Widyatama University Indonesia, Open University Indonesia and Open University Malaysia.

Townsend, L., & Wallace, C. (2016). *Social Media Research: A Guide to Ethics*. Aberdeen, UK: University of Aberdeen.

Weller, S. (2017). Using internet video calls in qualitative (longitudinal) interviews: Some implications for rapport. *International Journal of Social Research Methodology*, *20*(6), 613–625. https://doi.org/10.1080/13645579.2016.1269505

Wright, L. (2018). New perspectives in participatory arts key themes from the AHRC connected communities programme. University Report. East Anglia, UK: University of East Anglia.

Integrating the arts with collaboration and co-production

I know using the arts can help to understand participant experience, but how does it work? For socially just research, adapting and integrating new approaches and ways to work together to better understand others' voices and knowledges is fundamental. The arts provide opportunities for researchers interested in equity, inclusion, and social justice (Leavy, 2009, 2015, 2020; Mertens et al., 2013). In this chapter, we focus on using arts as a research method and tool to enhance understanding, knowledge, and communication. We explore how it can be used as a methodological practice and the potential for it to be integrated within collaborative and co-produced research. The use of these approaches is explained and understood in different ways by both researchers and also participants. Broadly, here's a way to consider arts-based research:

> *Arts-based research is a purposeful use of arts in research to promote participant voice and/or to enhance inquiry in the design, data collection, and/or dissemination.*

If we decide to use arts-based research and ask a participant to draw a picture of their experience, a typical first response is surprise or concern about their ability to draw. And this is okay. So, we can back up and help set the stage for participants. For example, when leading focus groups with ethnic minority middle school students, the research team started by passing out papers and colors and explaining: *You don't have to know anything about art, you can even just draw stick figures or use shapes or words to describe your work* (CohenMiller et al., 2021).

For those from marginalized communities, we can look at how arts can bridge language, sociocultural and economic barriers in research. As Finley (2011) notes, such practices can create collaborations with participants and stakeholders on equal footing with the primary researchers. The arts can be incorporated in various ways, such as within research method or to connect communities (e.g., working with artists, community, and participants): "Art is a process, and here we think about how things emerge – stuff comes from stuff: trying, helping, working, making, talking – new ideas come from doing" (Pahl & Pool, 2011, pp. 151–152). In this way, the arts can act as knowing, inquiry, and/or communicating (Bell & Pahl, 2018).

Using the arts in qualitative research offers opportunities to deeply engage with participants and communities. It can allow for "the systematic use of the artistic process, the actual making of artistic expressions in all of the different forms of the art, as a primary way of understanding and examining experience by both researchers and the people that they involve in their studies" (McNiff, 2007, p. 29). The arts can facilitate hearing, seeing, and understanding experiences across several sensitive issues such as gender, race, ethnicity, and sexuality at the global and local levels (Campbell & Pahl, 2018). Multimodality, including art-based practices and research, has been utilized with marginalized groups (Jewitt, 2005; Mills, 2015; Narey, 2008; Binder & Kotsopoulos, 2011). Using various modes of communication can promote participants' expression of ideas, such as with those with limited language skills. For example, Vist (2019) explored interactions with toddlers, moving away from an emphasis on verbal language, and instead integrated arts into the "aesthetic interviews." And now, with the need for socially distanced research and practice, the arts provide an opportunity, for instance, in using digital and online multimodal tools.

1. Arts in research

While there are many terms referring to the use of arts in research, we are guided by the work of Leavy (2015), who has written extensively on the topic of arts in social sciences and suggests the "umbrella category" of "arts-based research practices" (p. 5). **Arts-based research** (ABR) can be approached in various directions, including the researcher using arts, the participants using arts, or together co-producing research with arts, to name just three options. Leavy (2009) define arts-based research practices as the following:

178

Arts-based research practices are a set of methodological tools used by qualitative researchers across the disciplines during all phases of social research, including data collection, analysis, interpretation, and representation. These emerging tools adapt the tenets of the creative arts in order to address social research questions in holistic and engaged ways in which theory and practice are intertwined.

(pp. 2–3)

For example, in the classroom, the arts can be used to understand student experiences better, or even to encourage agency (Rolling, 2011). Using the arts can be a way for people to represent their ideas in various ways, moving beyond just words (Barone & Eisner, 2011; Derr, 2015). With ABR, multiple ways of knowing can be supported (Gerber et al., 2012). The sustained use of various ways of knowing, especially art-making, as instructional strategies can shape students' ability to be present and open (Lindgren & Johnson-Glenberg, 2013). Art as a way of knowing can help students let go of a kind of rigidity in their thinking and respond to others, offering opportunities for research into pedagogical practice and learning. So, you can ask yourself, *as a learner,* **how might I want to demonstrate my learning? As a researcher, can I incorporate this same approach?**

At times, ABR practices could be used when using participatory approaches, including with research relating to teaching and learning, or within community-based research. Visual methodologies connect academic research practices with public outcomes (Pink, 2012), offering opportunities for innovation and creativity (Hesse-Biber & Leavy, 2008). Creative, engaging methods promote opportunities for self-expression, dialogue with each other and with the broader community, and for feeling heard and empowered to make change in the community (Derr, 2015, p. 13). In addition to art used in research, art can also be the research itself as well as there being research about art.

As Conrad and Sinner (2015) explain, the arts can help us understand more than through a conventional approach on its own: "The personal voice that is part of arts-based research has the power to move us towards recognizing tacit knowledge, something that objective-based research methods often miss" (p. 195). For Barone and Eisner (2011), they define arts-based research centering on uncovering lived experienced:

Arts-based research is an approach to research that we define as a method designed to enlarge human understanding. . . . the aim is to create an expressive form that will enable an individual to secure an empathetic participation in the lives of others and in the situations studied.

(pp. 8–9)

We can look at an example when Anna asked participants to draw their experiences and thoughts of becoming a mother for the first time in their doctoral program. Anna found that using drawings with participants in addition to interviews led to a quicker understanding of their experiences (CohenMiller, 2018). As she continued working with motherscholars (mothers in academia), Anna saw that the arts continued to be useful to understanding experience and encouraging well-being (CohenMiller & Demers, 2019).

However, arts-based approaches, while growing in use and recognition, have also disrupted previously accepted "assumptions about what constitutes research and knowledge" (Leavy, 2015, p. 11). So, you might wonder, *is it worth using the arts if everyone does not fully understand it?* For us and many others, we see the vast potential of the arts in research in particular as a means to speak to issues of social justice. The underlying philosophy of arts-based research practices draws from "justice movements" (Leavy, 2015, p. 19).

2. Arts as practice

In both community and classroom research settings, arts-based approaches can open up discussion and create spaces for collaborating with participants providing voice, such as when participant-researchers are of a cultural or linguistic minority (Boivin, 2019; Boivin, 2021; Campbell & Pahl, 2018; CohenMiller, 2020; CohenMiller et al., 2021). Integrating approaches such as drawing, performance, music, moviemaking, or photography can help participants explain their lives, offering researchers (and educators) tools to understand someone else's lived experience (Boivin, forthcoming).

Categories for arts-based practices vary based upon which theoretical perspective and school of thought you're focused on (see Leavy, 2009, 2015, 2020; Wang et al., 2017). Arts-based research practices can be approached in many directions, including the researcher using arts, participants using art, or together in a co-producing approach or methodology (Campbell &

The arts, collaboration, and co-production

Pahl, 2018; Beebeejaun et al., 2014). Arts can also be used for social impact, such as in collaborative arts ethnography (Lassiter, 1998; Campbell & Lassiter, 2014). When choosing an ABR practice, we can think about how the particular mode fits our abilities and interests and our participants. In arts-based methods, the practices are a means to open space for participants to have voice and collect data. However, not all participants are equally comfortable in the same modes of creative expression. So, you can ask yourself, **which ABR practices fit the needs of my participants? Why and in what context am I utilizing art?**

Some types of ABR developed to work with vulnerable and marginalized populations, such as **body-mapping** and photovoice. Both these approaches directly involve collaboration with participants in data generation, interpretation, and dissemination.

Body-mapping is a qualitative research approach engaging participants in active drawing on a representation of a body, producing and interpreting data about their lives.

Body-mapping developed to "visually represent aspects of people's lives, their bodies and the world they live in" (Gastaldo et al., 2018, p. 5). It's an approach supporting voices of marginalized and vulnerable populations (Mitchell, 2006a, 2006b). The production of research data and interpretation can encourage greater agency for participants (Naidu & Prose, 2018) and reduce the power imbalance between researcher and participant (Sweet & Ortiz Escalante, 2015). Using such an approach can encourage engagement with young people for sensitive topics, such as sexual health (Chenhall et al., 2013; Senior et al., 2014). The use of body-mapping can help develop collaborative relationships with students as researchers, promoting equity and inclusion in higher education (CohenMiller, 2020; CohenMiller et al., 2021). So, now think for yourself, **how might you be able to use body-mapping for a topic you're interested in?**

Now, let's take a moment to look at another participatory arts-based practice supporting working with diverse communities, **photovoice**. Here's a simple definition:

Photovoice is a qualitative research approach involving participants in data creation through taking photos, data interpretation, and representation.

The arts, collaboration, and co-production

Wang and Burris (1997) describe the approach they solidified from health education and Freirean methods:

> Photovoice is a process by which people can identify, represent, and enhance their community through a specific photographic technique. It entrusts cameras to the hands of people to enable them to act as recorders, and potential catalysts for change, in their own communities. It uses the immediacy of the visual image to furnish evidence and to promote an effective, participatory means of sharing expertise and knowledge.
>
> (p. 369)

A typical outcome of a photovoice project is a visual presentation of the photos in an area agreed upon by all research members. In particular, the imagery tends to be shown in a shared space where communities gather (e.g., community centers, university halls, government halls). Such approaches in using photovoice had to be adapted in socially distanced research (CohenMiller & Izekenova, 2020). In this collaborative approach, the arts are embedded throughout the research process with researchers and participant-researchers.

As a researcher using ABR, Leavy (2015) suggests it's important to "act like both a researcher and artist" (p. 27). Yet, this does not mean that you have to *be* an artist. Instead, you can consider the ways creativity can be conceptualized within your work and with others. For example, Butler-Kisber (2018) describes how using poems as a form of data collection, analysis, or dissemination offers potential for understanding participant voice. Using poetry as method has been used across multicultural contexts, such as with African American high school students and their mothers (Corley, 2019), with academic mothers (CohenMiller, 2016), and with transnational women (Bhattacharya, 2013). As Bhattacharya (2013) explains, the use of poetry inquiry allowed her see experiences of colonization and oppression: "By identifying the spaces where those meanings functioned – and how – I was able to identify the intersection of multiple sociocultural discourses that operated on the Brown female in the United States" (p. 624).

Other forms of arts, such as drawing, can be used as collaborative tools with participants through data production or to elicit more understanding. Drawing as methodology (Theron et al., 2011) has been shown useful to hear the experiences of often overlooked populations, including young

The arts, collaboration, and co-production

participants (Brown & Johnson, 2015; Facer & Enright, 2016; Nomakhwezi Mayaba & Wood, 2015; Tay-Lim & Lim, 2013). Another use of drawings in arts-based research practices is portraiture (Lawrence-Lightfoot & Davis, 1997). As Lawrence-Lightfoot (2016) explains, the practice

> is very much written for multiple and diverse audiences. It is intentionally inclusive. That is, it is not just written for members of the Academy, for my colleagues and my students, but for broader eclectic audiences. The idea is to get people interested in thinking about important questions in complicated, grounded thoughtful ways.
>
> (pp. 19–20)

For example, participants might be invited to collaborate on data generation through developing portraits of their experience. Such an approach was used in the Philippines to unpack the experiences of graduate student mothers (Rosario & Obo-Rayos, 2019). Understanding Indigenous knowledges can incorporate various types of methodologies (Smith, 2012; Mertens et al., 2013). Creating can also be used to understand historically marginalized populations, affording chances for collaboration. In a special issue focused on crafting as research method, Fitzpatrick and Reilly (2019) highlight the work of scholars around the globe who explore and examine traditional and Indigenous notions of "craft" through collaborative processes such as *storymaking as belonging* (Bunda et al., 2019); *storywork* (Smith, 2019); *culturally responsive pedagogies* (Brien, 2019); *quilting with children* (Peterken, 2019); and *weaving* (Demecs & Miller, 2019). So, you can ask yourself, **which types of arts-based research practices speak to you?** *Can you imagine yourself using photographs, drawings, or poems with participants?*

3. Arts as knowledge

For those interested in working with marginalized groups whose sociocultural and linguistic practices differ from the majority community, the arts and co-produced research can provide socially just approaches. In this chapter, we consider the ways arts-based research, participatory arts research, and co-production of research with arts can be threaded throughout the whole research process. Arts can act as a mode of communication and a tool for

183

inquiry that is not reliant on culture or language within a multicultural research context (Wright, 2018).

Co-production is an approach to overcome the issues of power related to marginalized communities. Researchers in many countries have utilized arts to gather, create, and communicate knowledge with participants as collaborators and co-researchers. Activist and self-identified marginalized immigrant and academic Zanib Rasool, working with Kate Pahl, notes the need to break down barriers and respect everyday knowledge, including the arts (Rasool, 2017).

In these examples, we've seen several approaches using arts including in participatory research (Chevalier & Buckles, 2019), for co-production (Pahl & Pool, 2018; Degarrod, 2013; Liamputtong & Rumbold, 2008), and in co-creation (Voorberg et al., 2015). Defining these approaches can vary, but here are a few simple definitions of the three approaches. Collaborative qualitative research encourages working together with participants to improve understanding. In **participatory research**, we can consider the active integration of participants in the process, often as collaborators:

> Participatory research is an approach in qualitative research that actively involves participants in the research process.

In a team of researchers working with a local community, people may be involved throughout all stages of the research or in only certain portions. In collaborative research, the purpose is to integrate participants in the research, but the intention is not necessarily to become co-researchers. And collaboration can also be seen in **co-produced research** and in co-created research. In co-produced research, the emphasis is on the participants' becoming part of the research process from the beginning, such as developing research questions, data collection, analysis and representation/dissemination. In **co-created research**, there is a democratic approach.

> Co-produced research is a qualitative research approach that embeds participant and stakeholders as equal partners in the research process.
>
> Co-created research is a democratic, qualitative approach that views the participant as co-researcher from design, collection of data, and including analysis of data.

The arts, collaboration, and co-production

These are approaches that can use the arts. Next, we can explore **why and in what research contexts and perspectives arts are employed?**

If you've been reading through the other topics in the book, you'll know that there is no *one* method or recipe for the use of any methodological approach or tool. The process and approach of co-production can integrate arts-based research practices and directly speak to issues of social justice and decolonizing knowledge. A co-produced arts approach situates knowledge as mediated, shared, negotiated, and co-constructed through collaborative multimodal and sociocultural practices. As Rasool (2017) explains, "Co-production is a democratic form of knowledge creation and a more ethical way of working with communities that feels less like "doing things to communities" (p. 310). As qualitative researchers we can focus on a paradigm of research emphasizing social justice (Denzin, 2009). In this way, we can emphasize inclusion and collaboration as "knowledge integration focused on identifying and sharing different types of knowledge and expertise, and creating common understandings and frames of reference that include different sources of knowledge" (Polk, 2015, p. 113).

We can now look at an example of co-production in an arts-based ethnographic project. An example of research with artists collaborating with community stakeholders is in the Imagine and *Re-Imagining Contested Communities* project (2018). The work took place in two marginalized Muslim communities in northern England. The team integrated **arts methodologies for social cohesion** in partnership with voluntary sector researchers including a school, an adventure playground, and a Muslim women's group. Collaborative spaces of knowledge production, referred to as critical thinking groups, included social cohesion experts from across the city region's communities. The researchers worked with poets, visual artists, and activists. The project co-produced relevant and useful resources to illustrate critical approaches of creative and artistic methods within community/university knowledge production. Through the use of arts-based ethnography, "art making has the potential of becoming the means by which the participants, and the artist, and research can become aware of their views and understanding of each other" (Degarrod, 2013, p. 410).

If one of the aims of ethnographic research is an understanding of the other, art making has the potential of becoming the means by which the participants, and the artist, and research can become aware of their views and understanding of each other (p. 410).

185

The arts, collaboration, and co-production

Art in a co-produced project can then be a point of inquiry and voice for marginalized groups. So, you can ask yourself, **how might I incorporate the arts as a process within the research?**

Before we delve into the details of the ways co-produced research could be approached and carried out, let's get on the same page about what production and co-production can refer to. In collaborating with participants, co-produced research purposefully situates participants within the research study as key research members. The idea of co-researching is central for a participatory approach: the knowledge is produced together with the various stakeholders (local residents, but also local service providers, representatives of local elderly, activists, and invited artists) as co-researchers and co-actors (Lavrinec, 2014, p. 64).

When people of different ages, identities, and linguistic capital utilize arts, it's a way to provide justice in communicating ideas, beliefs, and feelings toward social cohesion. Participants and communities can then move from just collaborators within data collection into equal research partnerships (Escott & Pahl, 2017; Facer & Pahl, 2017; Pahl, 2016). Projects utilizing co-production can produce extensive usable and relevant knowledge (Hellstrom, 2015). And here, we can see the overlap in what some people refer to as co-production and others would classify as arts-based research informed by participatory practices. As Finley (2011) notes, such practices can create collaborations with participants and stakeholders that are on equal footing with the primary researchers.

Co-production can mean that participants are active in the overall research process rather than just in a collaborative event or specific activity. We can also think about how stakeholders could be involved in qualitative research as co-researchers and co-creators of data. By bringing in outside knowledge, recognizing its importance and asking for collaboration and co-production throughout the research process, we can aim to break down the fourth wall in research (Boivin & CohenMiller, 2018). In other words, "breaking the fourth wall in research" encourages researchers to push aside their own interpretation of events and experiences and let in others. So, let's think about this in practice. *How could participants co-produce data?* One such approach could involve participants being provided with the means to collect data.

Perhaps this means giving participants a camera to take photos, videos, or collect audio, or having them use their own if available, and setting up a secure way to share such information. In this way, participants can

The arts, collaboration, and co-production

individually emphasize their own voice as the co-researchers, embodying the power to choose what, when, who, and how to record the process. Participants can co-research and co-produce knowledge, enabling participants and researchers to move past the "invisible hierarchy of knowledge" (Bell & Pahl, 2018, p. 106). The goal in such an approach is to present multiple voices and identities and promote greater inclusivity and diversity. So, you can ask yourself, **how and when might you want to include participants as co-researchers in your work?**

4. Arts as communication

One form of using arts in research with co-production in mind is the use of collaborative arts ethnography. Such projects can incorporate participants as producers of knowledge and meaning, rather than researchers inferring meaning (Pahl, 2016; Escott and Pahl, 2017; Facer & Enright, 2016). In co-producing arts with participants, this approach can also help to build community (Facer & Enright, 2016; Escott & Pahl, 2017). It also provides a different mode of communicating. For multicultural and marginalized communities to have space to speak, have a voice, and represent their feelings is key for community research. One example is the use of co-production in an arts-based ethnographic project. The rationale for utilizing this approach is that "utilizing cretive arts methods is an effective way to engage the voices of marginalized women and girls by bringing them into research through artistic approaches, such as poetry, art, photography, and drama" (Rasool, 2017, p. 310).

Moreover, arts methodologies helped the researchers create ways of visualizing community knowledge rather than relying on local first language knowledge. It provided the bridging for multicultural/multilingual communities to have agency within the project (Rasool, 2017). Arts practices can help researchers create ways of visualizing community knowledge rather than relying on local first language knowledge. For example, it provided bridging of multicultural/multilingual communities to have agency within a project (Rasool, 2017). Back and Puwar (2012) emphasize the power of ABR in "developing creative, public and novel modes of doing imaginative and critical sociological research" (p. 6). Such projects can become opportunities for a point of inquiry and voice for marginalized groups. So, you can ask yourself, **how can I incorporate co-production within my research?** *How might I incorporate the arts as a process within the research?*

The arts, collaboration, and co-production

We can think about the use of arts as a mode of communication, allowing people to share their experiences whether they have proficiency in the primary language of the research study. It's important to cultivate and promote collaborative engagement and participatory stances grounded in solidarity with community. Involvement in community creative arts can have many positive outcomes, such as a sustained and positive impact on the mental and social well-being of participants (Argyle & Bolton, 2005), the inclusion of marginalized populations (Maidment & Macfarlane, 2011), and a vehicle for community development and social cohesion (Pahl & Pool, 2018).

Art in collaborative ethnography approach can support participants' communication through creating an alternative mode not purely focused on proficiency in linguistic skills (Boivin, 2021). As Derr (2015) explains, the use of creative, engaging methods can provide important opportunities for self-expression, dialogue with each other and with the broader community, and for feeling heard and empowered to make a change in the community.

By engaging artists and arts in the process of research, the question of whose knowledge is mitigated. As Pahl and Pool (2018) explain, the arts can be viewed as not just a method but a process bridging various stakeholders. They view art as resituating knowledge production practices within communities. Arts as a method, methodology, practice, or tool can be situated in previously unimaginable contexts. As researchers, we may have a chance to work with the arts and artists across contexts. In doing so, we can ask ourselves, **how do artists contribute to qualitative community research?** Below are a few directions for how to incorporate arts: community arts, social engaged arts practice, relational aesthetics, participatory arts, arts for health, artists in schools, art outside the gallery, and de-materialized artists (Facer & Pahl, 2017).

In working with others, such as participants, artists, and communities, collaboration in research can be conducted in different ways and spaces. At times it may involve solely working together, whereas it can be a process to enable agency and space for disparate views. Mutually beneficial outcomes are ideal, but at times typical hierarchies of power may be disrupted. Consider your own academic institution or work environment. *In meetings or classes, who is the first to speak? Do you sit at the same level, or do some people stand? Who makes the decisions?* When conducting research in the field, we can consider such interactions as representations of power. So, you can ask yourself, **how can I work with participants to highlight their experiences without imposing my power?**

The arts, collaboration, and co-production

Using a co-production approach can enable cross-community collaboration, as it often begins from the bottom up, even from the writing of a funding application (Pahl, 2016). Such collaborative practices can have a sustained and positive impact on the mental and social well-being of participants, including supporting the inclusion of marginalized populations (Maidment & Macfarlane, 2011), acting as a vehicle for social cohesion (Clover, 2006), and creating active citizen involvement (Brandsen & Pestoff, 2006; Verschuere et al., 2012). If one of the aims of arts ethnographic research is an understanding of the other, art-making has the potential of becoming how the participants, and the artist and research can become aware of their views and understanding of each other (Degarrod, 2013, p. 410). In collaborative research, the purpose is to integrate participants in the research, but the intention is not necessarily to have them become co-researchers.

So, **what happens when a project uses co-production, collaborative arts ethnography, and the arts?** For the Connected Communities initiative (Wakeford & Sanchez Rodriguez, 2018), they used participatory arts research across approximately 80 projects internationally. One of its primary goals was to respond to the emerging needs of various multicultural contexts. Wakeford and Sanchez Rodriguez (2018), working with others, integrated contemporary arts, foregrounding participatory processes as artistic outcomes and concerns in and of themselves. The initiative included communities, institutions, municipal stakeholders, and academic institutions that attempted to respond to the ideas and needs of all participants. The potential for openness and methodological breadth is one of the key strengths of the participatory arts, which can otherwise prescribe preformulated responses. In their research, Wakeford and Sanchez Rodriguez (2018) and others found several relevant themes that highlight the power of working with multicultural contexts using participatory arts:

- Being responsive to the needs of the community and not prescriptive.
- Encouraging diversity of perspective and experiences.
- Valuing alternative ways of knowing.
- Fostering multi-way dialogue.
- Unpacking structures of validation.
- Emphasizing sustainable outcomes.
- Valuing supportive collaboration.
- Bridging local to global, incorporating transnational perspective.
- Understanding affordances of digital technology.

The arts, collaboration, and co-production

In this participatory arts research approach, a space was created for diverse participants to negotiate their place (Wakeford & Sanchez Rodriguez, 2018). The approach can enable greater inclusion of expertise across various institutional and community stakeholders, such as with universities, arts organizations, educational institutions and organizations, cultural institutions (museums, theatres), hospitals, and formal and informal community groups. Responding to the conditions and needs of a diverse and multicultural society can involve creating opportunities for individuals who might not ordinarily be represented in research to be heard and acknowledged, including women, members of minority groups, and those from lower socioeconomic strata (Wakeford & Sanchez Rodriguez, 2018).

As we look further at co-production, it can mean participants are co-researchers in the overall research process rather than just in a collaborative event or specific activity. We can also think about how stakeholders can be involved in qualitative research as co-researchers and co-creators of data. By bringing in outside knowledge, recognizing its importance, and asking for collaboration and co-production throughout the research process, we can aim to break down the fourth wall in research (Boivin & CohenMiller, 2018). In other words, breaking the fourth wall encourages researchers to push aside their own interpretation of events and experiences and let in others. The concept draws from theatrical work, what Diderot termed as the "fourth wall" or the barrier between performer and audience – or in this case, researcher and participant.

For example, in a study Nettie conducted, she asked participants what and how they wanted to communicate. Instead of prescribing a type of art, the young students selected their means for communication (e.g., drawing, acting, making sound effects) to facilitate their voices to be heard and included (Boivin, 2021). In this way, Nettie explains, I used creative practices as data, and in a co-creation approach, where both children and researchers videotaped the moviemaking research process (Boivin, 2021). Such projects can incorporate participants as producers of knowledge and meaning, rather than researchers inferring meaning (Pahl, 2016; Escott & Pahl, 2017), and can build community (Facer & Enright, 2016).

So, you can ask yourself, **how can I create space in face-to-face or online environments for engaged participation and co-produced research?** Participatory arts projects enable diversity as it applies across institutional and community stakeholders throughout the process, rather than just as the end product. Responding to the conditions and needs of a diverse and multicultural society can involve creating opportunities for individuals who might not ordinarily be heard and acknowledged, including women, members of minority groups, and those from lower socioeconomic strata (Wakeford & Sanchez Rodriguez, 2018). Projects utilizing co-production can produce extensive usable and relevant knowledge (Hellstrom, 2015). This power sharing, which is negotiated throughout the research process, can provide agency for those previously marginalized (Wright, 2018). Therefore, while researching transnational, diverse, and multicultural contexts, a goal can be to facilitate and create space (literally and figuratively) for community partners to bring their expertise.

5. What ethical dilemmas should we be prepared for relating to using the arts in research?

Designing projects to allow space for marginalized groups to express and state their position is particularly noticeable and useful in a globalizing, transnational world. While creating arts-based research, collaborative projects, and co-produced work can be valuable, it's essential to consider potential ethical challenges as related to the multicultural context in which we're working. We can think about how our own vision, sense of aesthetics, or social agenda for participants could downplay community interests and needs, undermining authentic community cultural development (Goldbard, 2006). We can work to cultivate skills promoting collaborative engagement and participatory stances grounded in an experience of working in solidarity with the community, undoing injustice (see Glass & Newman, 2015). For instance, we can use co-produced research involving participants as co-researchers throughout the research study to enhance inclusivity, equity, and ethical and moral research.

As we've been exploring here, the use of the arts and co-production offer a chance to engage deeply with communities and hear voices that are often excluded, making participants equal researchers. Yet co-production also has its unique challenges. To create such a relationship takes work and effort to ensure all are on equal footing, that others feel they have a voice, feel protected, can trust, and can push back, to name just a few considerations. So, you can ask yourself, **What steps can I take to help my participants/co-researchers feel they can push back in the research process?**

The arts, collaboration, and co-production

In arts-based research, morality is a key tenet (Finley, 2011). While these are incredibly valuable and important approaches for socially just research, they also provide ethical considerations to address within the research and for external reviewers. For instance, ethical review boards are not always familiar with arts-based or participatory practices that afford co-production. At other times, academic journals or reviewers may struggle in understanding the use of arts. Fortunately, the world of research is rapidly changing and embracing the arts. We can see this in calls for papers emphasizing narrative and poetry, creation of journals of arts, and expanded editions of arts-based method texts.

So, *what happens when we work with a community when the research is done?* This is a central ethical dilemma faced by qualitative researchers. While funders are becoming more aware of co-produced research and even emphasizing such work to engage with stakeholder communities (see Global Challenges Research Fund, 2021), there remain ethical concerns to such work. A concern for our work with and across multicultural contexts, particularly for those oppressed or historically marginalized, is how and from scholarship is heard when the research is complete. For example, Hinton-Smith et al. (2017) embedded reflexivity into their co-produced scholarship with Roma, a marginalized minority group. They mention needing to be "acutely aware of the danger of occupying a position of 'speaking for' other women" (Hinton-Smith et al., 2017, p. 817).

So, you can ask yourself in conducting such research, **what steps do I need to take to establish a continued benefit for the community even after the research has "ended"?** In this way, we can move from building short-term relationships to creating strategies that establish sustainability. (See *Action Research 2021* journal for extensive examples of sustainability in participatory and action-based research.)

6. Reflections from the field: arts in research with collaboration and co-production

The following two *Reflections from the Field* explore ideas and approaches using the arts and collaboration in research. The first reflection is from research methods and arts-based specialist Patricia Leavy. In her critical self-reflection, she explains her move from traditional academic scholarship to the arts. Leavy leads us through turning research into fiction and the

The arts, collaboration, and co-production

reception and lessons learned. Through those experiences and others, she shares slips and offers suggestions for other researchers, artists, and practitioners about becoming centered and pleased with our own work, letting others' opinions fade away.

Reflection from the field

Patricia Leavy

I'm a sociologist turned arts-based researcher and novelist. Arts-based research (ABR) exists at the nexus of the arts/humanities and research/science. ABR involves researchers in any discipline adapting the tenets of the creative arts in order to address research questions. An arts practice may be used during project conceptualization, data collection, data analysis, and/or to represent research findings. These approaches to research are useful for producing new insights and learning; description, exploration, discovery, or problem-solving; forging macro-micro connections; evocation and provocation; raising critical consciousness or awareness; cultivating empathy; unsettling stereotypes; opening up multiple meanings; and contributing to public scholarship. Why did I turn to the arts? Like many, I was frustrated with the limitations of traditional ways of doing and sharing social science research. Peer-reviewed journal articles are totally inaccessible to the public because they're loaded with discipline-specific jargon and they only circulate in academic libraries. I turned to the arts in my own work to develop new insights and make my work more accessible, including to public audiences. But there was something I hadn't considered before leaping into this kind of work: how people respond to arts-based research.

With conventional academic publishing, you don't have to worry all that much about how people will respond to your work. First of all, very few people will actually read it. Even inside the academy, journal articles have tiny audiences, typically only a few readers. Second, a lot of time generally passes between when you do the research, when it is published, and when you receive any reader feedback (if you do at all), and that feedback is typically only in the form of citations

193

in other people's work, which also takes years to come out. Usually when we're several years out from a project, we're less emotionally invested. We have distance. The format of audience feedback – citations – is also just about as sterile and impersonal as can be. In short, with traditional academic writing there's a huge buffer between the researcher and the audience. With ABR, it's different.

When you engage in ABR, many people might be exposed to your work, both inside and outside of the academy. People may also have strong, visceral, and emotional responses. People may respond quickly, even immediately in the case of a visual art display or performance (theatrical, dance, music). In my own work as a novelist, sometimes the very day a novel is released readers leave reviews on vendor sites and comments on social media. On top of all of this, as the creator you are likely to feel deeply connected to your artistic work. My novels are an expression of who I am in a way that nothing else is. The characters are like close friends and I feel protective of them. In short, the stuff people say about your artistic work can hurt. Even when the feedback is positive, it can feel overwhelming. When I began doing arts-based work I hadn't considered any of this. Let me tell you briefly about my first novel, *Low-Fat Love*.

For nearly a decade I collected interviews with women about their relationships, identities, body image, and pop-culture consumption. I also taught courses in which students routinely shared their personal experiences. Over time I developed cumulative insights about how some women settle in life and love because they don't think they deserve more. I was frustrated with the limitations of traditional academic writing for expressing what I had learned and reaching relevant audiences, so I turned to fiction. *Low-Fat Love* is underscored with a commentary about female identity-building and self-acceptance and how, too often, women become trapped in limited visions of themselves. Women's media is used as a signpost throughout the book in order to make visible the context in which women come to think of themselves as well as the men and women in their lives. In this respect, *Low-Fat Love* offers a critical commentary about popular culture and the social construction of femininity. Ultimately, the novel explores women's identity struggles in relation to the men in their lives

The arts, collaboration, and co-production

and how women often develop myopic images of themselves as a part of "face-saving" strategies employed to cover up shame and a learned devaluation of self. *Low-Fat Love* suggests women seek new ways to see that are not dependent on male approval so that they will value themselves and reject degrading relationships. Moreover, as the main characters in the book learn, the most toxic relationship a woman may participate in is often with herself. So, too, the men in *Low-Fat Love* learn that one must find one's voice or suffer the consequences. In terms of the title, "low-fat love" is a concept. It's like "love lite." It's about settling for less than we really want and trying to pretend it's better than it is.

I was incredibly lucky, and *Low-Fat Love* became a bestseller for my publisher. However, that doesn't mean I didn't make mistakes.

I'm embarrassed to admit that regretfully, I didn't seek feedback from peers before I published *Low-Fat Love*. Writing the book was experimental for me and I was nervous about it. As a result, I kept it private. I wish I had sought feedback during the drafting, when there was still time to make revisions. I never made that mistake again. Now I seek ample feedback during the writing process. Fortunately, *Low-Fat Love* was successful and my publisher released an expanded anniversary edition that allowed me to make some revisions, but I know it would still be a stronger book had I received feedback during the initial writing process.

The biggest lesson I learned publishing this novel, and all of my subsequent novels, centers on negotiating audience response. *Low-Fat Love* struck a chord in a way I never could have anticipated. It's raw, honest, and it tapped into something that resonated. When it was released I was inundated with emails from readers. At book talks and conferences, readers lined hallways to whisper their stories to me. In all of these situations, people shared incredibly personal stories including battles with self-esteem, depression, toxic relationships, alcohol abuse, domestic violence, eating disorders, and even suicide attempts. Many readers saw things in the book I had never intended. I learned quickly how important it is to allow readers their interpretations and not to impose my own. I'm not a therapist, and so I also learned that in order to take in all of these people's personal and often emotionally charged experiences, I would need to ground myself. I created a space for people to have their relationship with my work, and I had my own. This also helped when the comments were unkind.

Based on my experiences, here's my advice. Develop a relationship with your artistic work that isn't dependent on external opinions, good or bad. It's vital for any artist or scholar. Get lots of feedback while you're working on a project and learn to look at it as objectively as you can, to make your work stronger. But once you release the work, let it go. How others feel about it isn't really your business. Do not read reviews. I know people say that and no one believes them, but reviews are unhealthy. I make a concerted effort not to read them. As for practical advice, here's something that's been helpful to me. Go on Amazon and look up a couple of your favorite artists who have been successful; musicians, authors, whatever. Click on their one- and two-star reviews. You will disagree with them when you read them because you love this artist. What you will realize is that no one is immune from criticism. That doesn't mean it's correct or valid. It's just someone's opinion. If you do this exercise, you will see no one who has had an impact – from Beyoncé and Taylor Swift to Neil Gaiman and Jodi Picoult – is immune from criticism. If many people read or experience your creative work, some won't like it, and some will interpret it differently than you do. That's inevitable. Allow people to interpret your art in their own ways, bringing their perspectives and experiences to bear. Just remember, the goal was for your work to reach people and provoke some sort of engagement. You can't control how that unfolds. The truth is that every strength of working with the arts – reaching diverse audiences, provoking strong responses, opening up a multiplicity of meanings – bears a shadow side. Be ready for it. And don't let anyone discourage you.

The following reflection is from Nadia Dresscher-Lambertus, a sociologist from the University of Aruba, who explores research with students during lockdown. Through her critical self-reflection, Dresscher-Lambertus discusses how she collaborated with multicultural, first-generation students to move through crisis with collaborative autoethnography. Ultimately, through this work, we can see how participant-researchers were provided with space to learn about themselves and contribute their unique voice to the project.

"Sitting with the uncomfortable" as a research topic and reflective praxis

Nadia Dresscher-Lambertus

As I'm writing this, I'm in the middle of assembling a collaborative sociological autoethnographic project – a project I undertook together with 16 university students during the first three months after the pandemic hit the small Caribbean island of Aruba. The research project focused on how we, as a very diverse group, sat with the *uncomfortable* while learning to write ourselves into data. Autoethnography not only acted as a way of documenting our lived visceral experiences, but the practice of teaching, learning, and applying this method acted as a pedagogy of (self-)compassion, a way to reclaim ourselves. In that sense, the research project had a strong pedagogical component: we were learning and exploring our positionality during the crisis, and how to create self-data.

Aruba is a multicultural society, and this is reflected in the multiethnic composition of our group (from Aruba, Venezuela, Colombia, the Netherlands, and the Philippines). Students also varied in social background and university program background – social work students and organization and management study students. One commonality was that most of the students were first-generation college students – something I could identify with, since I also was the first in my family to go to college.

As I reflect on the project, I realize that one of the strengths of the project was that it created space for contemplation. At the beginning of the pandemic (March–May 2020), we were caught up in the rapid changes that also had the rest of the world in its grip. This made the project a sort of self-care container where we could pause and become consciously slow amid the turmoil, to talk and write. Self-reflection was not only the topic – how the pandemic is affecting each of us personally – but also how we navigated the project.

In hindsight, it was this *spaciousness-as-approach* that made it possible to attune to our shifting emotional geography, to sit with the uncomfortable, as we reflected on themes such as the changing dimensions of home and education, the interruption of our daily routines, the emerging of new habitual practices, the fear for our health and the health of our loved ones, the intensification of inequalities, and the precarity of a small island economy and the dependence on postcolonial ties for aid. It is noteworthy that the slowing down was a sort of antidote to rapid changes that were taking place during those first three months. It was a needed temporality to awaken the sociological introspection necessary for making sense of our positionality amid social change and how this is entangled into the changing structures of feelings that were taking place.

For me, the most challenging part was managing a research group of 16 students and teaching at the same time. Again, consciously pausing to reflect was the only way to envision the next steps and to feel what was possible: sifting between the expectations we all had, opening up to working with what we actually had and could co-create during a pandemic, and, most importantly, cultivating a trusting space. This all requires pause, time, and conversations.

For instance, an important thread in the whole process is approaching ethics as a continuous process. Teaching the ethics of autoethnography took time. A bit more than anticipated. Navigating the productive tension between the ethics of writing autoethnography and protecting all involved (as the teacher) and writing ourselves into data is a major responsibility. It's not easy, but it's fruitful, and it's only possible when making space to reflect on each step of the process, involving all.

There were times I felt anxious, sad, and exhausted; the pandemic was taking its toll on my personal life as I was stretching myself to fulfill all the collapsing roles at home and work (parenting small children, teaching online, homeschooling). I found refuge in autoethnography as a mechanism of resilience. I remember the days when lots of cameras were off during our Zoom encounters; these were the hardest for me. I couldn't assess how they were doing as I'm used to in a physical classroom. But then I realized, this is also an experience, and thus writing this into data was also a way to process and sit with the grief that a pandemic brings. This expanded my capacity for empathy, and I could meet students at the place where they were when they were anxious, sad, and exhausted, and cameras turned off sometimes signaled this.

The most exciting part of the project was analytically assembling the data into a multivocal story. Since the autoethnographic form was not fixed from the beginning, it was a process that was both messy and full of possibilities. I chose an emerging format to give all involved the room to write themselves into data in ways that felt possible at the moment and that were more aligned to their unique style of expression. The format for the collaborative autoethnography became a mix of evocative, analytical, and part performative. Some wrote a line a day, others made bullet points, a few students wrote poetry or made drawings, and others started painting. When working with diverse groups, I found that integrating multivocality – the multilayered process of assembling, rereading, commenting, co-iterating, and co-producing – allows room for richness in different data formats and also in voices to emerge.

7. Engaging more deeply: concluding thoughts on arts, collaboration, and co-production

So, **how might we use the arts to engage and provide voice for marginalized communities? How might we use these approaches in online environments?** They can be used as a research method and tool to enhance understanding, knowledge, and communication. For those interested in working with marginalized groups whose sociocultural and linguistic practices differ from the majority community, the arts, collaboration, and co-produced research can provide socially just approaches. In this chapter, we considered ways such approaches can be threaded throughout the whole research process to address issues of equity, inclusion, and social justice. Collaborating with participants can involve their unique and diverse voices, speaking to key issues of social justice. Integrating approaches such as drawing or photography can help participants explain their lives, offering tools for researchers to understand someone else's lived experience.

We saw how participatory arts projects can create unity in the research relationship by providing environments for constructing new community teams

The arts, collaboration, and co-production

dedicated to a common aim. The goal then is to respond to disparate ideals by finding congruence between multiple stakeholders. Highlighting large initiatives, such as Connected Communities, which incorporated collaboration with several universities, institutions, governmental organizations, artists, and community groups, can enable an increased acceptance of the role of artists concerning knowledge generation and analysis. Such an approach can promote discourses and negotiation, which can enable partners to feel represented, respected, and recognized for their value and contribution.

Reflective questions about arts with collaboration and co-production

The chapter raises several questions to reflect upon regarding arts-based research practices, collaboration, and co-produced research in multicultural contexts. We've discussed some ways researchers have incorporated the arts to better understand and work with those across multicultural and vulnerable populations. While not a simple set of steps or approaches, the potential is immense to bring together insights and understandings. Now, here are a few questions to guide you through thinking about these ideas as a whole as arts, collaboration, and co-production in relation to research to support participant voice and dissemination of research.

Topic	Questions
Arts in research	• How can you explain the importance of the arts in research for academic audiences? To non-academic public audiences? • What types of research projects can you envision that the arts mesh well with? Which ones would not fit well with arts-based research practices?
Incorporating arts	• Consider a research project using arts-based research practices. In which stage of the research will you incorporate ABR (e.g., planning, data collection, data analysis, representation), and why? • How can you use the arts to include a community beyond your academic discipline? What resources, tools, or connections might you need to make that possible?
Considering arts and co-production in publications	• If you were a reviewer, what are some key aspects, concepts, or descriptions you would want to see explained or visualized? • What would make you question the value of the work? • What would convince you of the value and strength of the work?

200

Topic	Questions
Co-production in research	• How could you incorporate participants as co-producers of questions, methods, data, and representation? • When would this be important? What challenges could you expect to face?

References

Action Research. (2021). Retrieved January 22, 2021, from https://journals.sagepub.com/home/arj

Argyle, E., & Bolton, G. (2005). Art in the community for potentially vulnerable mental health groups. *Health Education*, *105*(5), 340–354. https://doi.org/10.1108/09654280510617178

Back, L., & Puwar, N. (2012). A manifesto for live methods: Provocations and capacities. *The Sociological Review*, *60*(1, suppl), 6–17. https://doi.org/10.1111/j.1467-954X.2012.02114.x

Barone, T., & Eisner, E. (2011). *Arts Based Research*. Thousand Oaks, CA: Sage.

Bell, D. M., & Pahl, K. (2018). Co-production: Towards a utopian approach. *International Journal of Social Research Methodology*, *21*(1), 105–117. https://doi.org/10.1080/13645579.2017.1348581

Bhattacharya, K. (2013). Voices, silences, and telling secrets: The role of qualitative methods in arts-based research. *International Review of Qualitative Research*, *6*(4), 604–627. https://doi.org/10.1525/irqr.2013.6.4.604

Binder, M., & Kotsopoulos, S. (2011). Multimodal literacy narratives: Weaving the threads of young children's identity through the arts. *Journal of Research in Childhood Education*, *25*(4), 339–363.

Boivin, N. (2019). Collaboration, construction, reflection (CCR) approach: 21st Century EYL teacher professional development. In S. Garton & M. Subhan Zein (Eds.), *Early Language Learning and Teacher* (Ch. 9). Bristol, UK: Early Language Series in Multilingual Matters.

Boivin, N. (2021). Intergenerational multimodal oral storytelling: Shifting preschool digital nativist expectations, *Journal of Early Childhood Literacy*. https://doi.org/10.1080/13645579.2017.1348581

Boivin, N. (forthcoming). Transmodalities: Co-constructing agency for transmigrant children. In J. Ennser-Kananen & T. Saarinen (Eds.), *(New) Materialist Approaches in Language Education* (Ch. 8). Cham, Switzerland: Springer.

Boivin, N., & CohenMiller, A. (2018). Breaking the "fourth wall" in qualitative research: Participant-led digital data construction. *The Qualitative Report*, *23*(3), 581–592.

Brandsen, T., & Pestoff, V. (2006). Co-production, the third sector and the delivery of public services: An introduction. *Public Management Review*, *8*(4), 493–501.

Brien, J. (2019). Stitchery me, stitchery do. *Art/Research International: A Transdisciplinary Journal*, *4*(1), 22.

Brown, J., & Johnson, N. F. (Eds.). (2015). *Children's Images of Identity: Drawing the Self and the Other*. Rotterdam, the Netherlands: Sense Publications.

Bunda, T., Heckenberg, R., Snepvangers, K., Phillips, L. G., Lasczik, A., & Black, A. L. (2019). Storymaking belonging. *Art/Research International: A Transdisciplinary Journal, 4*(1), 153–179. https://doi.org/10.18432/ari29429

Butler-Kisber, L. (2018). *Qualitative Inquiry: Thematic, Narrative and Arts-Based Perspectives* (2nd ed.). Sage. https://doi.org/10.4135/9781526417978

Campbell, E., & Lassiter, L. E. (2014). *Doing Ethnography Today: Theories, Methods, Exercises*. West Sussex: John Wiley & Sons.

Campbell, E., & Pahl, K. (Eds.). (2018). *Re-Imagining Contested Communities: Connecting Rotherham through Research*. Bristol UK: Policy Press.

Chenhall, R., Davison, B., Fitz, J., Pearse, T., & Senior, K. (2013). Engaging youth in sexual health research: Refining a "youth friendly" method in the Northern Territory, Australia. *Visual Anthropology Review, 29*(2), 123–132. http://doi.org/10.1111/var.12009

Chevalier, J. M., & Buckles, D. J. (2019). *Participatory Action Research: Theory and Methods for Engaged Inquiry*. London: Routledge.

Clover, D. E. (2006). Culture and antiracism in adult education: An exploration of the contributions of arts-based learning. *Adult Education Quarterly, 57*(1), 46–61.

CohenMiller, A. S. (2016). Artful research approaches in #amwritingwithbaby: Qualitative analysis of academic mothers on Facebook. *Artful Inquiry: Transforming Understanding Through Creative Engagement, 9*(2), 181–196. http://doi.org/10.36510/learnland.v9i2.770

CohenMiller, A. S. (2018). Visual arts as a tool for phenomenology. *Forum Qualitative Sozialforschung/Forum: Qualitative Social Research, 19*(1), Art. 15. http://dx.doi.org/10.17169/fqs-19.1.2912

CohenMiller, A. S. (2020). *Body-mapping: Encouraging equity and inclusion in higher education*. Presentation for the Asian Qualitative Research Association (AQRA) virtual colloquium #6. October 8.

CohenMiller, A. S., & Demers, D. (2019). Conflicting roles of mother and academic? Exploring the use of arts-based self-care activities to encourage wellbeing. *Art/Research International: A Transdisciplinary Journal, 4*(2), 611–645. https://doi.org/10.18432/ari29391

CohenMiller, A. S., Kataeva, Z., Durrani, N., & Makhmetova, Z. (2021). Conducting inclusive focus groups in educational multicultural contexts. *20th Annual Thinking Qualitatively – Virtual*. July 8.

CohenMiller, A., & Izekenova, Z. (2020). *Adapting Photovoice for Online Use During Times of Disruption: Addressing Issues of Equity and Inclusion in Higher Education*. NVivo Virtual Conference – Qualitative Research in a Changing World. September 24. https://doi.org/10.13140/RG.2.2.18500.24961

CohenMiller, A., Rakisheva, A., & Smat, N. (2021). *Pedagogy of Body-Mapping: Exploring Salient Cultural and Institutional Issues for Student-Researchers*. Washington, DC: American Educational Research Association (AERA) Virtual Conference.

The arts, collaboration, and co-production

Conrad, D., & Sinner, A. (2015). *Creating Together: Participatory, Community-Based, and Collaborative Arts Practices and Scholarship Across Canada*. Waterloo, ON: Wilfrid Laurier University Press.

Corley, N. A. (2019). Exploring poetry as method: "Representing faithfully" the narratives of African American high school students and their mothers. *Qualitative Social Work, 19* (5–6), 1022–1039. https://doi.org/10.1177/1473325019888010

Degarrod, L. N. (2013). Making the unfamiliar personal: arts-based ethnographies as public-engaged ethnographies. *Qualitative Research, 13*(4), 402–413.

Demecs, I. P., & Miller, E. (2019). Woven narratives: A craft encounter with tapestry weaving in a residential aged care facility. *Art/Research International: A Transdisciplinary Journal, 4*(1), 31.

Denzin, N. K. (2009). The elephant in the living room: Or extending the conversation about the politics of evidence. *Qualitative Research, 9*(2), 139–160.

Denzin, N. K. (2017). *Qualitative Inquiry Under Fire: Toward a New Paradigm Dialogue*. New York: Routledge.

Derr, V. (2015). Integrating community engagement and children's voices into design and planning education. *CoDesign, 11*(2), 119–133.

Escott, H., & Pahl, K. (2017). Learning from Ninjas: Young people's films as a lens for an expanded view of literacy and language. *Discourse: Studies in the Cultural Politics of Education*, 1–13.

Facer, K., & Enright, B. (2016). *Creating Living Knowledge. The Connected Communities Programme, Community University Relationships and the Participatory Turn in the Production of Knowledge*. Bristol: University of Bristol/AHRC Connected Communities.

Facer, K., & Pahl, K. (Eds.). (2017). *Valuing Interdisciplinary Collaborative Research: Beyond Impact*. Bristol: Policy Press.

Finley, S. (2011). Critical arts-based inquiry. In N. K. Denzin & Y. S. Lincoln (Eds.), *The SAGE Handbook of Qualitative Research* (4th ed., pp. 435–450). Thousand Oaks, CA: Sage.

Fitzpatrick, E., & Reilly, R. C. (2019). Special issue: Making as method: Reimagining traditional and Indigenous notions of "craft" in research practice. *4*(1), 16. https://doi.org/10.18432/ari29464

Gastaldo, D., Rivas-Quarneti, N., & Magalhães, L. (2018). Body-map storytelling as a health research methodology: Blurred lines creating clear pictures. *Forum Qualitative Sozialforschung, 19*(2). https://doi.org/10.17169/fqs-19.2.2858

Gerber, N., Templeton, E., Chilton, G., Cohen Liebman, M., Manders, E., & Shim, M. (2012). Art-based research as a pedagogical approach to study intersubjectivity in the creative arts therapies. *Journal of Applied Arts and Health, 3*(1), 39–48.

Glass, R. D., & Newman, A. (2015). Ethical and epistemic dilemmas in knowledge production: Addressing their intersection in collaborative, community-based research. *Theory and Research in Education, 13*(1), 23–37.

Global Challenges Research Fund. (2021). Strategic advisory group. Retrieved January 22, 2021, from www.ukri.org/our-work/collaborating-internationally/global-challenges-research-fund/strategic-advisory-group/#contents-list

Goldbard, A. (2006). *New Creative Community: The Art of Cultural Development*. New York: New Village Press.

Hellstrom, T. (2015). Formative evaluation at a transdisciplinary research center. In *Co-Producing Knowledge for Sustainable Cities* (pp. 162–181). London: Routledge.

Hesse-Biber, S. N., & Leavy, P. (Eds.). (2008). *Handbook of Emergent Methods*. New York: Guilford Press.

Hinton-Smith, T., Danvers, E., & Jovanovic, T. (2017). Roma women's higher education participation: Whose responsibility? *Gender and Education*, 1–18.

Jewitt, C. (2005). Multimodality, "reading," and "writing" for the 21st century. *Discourse: Studies in the Cultural Politics of Education*, *26*(3), 315–331.

Lassiter, L. E. (1998). *The Power of Kiowa Song: A Collaborative Ethnography*. Arizona: University of Arizona Press.

Lavrinec, J. (2014). Community art initiatives as a form of participatory research: The case of street mosaic workshop. *Creativity Studies*, *7*(1), 55–68.

Lawrence-Lightfoot, S. (2016). Commentary: Portraiture methodology: Blending art and science. *LEARNing Landscapes*, *9*(2), 19–27. https://doi.org/10.36510/learnland.v9i2.760

Lawrence-Lightfoot, S., & Davis, J. H. (1997). *The Art and Science of Portraiture*. San Francisco, CA: Jossey-Bass.

Leavy, P. (2009). *Method Meets Art: Arts-Based Research Practice*. New York: Guilford Press.

Leavy, P. (2015). *Method Meets Art: Arts-Based Research Practice* (2nd ed.). New York: Guilford Press.

Leavy, P. (2017). *Research Design: Quantitative, Qualitative, Mixed Methods, Arts-Based, and Community-Based Participatory Research Approaches*. New York: Guilford Press.

Leavy, P. (2020). *Method Meets Art: Arts-Based Research Practice* (3rd ed.). New York: Guilford Press.

Liamputtong, P., & Rumbold, J. (2008). *Knowing Differently: Arts-Based and Collaborative Research Methods*. New York: Nova Publishers.

Lindgren, R., & Johnson-Glenberg, M. (2013). Emboldened by embodiment: Six precepts for research on embodied learning and mixed reality. *Educational Researcher*, *42*(8), 445–452.

Maidment, J., & Macfarlane, S. (2011). Crafting communities: Promoting inclusion, empowerment, and learning between older women. *Australian Social Work*, *64*(3), 283–298.

McNiff, S. (2007). Art-based research. In J. G. Knowles & A. L. Cole (Eds.), *Handbook of the Arts in Qualitative Research: Perspectives, Methodologies, Examples, and Issues* (Ch. 3). Thousand Oaks, CA: Sage.

Mertens, D., Cram, F., & Chilisa, B. (2013). *Indigenous Pathways into Social Research: Voices of a New Generation*. Walnut Creek, California: Left Coast Press.

Mills, K. A. (2015). *Literacy Theories for the Digital Age*. Bristol, UK: Multilingual Matters.

Mitchell, L. M. (2006a). Body and illness: Considering Visayan Filipino children's perspectives within local and global relationships of inequality. *Medical Anthropology*, *25*(4), 331–373. https://doi.org/10.1080/01459740601025856

Mitchell, L. M. (2006b). Child-centred? Thinking critically about children's drawings as a visual research method. *Visual Anthropology Review*, *22*(1), 60–73. https://doi.org/10.1525/var.2006.22.1.60

Naidu, T., & Prose, N. (2018). Re-envisioning member checking and communicating results as accountability practice in qualitative research: A South African community-based organization example. *Forum Qualitative Sozialforschung / Forum: Qualitative Social Research*, *19*(3), Art. 26. http://dx.doi.org/10.17169/fqs-19.3.3153

Narey, M. (Ed.). (2008). *Making Meaning: Constructing Multimodal Perspectives of Language, Literacy, and Learning Through Arts-Based Early Childhood Education* (Vol. 2). New York: Springer Science & Business Media.

Nomakhwezi Mayaba, N., & Wood, L. (2015). Using drawings and collages as data generation methods with children: Definitely not child's play. *International Journal of Qualitative Methods*, *14*(5). https://doi.org/10.1177/1609406915621407

Pahl, K., & Pool, S. (2011). Living your life because it's the only life you've got. *Qualitative Research Journal*, *11*(2), 17–37. https://doi.org/10.3316/QRJ1102017

Pahl, K., & Pool, S. (2018). Re-imagining artistic subjectivities within community projects. *Imaginaries of the Future 01: Bodies & Media*, *4*(2), 1–22.

Pahl, K. H. (2016). The university as the "imagined other: Making sense of community co-produced literacy research. *Collaborative Anthropologies*, *8*(1–2), 129–148.

Peterken, C. (2019). Crafting living inquiry with a quilt of children's images. *Art/Research International: A Transdisciplinary Journal*, *4*(1), 16.

Pink, S. (2012). *Advances in Visual Methodology*. Sage. https://doi.org/10.4135/9781446250921

Polk, M. (2015). Transdisciplinary co-production: Designing and testing a transdisciplinary research framework for societal problem solving. *Futures*, *65*, 110–122.

Rasool, Z. (2017). Collaborative working practices: Imagining better research partnerships. *Research for All*, *1*(2), 310–22.

Rolling, J. H. (2011). Arts practice as agency: The right to represent and reinterpret personal and social significance. *Journal of Cultural Research in Art Education*, *29*, 11–24.

Rosario, A. H., & Obo-Rayos, E. (2019). The portrait of a superwoman: Finding compatibility and balance between motherhood and graduate school. *International Forum*, *22*(2), 5–23.

Senior, K., Helmer, J., Chenhall, R., & Burbank, V. (2014). "Young clean and safe?" Young people's perceptions of risk from sexually transmitted infections in regional, rural and remote Australia. *Culture, Health & Sexuality*, *16*(4), 453–466. https://doi.org/10.1080/13691058.2014.888096

Smith, L. T. (2012). *Decolonizing Methodologies: Research and Indigenous Peoples* (2nd ed.). London: Zed Books.

Smith, L. T. (2019). Foreword. In J. A. Archibald, J. Lee-Morgan, & J. D. Santolo (Eds.), *Decolonizing Research Indigenous Storywork as Methodology*. London: Zed Books.

Sweet, E. L., & Ortiz Escalante, S. (2015). Bringing bodies into planning: Visceral methods, fear and gender violence. *Urban Studies, 52*(10), 1826–1845.

Tay-Lim, J., & Lim, S. (2013). Privileging younger children's voices in research: Use of drawings and a co-construction process. *International Journal of Qualitative Methods, 12*(1), 65–83.

Theron, L., Mitchell, C., Smith, A., & Stuart, J. (2011). *Picturing Research: Drawing as Visual Methodology*. Rotterdam, the Netherlands: Sense Publishers.

Verschuere, B., Brandsen, T., & Pestoff, V. (2012). Co-production: The state of the art in research and the future agenda. *VOLUNTAS: International Journal of Voluntary and Nonprofit Organizations, 23*(4), 1083–1101.

Vist, T. (2019). Toddler encounters as aesthetic interviews? Discussing an arts-based data gathering. *Qualitative Inquiry, 25*(7), 604–614. https://doi.org/10.1177/1077800418801378

Voorberg, W. H., Bekkers, V. J., & Tummers, L. G. (2015). A systematic review of co-creation and co-production: Embarking on the social innovation journey. *Public Management Review, 17*(9), 1333–1357.

Wakeford, T., & Sanchez Rodriguez, T. (2018). *Participatory Action Research: Towards a More Fruitful Knowledge*. University of Bristol and the AHRC Connected Communities Programme.

Wang, C., & Burris, M. A. (1997). Photovoice: Concept, methodology, and use for participatory needs assessment. *Health Education & Behavior, 24*(3), 369–387. https://doi.org/10.1177/109019819702400309

Wang, Q., Coemans, S., Siegesmund, R., & Hannes, K. (2017). Arts-based methods in socially engaged research practice: A classification framework. *Art/Research International: A Transdisciplinary Journal, 2*(2), 5–39. https://doi.org/10.18432/R26G8P

Wright, L. (2018). New perspectives in participatory arts key themes from the AHRC connected communities programme. University Report. East Anglia, UK: University of East Anglia.

Applying social justice in research and practice in multicultural contexts

What does it mean to research across multicultural contexts? How do I "best" conduct research within and across such varied contexts? These types of questions are central to our work as qualitative researchers and prompted the writing of this book. Over the years, emerging researchers we have worked with have insightfully noted the challenges of these types of questions especially when conducting research across diverse linguistic, cultural, and social contexts. Presented in these chapters, we've seen that there aren't straightforward answers for this type of work. Instead, through questioning ourselves and our approaches individually and collectively, research processes and outcomes can become more adapted to local contexts, more inclusive, richer, and more rigorous. The journey into greater awareness and critical self-reflection in our work is an exciting beginning.

The chapters presented offered a chance to see dynamic answers to understanding how social justice is foundational is qualitative research. As researchers, whether as students or more seasoned scholars or practitioners, you have a chance to bring an important piece of the puzzle to the future of qualitative social justice research. Rather than assuming a novice audience that needs to be taught basic strategies of research, we see each individual as having great knowledge and need only to be guided in their approaches to find your answers. Just as we see *you* as offering insight from your own experiences and embodied knowledge, so too do all those you have worked with and *will* work with in the future. Each emerging research project and potential participant and co-researcher offers incredible opportunities for collective work to explore and unpack injustice, to move beyond binary definitions, and to allow for a way forward that can potentially rectify these worldwide issues.

DOI: 10.4324/9780429285691-9

Social justice in multicultural contexts

Our goals in this book were to raise awareness of the multidimensional aspects of researching within and across multicultural contexts, to connect theoretical and conceptual concepts, and to encourage researchers to move beyond simple classifications of individual and community identification. We aimed to provide a space to critically examine, challenge, reflect, and mediate issues for emerging researchers. Whether as novice or more experienced researchers and practitioners, we have sought to provide pathways for critical self-reflection of our practice as qualitative researchers to make our work and society more equitable, inclusive, and socially just. We hope that raising questions and issues and creating discussions is the starting point for researchers in diverse contexts.

We have put forth questions and reflections raising critical discussion, investigating perspectives, and aiming to incorporate new and inclusive practices for qualitative research. Whether you have read every chapter or selected individual ones to concentrate on, we're glad you've joined us. In reading and critically self-reflecting, you're taking important steps in becoming more reflexive and self-aware of your own practices and ways in which to enhance your research to work with others for a more socially just world. There is no one way to answer any of the questions we've shared. Instead, you may answer one question one way today, and when you return to it in another week or another year, you may find you'll have a whole new perspective.

As qualitative researchers, we want to do the best we can and not get bogged down in the rabbit hole of concerns in conducting research. In this way, through critical self-reflection and connecting with the research of others, we can grow in our focus on the fundamentals of social justice and yet not be mired in decision-making to take the next steps, albeit hesitatingly, to consider key themes of power and vulnerability, trust, and community work. We consider the next steps for moving critical self-reflection into application of social justice in research and practice. Included in this chapter are an overview of where we started, what we have learned to uncover rich answers and collective knowledge, and practical next steps for integrating social justice in research and practice. We include a *Reflection from the Field* bringing together key discussion of social justice with decolonizing and humanizing methodologies speaking to how principles from the Black Lives Matter are a clear example of a current context that intersects and informs global insights.

1. What have we learned? Uncovering rich answers and collective knowledge

The following sections offer an overview of the concepts and ideas brought to light throughout the book. The previous chapters have offered a means to focus back to your own work in meaningful ways. Weaving together theories of social justice, decolonization, power, globalization, and diversity from a conceptual level allows a way to see the integration for a real applied context. Each of the previous chapters brought to light important concepts about researching within and across multicultural contexts focusing on equity, inclusion, and socially just practices. Embedded within each chapter were questions to guide us on our journey of critical self-reflection to thinking deeply about conducting ethical and socially just research (e.g., Bhattacharya, 2013; Bell & Pahl, 2018; Leavy & Harris, 2018; Mertens, 2020; Smith, 2012). These are meant to be utilized throughout one's research process and journey.

From this perspective, the reflective, critical questions can enable us as researchers to shift our research practices from normative, learnt practices to inclusive, interdisciplinary practices. Considering that qualitative research has a variety of ways to conduct research, the struggle for many is that there is no *one* right of doing it. Thus, by sharing different ways to move forward and conduct qualitative research within and across multicultural contexts across intersectional constructs, such as ethnic, racial, religious, gendered, and linguistic contexts, we can see how each person has great knowledge and only needs to be guided in their approaches to work with diverse populations. We aimed to co-construct with emerging researchers, students, and practitioners embodied notions of collaboration, co-construction, and reflective inquiry. In order to reach these aims, we asked you to consider robust questions to engage and reflect upon your own research plans and practices, journeying in an exploration of self-reflection to provoke deep thinking for current and future research. We hope that you come out of reading these chapters feeling more confident about steps to consider and directions to take in your own practice in conducting qualitative social justice research in multicultural contexts.

In Chapter 1, "Owning Our Power," we saw how issues of privilege and power intersect and form a basis for becoming more reflexive, self-aware, and critically self-reflective in our research. There, we learned from Kakali

Bhattacharya in her *Reflection from the Field* about steps to use to uncover our power. We also heard from Polina Golovátina-Mora and Raúl Alberto Mora about the ways our reflexivity offers us a chance to envision a future of our research. These issues raised led us to examine aspects of trust in the research relationship.

In Chapter 2, "Unpacking the Meaning and Practice of Trust," concepts of trust and vulnerability were highlighted as central for building trusting relationships with individuals and in communities. There, we learned from Jennifer R. Wolgemuth about the way trust and issues of power and ethics can emerge in unexpected places. We also heard from Fatma F. S. Said about the way participatory research and trust connect when working with multi-lingual, multicultural, hard-to-reach populations. These voices illuminated the path toward better accepting the positionality notion of insider-outsider.

In Chapter 3, "Uncovering the Spectrum of Insider-Outsiderness," we explored the concept of being an insider and outsider beyond a dichot-omy and instead as a spectrum. We saw how these identity markers and membership roles affect the ways we interact, are seen by others, and how they affect our research. In the *Reflections from the Field*, we heard from Linda Tuhiwai Smith, who explored the histories of colonizing research and her movement through boundaries of roles, leading her to a love and joy for research with Indigenous communities and Indigenous methodologies. Then we heard from Arceli Rosario about returning to the field, as family, and the ways the insider-outsider divide can shift in an instant. These deep issues that are often superficially examined critically challenge emerging understandings.

In Chapter 4, "Awareness in Social Justice and Transformative Research," we applied topics from across the chapters, such as power, privilege, and local knowledges, to expand our understanding of conducting socially just, community-based, participatory, and transformative research. We learned from Donna M. Mertens about the origin story and process of developing transformative research and the ways the paradigm continues to expand based upon the needs of marginalized communities. Then Tineke A. Abma shared about researcher's reflexivity, offering ideas for developing ourselves through framing work and emotion work as the "researcher-as-instrument" when working in a multicultural context.

In Chapter 5, "Crossing Disciplinary Boundaries within the Research Team," we explored the ideas of working in varied ways for researching with those within and outside academia across disciplinary boundaries,

Social justice in multicultural contexts

such as to address complex societal problems. In the *Reflections from the Field* we heard from practitioners, activists, and scholars about cross-cultural and cross-disciplinary approaches for promoting voice. Agnes Atia Apusigah discussed key considerations for teams of whose knowledge is prioritized or glossed over. Akmaral Sman emphasized building trust with academic and community teams. And the team of Roxanne Henkin, Gopal Krishna Sharma, Purva Sharma, and Mashaba Mashala discussed the power of writing and the benefits and challenges of community-based work across multicultural contexts and countries.

Then in Chapter 6, "Moving between Face-to-Face and Online Engagement," we learned about how moving to research online or in using varied modes and platforms affords opportunities, such as reaching distant communities, but is also embedded with key considerations about power, access, and ethics. In the *Reflections from the Field*, Carolyn Ellis shares a discussion she had with Jerry Rawicki – a survivor of the Holocaust and a long-time participant, friend, and collaborator in research – about their interviews over the years and the potential of online video for interviewing. We also heard from Tamsin Hinton-Smith about an equalities perspective, "to shield participants at least partially from the vulnerabilities of the unequal research and unwelcome public exposure of personal lives," and its potential as applied to researching online with marginalized communities.

Finally, in Chapter 7, "Integrating the Arts with Collaboration and Co-production," we explored multiple uses of arts with collaboration and co-production in research to address issues of equity, inclusion, and social justice. We learned from Patricia Leavy in her *Reflection from the Field* about the potential of arts in scholarship and how to treat ourselves in the process. And in the critical self-reflection from Nadia Dresscher-Lambertus, we heard about the potential of coming together with students to co-create autoethnography during times of crisis.

2. Where do we go from here? Joining a journey for applying social justice in research and practice

The central tenets of social justice and compassion in qualitative research rely upon self-reflection and more importantly, critical self-reflection. Simply put, self-reflection is essential for qualitative researchers. The philosophical nature of self-reflection can be considered in various ways. For some, there has been an exploration of the process of self-reflection as a method (Franks, 2015), as a central part of autoethnography (Mahoney, 2007), or as connected to the research vignette (Langer, 2016). We can consider delving into these questions not as a philosophical-type exercise but working toward depth and breadth, as emphasized in anthropology by Clifford Geertz, going deeper to provide "thick description" (1973). Through thick description, we get to thick interpretation and "thick meaning" (Ponterotto, 2006). We get a chance to live, reflect, share and co-construct research with others in order to fully address social justice and to be inclusive of others within the community. As such, we have had the opportunity to discuss the importance of inclusivity, of involving others in meaningful ways and for us as qualitative researchers to act in accord with the needs of the community. Such ideas have been shared in the *Reflections from the Field* across the preceding chapters from researchers around the globe.

We started this book to help those who wanted answers to the complicated questions for those committed to social justice. Such questions as "How do I ensure I'm not harming my participants inadvertently?" and "How can I best share their voices?" were jumping-off points. These types of questions aren't unique to students or researchers but instead are central to ethical, socially just research in a globalizing world. We find ourselves continually asking ourselves these questions, sharing with others, and trying to better understand ourselves in relation to our research. And although it is uncomfortable at times to not have "the" answer, the benefit of improving our research to better address inequities, hear communities, and broadcast their voices is immensely rewarding.

There will always be questions that remain, aspects to consider, to reflect upon, and to work to develop. There will always be research that needs addressing to better hear and amplify the voices of those historically marginalized and oppressed. As we navigate through an increasingly shifting, globalizing multilingual and multicultural research context, it becomes apparent as researchers, our approaches, practices, and perspectives must shift too. The concepts addressed throughout the chapters help us as qualitative researchers to consider our own practice as a process of development and growing self-awareness.

Together with compassion, we are positioned then to make significant contributions within the framework of social justice. As qualitative researchers focused on conducting socially just work, we care and we're working

Social justice in multicultural contexts

toward effective ethical research. Yet, *we* are not the center of the work, however; our ego is not the important part, and neither are the publications. The move to focusing on the nature of the research and its outcome, then, become the focus and the academic institutional expectations are a benefit, instead of vice versa. The emerging patterns discussed across the chapters shift our stance as researchers from objectivity and invisibility of the "researcher" to research centering on social justice and inclusivity with the recognition of the centrality of co-produced practices. Through such a transformative research lens, qualitative research as a whole is better positioned to allow all voices and multiple truths to emerge. So, there isn't one particular way forward to conduct socially just qualitative research, and that's a good thing.

At times, questioning our research practice can feel challenging. It can bring up feelings of inadequacy; there is always more to question and more to answer. But the nature of qualitative research demands questioning our practice. The hope, though, is that we can move beyond *only* having concerns and a rabbit hole of questioning, to finding the air to conduct our work in a manner *we* feel is just and socially responsible. In this way, we can move from feeling *just okay* to even feeling good about our work. We can look back at our research study, at our corpus of work, and feel proud of how we have helped others to be heard and how we have been a conduit for communities to share their experiences, needs, and values. For instance, research practices can move away from Western normative practices. Attempting a shift away from Western language-centric practices can be one such direction to make research more inclusive. Recent research, such as in multisensory discourse resources (MDR) analysis, highlights the importance of often overlooked data in ethnographic observational evidence, to include intersecting sensory experiences (e.g., sight, sound, taste, smell, touch) to connect to emotional sense memory and identity (Boivin, 2020a, 2020b, forthcoming). Such an approach can enable the co-creation of decolonized ethnographic research practices (DERP) aimed at involving all the stakeholders with specific reference to facilitating voice for colonial, Indigenous, and marginalized people (Boivin, 2020a).

As we finish the chapters and see the overlapping concepts of power and privilege, of equity and inclusion, the questions we can consider don't stop, but extend. We can think more deeply, for instance, about who we are and how we can do our work better. And we can consider these questions as part of a growing community of qualitative researchers committed to social

Social justice in multicultural contexts

justice. Within higher education institutions, there are chances to discuss these ideas in courses, workshops, and lectures. Within organizations, we can join and find research-based groups committed to these ideas.

3. Practical next steps: improving equity, inclusion, and social justice in research and practice

In this chapter, we reflected on the ways the topics came together to offer opportunities to critically self-reflect on our research and the future of socially just qualitative research. We have highlighted the importance of learning across disciplinary boundaries for qualitative research in multicultural contexts. We have seen how interesting perspectives can work across fields of research.

Thus, when faced with questions, problems, or even "failures" in qualitative research (CohenMiller et al., 2020), we hope you'll be more comfortable considering your work in a practical, non-judgmental manner to move toward a purposeful shift to situate equity, inclusion, and social justice at the center. Across the chapters, there is a type of map presented, through actual successes and difficulties in the field, for how to bridge identity, power, status, inclusivity, voice, and agency. The reflective perspectives of researchers and future researchers were provided as examples for when we are faced with questions for ourselves. We hope this book has peeled back the sometimes closed, or siloed, institutional process of research to allow inclusion of stakeholders whose lives are socially impacted from the research. So when questions arise – such as **Am I taking the appropriate steps to engage in culturally sensitive and aware research? Have I had a chance to reflect on the research I'm conducting?** – you'll have a set of tools to critically self-reflect to find *your* answers informed by insights from qualitative researchers committed and practicing socially just research from around the globe.

4. Reflection from the field: social justice in action

As an example of bringing together these central tenets of qualitative social justice research, we can look to a highly contemporaneous example (Black

Lives Matter 2021). Our final *Reflection from the Field* offers insight to the practical nature of implementing a lens centered on equity, inclusion, and social justice in research and practice across contexts including international and local communities, in academic institutions, and in teaching and learning. Sharon M. Ravitch from the University of Pennsylvania addresses the connections between social justice and humanizing, decolonial, and anti-racist methodological approaches. Through this *Reflection from the Field*, we can see how social justice moves beyond improving inequalities and into research that supports and prompts structural societal change.

Black Lives Matter and humanizing methodologies for social justice

Sharon M. Ravitch

The 13 Principles of Black Lives Matter (BLM) are the starting point and the foundation of all of my research team orientations, research meetings, and research designs. This decision stems from seeing the harm caused by researchers' internalized logics, unquestioned assumptions, and limited interpretations and how they shape the research in ways that uphold White dominance, deficit orientations, and the imposition of worldview, implicit bias, and projection. Most often research team members are not able to recognize these invisible logics in themselves, which is where the most generative work of research teams begins.

One example of what this looks like in motion emerges from my applied research on intersectional identities, pluralism, and well-being at a women's home science school in Mumbai, India. Given the nature of intersectionality in this setting, and the need to understand the role of intersectional identities in schooling experiences for minoritized first-generation girls, different dimensions of identity and axes of oppression emerge as salient given national and local contexts. Watching researchers who work on these teams project Western institutional impositions onto this group of women surfaced the immediate need to engage in place-based intersectional racial literacy work and then to widen the aperture from there into a more global critical literacy of identities and pluralism in an educational setting. The tenets of BLM helped us as a team to address the underlying perspectival issues more holistically than otherwise would be possible, to criticalize our understandings of the relationship between identity, structure, and agency, and to center us as a team in terms of how we think about the relationship of identities to structural barriers and enablers as it relates to educational experience, opportunity, and wellness. This is a global movement given the coloniality of institutions.

My over two decades of doing, teaching, advising, and studying qualitative research helps me understand the need to address people's implicit biases and dysconscious racism as a foundational principle and process of research. Starting each project and new team with the BLM principals and then integrating them into how we ongoingly assess and address validity is deeply important and generative, opening up necessary opportunities for enacting criticality about race, engaging intersectional identities, enacting critical race theory as a theoretical framework and methodological approach, examining structural racism in field research and academia, interrogating White Western impositions in most research, positioning research as counter-narrative to dominating and deficitizing narratives, and cultivating critical identity and equity literacies. Anti-racism is central to humanizing and decolonial methodologies and to understanding ourselves as researchers who act as the primary instrument of our research (Ravitch & Carl, 2020).

The Black Lives Matter movement is guided by these principles:

1 *Restorative Justice* – We are committed to collectively, lovingly, and courageously working vigorously for freedom and justice for Black people and, by extension, all people.
2 *Empathy* – We are committed to practicing empathy; we engage comrades with the intent to learn about and connect with their contexts.
3 *Loving Engagement* – We are committed to embodying and practicing justice, liberation, and peace in our engagements with one another.
4 *Diversity* – We are committed to acknowledging, respecting, and celebrating difference(s) and commonalities.

Social justice in multicultural contexts

5 *Globalism* – We see ourselves as part of the global Black family, and we are aware of the different ways we are impacted or privileged as Black folk who exist in different parts of the world.

6 *Queer Affirming* – We are committed to fostering a queer-affirming network. When we gather, we do so with the intention of freeing ourselves from the tight grip of heteronormative thinking, or, rather, the belief that all in the world are heterosexual unless s/he or they disclose otherwise.

7 *Trans Affirming* – We are committed to being self-reflexive and doing the work required to dismantle cis-gender privilege and uplift Black trans folk, especially Black trans women who continue to be disproportionately impacted by trans-antagonistic violence.

8 *Collective Value* – We are guided by the fact all Black Lives Matter, regardless of actual or perceived sexual identity, gender identity, gender expression, economic status, ability, disability, religious beliefs or disbeliefs, immigration status, or location.

9 *Intergenerational* – We are committed to fostering an intergenerational and communal network free from ageism. We believe that all people, regardless of age, show up with the capacity to lead and learn.

10 *Black Families* – We are committed to making our spaces family-friendly and enable parents to fully participate with their children. We are committed to dismantling the patriarchal practice that requires mothers to work "double shifts" as they participate in justice work.

11 *Black Villages* – We are committed to disrupting the Western prescribed nuclear family structure requirement by supporting each other as extended families and "villages" that collectively care for one another, and especially "our" children to the degree that mothers, parents, and children are comfortable.

12 *Unapologetically Black* – We are unapologetically Black in our positioning. In affirming that Black Lives Matter, we need not qualify our position. To love and desire freedom and justice for ourselves is a necessary prerequisite for wanting the same for others.

13 *Black Women* – We are committed to building a Black women–affirming space free from sexism, misogyny, and male-centeredness.

In research projects, and on research teams, we discuss the structural and organizational conditions that create and perpetuate the need for these statements, for this and other social justice movements to take root in schools, to be centralized in inquiry and research, and to be lifted up in policy and civic life. I want to make sure everyone shares an understanding of these issues as a floor and not a ceiling of our research. This requires taking a critical learning stance on ourselves, our research, and the contexts – relational, structural, and sociopolitical, and economic – that shape research settings, research designs, and methodological processes. These processes require, as they evince, critical dialogic engagement, culturally responsive methods, humanizing and ethical research; they challenge norms in the field, in methods texts, and in our own embedded logics and ways of studying and interpreting the world (Ravitch, 2021).

Researchers must actively question the hegemonic codification of academic texts, research processes, norms of fieldwork and in the field as a whole, to critique assumptions and the potential for research to be transformational and/or oppressive, to be racist and sexist and uncritical around intersectionality. We must examine White logics and the colonization of inquiry and research, of our minds, of the ways that we relate even as we endeavor to design and conduct research. These conscious starting points and disruptions to White dominance and normativity matter. Specifically, interrogations of the expert-learner binary as a false White Western construction of knowledge and value are an antidote to authentic and humanizing teaching, learning, and inquiry. We must examine the ways that dominance is conferred upon so-called experts as an outgrowth of White supremacy – which must be disrupted at the very conception of our research and in the researcher within our core self – for research to be vital, valid, catalytic, ethical, and useful (Ravitch, 2021).

Anti-racist and critically inclusive researchers must work continuously to explore our social identities, power, and privileges and how they influence our worldviews, practices, and experiences as researchers. In our teams we explore social identities in terms of power and privilege, and hierarchy broadly, which inform the development of our mental models for how we think the world operates. We examine

Social justice in multicultural contexts

how those who exist uncritically in these nested systems of power and privilege often mistakenly subscribe to the meritocracy myth, deficit orientations, and disbelief of structural oppression (Pak & Ravitch, 2021). The uncritical acceptance of opportunity structures ignores the role of structural racism and discrimination in shaping the differential opportunities that people have, creating fertile ground for grand narratives of deficit, exceptionality, essentialization, and tokenism – concepts central to critical research. Deficitization is the foundational lie upon which most codified research is built, and our research can serve to unsettle and dismantle these problematic norms.

I strongly believe that all researchers, and especially White researchers, must engage racial literacy work and build our identity-based stress-navigation skills as a baseline for ethical and equitable research, as foundational to what it means to be a skilled researcher. This is necessary to being ethical co-learners and researchers who build our own critical literacies for interpretation and meaning-making as a primary responsibility. Relatedly, we must address inequities and microaggressions that arise in our work and on our research teams to model anti-racist pedagogy and challenge with care. It is our responsibility to validate and amplify non- and anti-dominant knowledges, value systems, points of view, and approaches to research (Ravitch, 2021). Everything sets us up as White people to impose our own hierarchies and values – we must resist and teach this resistance to our students precisely toward social justice processes and ends.

Researchers must continuously interrupt and address racism, sexism, microaggressions, and imposed deficit orientations with clarity and kindness while not tolerating behavior borne of White fragility and White grievance, assiduously challenging discriminatory views, unspoken assumptions, and projections as they emerge on our research teams and in our methods classes. It is important that we lead with this kind of critical anti-racist care and that we demystify research. This kind of team work is liberatory, disruptive, and affirming. Our own identities and positionalities mediate all of this in vital ways that must be attended to and named as part of this inquiry process. Critical possibilities abound for reconstructive research that helps to heal our world. Black Lives Matter provides a compass and set of coordinates for anti-racist humanizing methodologies that examine and foster social justice.

References

Black Lives Matter. Retrieved March 18, 2021, from https://blacklivesmatter.com/

Pak, K., & Ravitch, S. M. (Eds.). (2021). *Critical Leadership Praxis for Educational and Social Change*. New York, NY: Teachers College Press.

Ravitch, S. M. (2021). *Teaching Black Lives Matter principles to Shape Humanizing Research and Methods Pedagogy*. Sage MethodSpace. Retrieved from https://www.methodspace.com/teaching-black-lives-matter-tenets-to-shape-humanizing-research-and-methods-pedagogy/

Ravitch, S. M., & Carl, M. N. (2020). *Qualitative Research: Bridging the Conceptual, Theoretical, and Methodological*. Thousand Oaks, CA: Sage.

5. Reflective questions on improving equity, inclusion, and social justice in research and practice

These final sets of questions offer a chance to inventory and reflect on your work in a non-judgmental manner to move toward improving equity, inclusion, and social justice in research and practice. Together as researchers, we get a chance to learn more about our work, to understand ourselves, to work with others, to learn about local and embedded knowledges, and to work toward building a more equitable, inclusive, and socially just society.

Topics	Questions
Commitment to social justice	• How am I committing to working toward equity, inclusion, and social justice for all? • Where do I feel I am doing well regarding this topic? • Where could I improve? • Which tools, networks, or knowledge might I want/ need to incorporate?

Topics	Questions
Extending collaboration, compassion, and empathy	• How am I working toward extending collaboration for working with others? • Where do I feel I am doing well regarding this topic? • Where could I improve? • Which tools, networks, or knowledge might I want/need to incorporate?
Emphasizing diversity	• How am I emphasizing diversity in my research and practice? • Where do I feel I am doing well regarding this topic? • Where could I further enhance or expand these approaches? • Which tools, networks, or knowledge might I want/need to incorporate?
Critically self-reflection for research and practice	• After critically reflecting on my own research journey at this stage: • What do I feel like I am doing very well? • Where would I like to improve or feel confident about? • Which tools, networks, or knowledge might I want/need to incorporate?

References

Bell, D. M., & Pahl, K. (2018). Co-production: Towards a utopian approach. *International Journal of Social Research Methodology*, *21*(1), 105–117.

Bhattacharya, K. (2013). Voices, silences, and telling secrets: The role of qualitative methods in arts-based research. *International Review of Qualitative Research*, *6*(4), 604–627. https://doi.org/10.1525/irqr.2013.6.4.604

Boivin, N. (2020a). Multisensory discourse resources: Decolonizing ethnographic research practices. *Journal of Multilingual and Multicultural Development*. https://doi.org/10.1080/01434632.2020.1841215

Boivin, N. (2020b). Homescape: Agentic space for transmigrant families multisensory discourse of identity. *Linguistic Landscape Journal*, *7*(1), 37–59. https://doi.org/10.1075/ll.19019.boi

Boivin, N. (forthcoming). Foodscapes: Multisensory food discourse resources initiating reciprocal interactions. *Language, Culture and Society Journal*.

CohenMiller, A. S., Demers, D., & Schnackenberg, H. (2020). Rigid flexibility in research: Seeing the opportunities in "failed" qualitative research. *Special issue: Failures in Qualitative and Mixed Methods Research, Sousa and Clark (Eds)*.

International Journal of Qualitative Methods. https://journals.sagepub.com/doi/10.1177/1609406920963782

Franks, T. M. (2015). Purpose, practice, and (discovery) process: When self-reflection is the method. *Qualitative Inquiry, 22*(1), 47–50. https://doi.org/10.1177/1077800415603394

Geertz, C. (1973). *The Interpretation of Cultures*. New York: Basic Books.

Langer, P. C. (2016). The research vignette: Reflexive writing as interpretative representation of qualitative inquiry: A methodological proposition. *Qualitative Inquiry, 22*(9), 735–744. https://doi.org/10.1177/1077800416658066

Leavy, P., & Harris, A. (2018). *Contemporary Feminist Research from Theory to Practice* (1st ed.). New York: Guilford Press.

Mahoney, D. (2007). Constructing reflexive fieldwork relationships: Narrating my collaborative storytelling methodology. *Qualitative Inquiry, 13*(4), 573–594. https://doi.org/10.1177/1077800407300765

Mertens, D. M. (2020). *Research and Evaluation in Education and Psychology: Integrating Diversity with Quantitative, Qualitative, and Mixed Methods* (5th ed.). Thousand Oaks, CA: Sage.

Ponterotto, J. G. (2006). Brief note on the origins, evolution, and meaning of the qualitative research concept thick description. *The Qualitative Report, 11*(3), 538–549.

Smith, L. T. (2012). *Decolonizing Methodologies: Research and Indigenous Peoples* (2nd ed.). London: Zed Publishers.

Glossary

This glossary provides short definitions of key terms used throughout the book. These are informed by our multidisciplinary backgrounds and offer a quick reference for understanding major topics in qualitative social justice research in multicultural contexts.

Bias is a positive or negative belief or inference about a person or persons, group, or community based on emotional and normative understandings.

Capital (cultural, social, linguistic) is an immaterial (non-monetary) form of affordances enabling entrance or advantage within a community, society, or group.

Cultural brokers are people who can linguistically and culturally bridge between institutions and communities, groups, or families. Children who translate for immigrant grandparents can be considered language brokers.

Decolonizing research is an approach used to emphasize local and Indigenous knowledges that have been historically marginalized by dominant groups.

Diversity is a concept that centers awareness and attempts to provide space and inclusion for all regardless of gender, age, culture, ethnicity, linguistic, social status, nationality, socioeconomic status, education, cognitive, behavioral, or physical status/level.

Equality refers to being treated the same in status, rights, and opportunity without differences, yet does not consider fairness of outcomes.

Equity refers to being provided with equal opportunity in all segments of society, including support, fairness and equal outcomes.

Gatekeeper refers to a person who researchers connect with to facilitate entrance to an institution or community.

Glossary

Identity markers are different expressions of who we are. These labels embody characteristics that have meaning to us and the society in which we exist, such as culture, age, gender, ability, socioeconomic status, religion, sexual orientation, and the social construct of race.

Inclusion is the practice or policy of including all, providing opportunities for those who otherwise would be marginalized.

Insider is a person believed to be a member of a group or community.

Intersectionality is the interconnected nature of social categorizations, such as race, class, and gender as they apply to a given individual or group, creating overlapping and interdependent systems of discrimination or disadvantage.

Online research is a method of research that involves the collection of research from the internet or in the use of digital technologies.

Positionality is the social and political context that creates your identity, such as in terms of race, class, gender, sexuality, and ability status. It includes how we identify and views our perspective and possible biases of society as well as how others see us.

Power is a concept, a cultural construct, and a process that affects interactions and relationships with others.

Reflexivity is the concept and process of critical self-reflection to better understand ourselves and our effects on the research process.

Social justice in research is the purposeful commitment and advocacy to address systemic issues of equity and inclusion in particular for historically marginalized and oppressed peoples.

Stakeholders are people who have interests in the context or community in which one is doing research. These can include but are not limited to institutional, governmental, community, neighborhoods, social, family, and transnational communities.

Index

access, accessible xxiv, 10, 13, 22, 34, 53–56, 64, 67, 69, 70, 75–76, 78–79, 80, 89, 92, 96, 99, 102, 104, 106, 122, 138, 144, 152–153, 155, 157, (accessible, technology) 158, 160–164, 171–172, 193, 211

agency xxiii, 13, 15, 27, 39–41, 59, 66, 70, 103, 112, 121, 156, 164, 173, 179, 181, 187, 188, 191, 201, 205, 214, 216

applicability (or transferability) 48, 49

arts-based research (ABR) xxii, xxv, 7, 11, 40, 41, 92, 97–98, 136, 173, 177–181, 183, 185–187, 191–194, 200–206; see also body mapping; photovoice; poetry

arts methodologies 185, 187

autoethnography see ethnography

Bhattacharya, Kakali 6, 16, 26, 31, 40, 74, 77, 91–92, 182, 201, 209–210, 221

Black Lives Matter (BLM) 5, 208, 215–217, 219–220

bicultural, bicultural recruiter 52–53; see also cultural broker

body-mapping, body mapping xxv, 181, 202; see also arts-based research

Burris, Mary Ann 182, 206; see also photovoice; Wang, Caroline

co-constructed research, co-construction xxiii, 19, 24, 41, 44, 58, 63–65, 74, 90, 133, 173, 185, 201, 206, 209, 212

co-create, co-created research 118, 184, 198, 211

collaboration xxvi, 5, 9, 43, 102, 122, (collaboration, ethical research) 125, 126, (collaboration, interdisciplinary) 127, 129, 133–136, 146, (collaboration and investment) 147), 148–150, 152, 164, 170, 177–178, 181, 183, (collaboration, co-produced research) 184, 185–186, 188–190, 192, 199–201, 209, 211, 221

colonization 27–28, 38, 106, 182, 218; see also decolonization

community-based, community-based participatory research (CBPR) xxiii, 43, 97, 104, 121, 203–304, 210, 211; see also participatory research

confirmability 49; see also neutrality

consistency 48–49; see also dependability

contemplative practice 31, 179, 182; journeying and imagination 31–32; metamorphosis and impermanence 31–33; shadow work 31

co-produced research, co-production 55, 58, 83, 90, 98, 100, 105, 128,

225

133, 136, 142, 148, 177–178, 180, 183–187, 189–192, 199–201, 204–206, 211, 213, 221

credibility (or truth value) 22, 48–49, 53, 79

critical dialectical pluralism 1.0 104

critical reflexivity 23, 31, 73, 110, 219; *see also* reflexivity

critical self-reflection xxii, (critical self-reflection, definition of) 2, 5–6, 14–15, 22, 39, 60, 73, 99, 118, 123, 133, 160, 192, 196, 207–209, 211, 224

cross-disciplinary research 29, 124, (cross-disciplinary research, definition of) 126, 127, 129, 137–143, 211

cultural broker 52, 223

cultural frames 112; emotion work 113–114, 210; framing work 111–114, 210

culturally competent 56, 94

decolonization 96, 108, 121, 160, 209; *see also* colonization

decolonizing research 25, 75, 206, 223

dependability 48–49; *see also* consistency

digital technology 54, 154–156, 164, (digital technology, affordances of) 189; *see also* social media; video conferencing, YouTube; Zoom

disability xxiii, 20, 63, 102, 104, 217

dissemination 103, 156, 158, 161–162, 174, 177, 181–182, 184, 200

diversity xxiv, 2, 6, 9, 12, 21, 40, 42, 44, 52, 66, 68, 71, 110, 112–113, 119, 121, 127, 150, 169, 187, 189, 190, 207, 209, 216, 221–223; superdiversity, super-diversity 70, 93, 98, 119, 122

duoethnography *see* ethnography

Ellis, Carolyn 7, 79, 83, 93, 134, 148, 164–165, 174, 211

emotion work 111, 113–114, 210; *see also* cultural frame

emancipatory research 15, 101, 103–104

empathy 4, 25, 32, 59, 66, 68–69, 114, 117, 193, 198, 216, 221

engagement xxii, 4–5, 7, 11, 49, 102, 122, 132–133, 150–152, 154–155, 164, 171–172, 181, 188, 191, 196, 202–203, 211; engagement, loving 216, 218

epistemological reflexivity *see* reflexivity

ethics, ethical xxii, xxiii, xxiv, xxv, xxvii, 1, 4, 6, 9, 15, 23, (ethical dilemmas, relating to power) 28–31, 33–34, 42–47, 52, 55–56, (ethical dilemmas, trust) 57–59), (ethical dilemmas, sharing power) 60, 63, 67–68, 70–71, 73, 75, 82, (ethical dilemmas, insider-outsider) 83–85, 89–90, 100, (ethical dilemmas, social justice and transformative research) 106–108, 110, 112–114, 125, 131, (ethical dilemmas, working across disciplines) 134–136, 147–148, 152–154, 156–158, (ethical dilemmas, online research) 160–163, 167, 169, 171–176, 185, (ethical dilemmas, arts in research) 191–192, 198, 203, 209–213, 218–219; micro-ethics 29, 45; societal ethics 29; *see also* GDPR

ethnicity xxiii, 2–3, 14, 17–20, 25–26, 52, 58–59, 69, 71, 73, 81, 83, 90, 95, 97, 101, 104, 110, 134, 178, 223

ethnography 8, 17, 40, 42–43, 51, 71, 83, 153, 181, 185, 187–189, 204; autoethnography 40, 83, 92–93, 164, 174, 196–199, 202, 211–212; duo-ethnography 25, 43–44

equality, inequality 19–21, 24, 26, 29, 75, 96, 136, 205, 223

equity, inequity xxii, xxviii, 2, 4, 6, 8, 12, 19, 24, 39, 41, 45, 71, 96–99,

103–105, 115, 117, 120, 133, 135, 140, 147, 161, 167, 171, 173, 177, 181, 191, 199, 202, 209, 211, 213–216, 220, 223–224

Facebook xxiv, 11, 153, 158, 161–163, 174–176, 202; *see also* social media
feminist reflexivity *see* reflexivity
feminist research 11, 19, 26, 39, 43, 59, 71, 168, 222
fourth wall 24, 41, 148, 186, 190, 201
funding 27, 53, 123–125, 129–130, 134, 138, 140–141, 144, 162, 189

gatekeeper xxii, 19, 46, 55–57, 67, 69, 71–72, 140, 223
gender xxiii, 3, 8, 9, 14, 16–19, 21, 23, 26, 41–42, 52, 54, 57–59, 63, 65, 69–71, 74, 76–77, 82, 85, 90, 92, 99, 104, 110, 120–122, 125, 134, 140–142, 168, 170, 178, 204, 206, 209, 217, 223
General Data Protection Regulation (GDPR) (see *also* ethics) 153, 155, 162–163, 174
globalization, globalism 15, 38–39, 129, 209, 217

hegemony, cultural 29; *see also* power
Hesse Biber, Sharlene 43, 155, 174, 179, 204
humanizing methodologies 208, 215–216, 218, 220

identity markers xxiii, 52, 73, 79, 210, 224
inclusion, inclusive xxii, xxv, 1–4, 8–9, 16, 18–20, 23–24, 26–27, 30, 38–39, 41, 67, 79–80, 96–97, 101–102, 108, 110–111, 114–115, 117, 122, 131, 133–134, 138, 147, 171, 173, 177, 181, 183, 185, 188, 189–190, 199, 202, 204, 207–209, 211–215, 218, 220, 223–224

inequality *see* equality
inequity *see* equity
insider xxii, xxiii, 5, 6, 40, 42, 51, 59, 70–71, 73–94, 103, 108, 137, 139, 210, 224; *see also* outsider
interdisciplinary xxiv, 3–4, 16, 41, 79, 92–93, 124, 127–128, 130–133, 135–136, 145–146, 148–151, 203, 209; interdisciplinarity 7, 124, 127, 129–130, 134–135, 149–150
interdisciplinary research (IDR) 127–128, 130, 132, 135, 148–151
intersectionality 18–19, 21, 40–41, 45, 95, 99, 215, 218, 224

Janesick, Valerie J. 102, 121, 133, 149
Justice, restorative 216; *see also* social justice

label, labeling 20, 29, 74, 98, 107–108, 112, 224
Lawrence-Lightfoot, Sara 183, 204
Leavy, Patricia 2, 7, 11, 24, 43, 97, 104, 121, 155, 174, 177–180, 182, 192–193, 204, 209, 211, 222
lived experience 1, 9, 20, 59, 83, 109, 143, 152, 158, 164, 179–180, 199

membership roles 73–74, 77, 82–84, 87, 90–91, 210
Mertens, Donna M. xxv, 2, 7, 12, 15, 24, 44, 57, 71, 96–97, 101–104, 108–109, 118, 121–123, 137, 149–150, 177, 183, 204, 209–210, 222
multiculturalism 2, 15, 19, 40, 44–45, 69, 98
multidisciplinary, multidisciplinary research 9, 77, 124, 126–127, 131, 133, 151, 223
multimodal 36–37, 41, 133, 154, 173–175, 178, 185, 201, 204–205

neutrality 48–49; *see also* confirmability

Index

objectivity 17, 24, 26–27, 49, 213
online research 67, 83, 152, 155–157, 159–161, 164, 167–168, 171–175, 224
Onwuegbuzie, Tony 104, 122
outsider xxii, xxiii, 5–6, 8, 40, 42, 49, 51, 55, 59, 69–70, 73–95, 98, 103, 108, 137, 139, 210; *see also* insider

Pahl, Kate 14, 30, 40, 98, 120, 133, 148, 150, 178, 180–181, 184, 186–190, 201–203, 205, 209, 221
paradigm 24–26, 42–43, 69, 86, 103–105, 107, 110, 119, 121–122, 128, 185, 203, 210
participant voice *see* voice
participatory research xxiii, 26, 43, 45, 63, 97, 101, 104, 111, 114–115, 118, 121, 149, 184, 204, 210; *see also* community-based participatory research
partnership 28, 51, 53, 68, 94, 128, 132, 136, 150, 185–186, 205
personal reflexivity *see* reflexivity
photovoice xxv, 181–182, 202, 206; *see also* arts-based research; body-mapping; poetry
poetry, poetic inquiry, poet xxv, 182, 185, 187, 192, 199, 203
positionality 7, 9, 14–15, 17–18, 21, 26, 29, 38, 40, 42, 47, 52, 55–56, 59, 68, 70–72, 74, 91, 103, 197–198, 210, 224
postmodern 22, 24, 26, 45; *see also* paradigm
power 4–6, 13–40, 42, 44, 47, 55–56, 60–64, 67, 69, 74–75, 82–83, 85–86, 89–90, 99, 103–105, 108, 111, 115, 128, 130, 140, 144, 152, 154, 158, (democratizing power) 160, (power dynamics, acknowledging power) 168, 171, 179, (power imbalance) 181, (issues of power) 184, 187, (hierarchies of

power) 188, 189, (power sharing) 191, 204, 208–211, 213–214, 218, (nested systems of power) 219, 224; decentralize power 24–25, 30; institutional power 20, 85; participant power 19
praxis 12, 22, 42, 197, 220
privilege xxii, xxiii, xxiv, 18, 20–22, 24, 29–31, 38, 59, 64, 67, 73, 84, 86, 96, 98–100, 103, 108, 113, 134, 146, 152, 156, 168, 171, 209–210, 213, 217–219

race xxi, xxiii, 8, 14, 17–18, 20–21, 25, 41, 58–59, 63, 69, 71, 74, 85, 91–93, 99, 104, 110, 134, 178, 216, 224
Ravitch, Sharon M. 5, 7, 12, 105, 120, 215–216, 218–220
reflexivity 22–24, 30, 36–37, 42, 44–45, 48–49, 59, 66, 70, 92, 97, 111, 118, 146, 156, 192, 210, 224; critical reflexivity 73; epistemological reflexivity 23; feminist reflexivity 23–24; personal reflexivity 23
relationships (also reciprocal relationship) xxii, 13–16, 18, 23–26, 28–30, 32–33, 38, 46–47, 51–59, 62, 64–70, 72, 75, 77, 79, 82, 84, 86, 90–91, 98, 100, 102, 105, 111, 120, 132, 141, 155–156, 158, 168, 171, 175, 181, 191–192, 194–196, 199, 203, 205, 210, 216, 222, 224
research *see* decolonizing research; feminist research; participatory research; rights-based research
rights-based research 26
Rigor, rigorous 27, 30, 45, 47, 50, 64, 69–70, 151, 207
Roulston, K. 60, 63, 79, 94

self-reflection 81, (continuous self-reflection) 147, 150, 209, 211–212; *see also* critical self-reflection
self-reflexive 23, 40, 217

Skype 158, 165, 175

Smith, Linda Tuhiwai 2, 6, 12, 25, 27, 30, 42, 44–45, 57, 75, 85, 95, 97, 102, 108, 121–122, 137, 150, 183, 205–206, 209–210, 222

social capital 53–54, 67–68, 71

social construct, social construction 23, 102, 194, 224

social inclusion 115, 117, 138

social justice xxi–xxv, 1, (definition) 4, 5–9, 11–14, (social justice positions) 21, 25–26, 29, 41, 43, 49, 57, 69, 71, 77, 84, 91, 94, (social justice, transformative approach) 96, 97–99, 101, (social justice and transformative research) 102, 103–106, 108–111, 114, 117–122, 125, 136–137, 147, 171, 177, 180, 185, 199, 207–215, 218–220, 223, (definition) 224

social media xxiv, 51, 153–159, (social media, ethics) 160–164, 165, 172–176, 194

stakeholder xxiii, 15, 18–20, 29–30, 46, 48–49, 54, 58, 70, 73, 83, 113, 119, (stakeholders, collaboration with) 124, 129, 133, 136, 147–148, 178, 184–186, 188–190, 192, 200, 213–214, (stakeholders, definition of) 224

texting xxiv, 106–107, 120, 154–155, 160, 172–174

transdisciplinary research (transdisciplinary, definition of) 128, 129, 132–133, 149, 151, 204–205

transferability 48–49; *see also* applicability

transnational 8–9, (transnationalism) 15, 38, 69, 119, 156, 182, 189, 191, 224

trust: breaking trust 50; co-constructing trust 64–65; truth-value 48 (*see also* credibility); trustworthiness xxii, 45–49, 53, 57, 68–72, 83

video conferencing 167, 172

voice xxiii, xxvii, 1–2, 4–7, 10, 13–15, 19–21, 24, 27, 30, 38, 49–50, 59, 74, 84, 86, 89–90, 97, 102, 105, 107–108, 115–119, 121, 124, 129, 131, 134, 136–137, 142, 146–147, 156, 165–166, 171, 173, 177, 179–181, (photovoice, voice) 186, 187, 190–191, 195–196, 199–200–201, 203–206, 210–214, 221

Wang, Caroline 180, 182, 206

WhatsApp xxiv, 120, 153, 160, 174, 176; *see also* texting

Wolgemuth, Jennifer R. 6, 60, 71, 150, 210

YouTube 163, 175; *see also* social media

Zoom 10, 144, 158, 165, 169, 173, 198; *see also* video conferencing, social media